EDUCATIONAL SERIES

D0127300

Stock Selection Handbook

Written by Bonnie Biafore
for the National Association of Investors Corporation

Published by National Association of Investors Corporation (NAIC)
Madison Heights, Michigan

First published in the United States of America by
National Association of Investors Corporation (NAIC)
711 West 13 Mile Road, Madison Heights, Michigan 48071
1-877-275-6242 • www.better-investing.org

Manufactured in the United States of America
Edition #1
ISBN # 0-9678130-4-2

Biafore, Bonnie.
    NAIC stock selection handbook / written by Bonnie
Biafore for the National Association of Investors
Corporation.
    p. cm. -- (NAIC Better Investing Educational Series)
    Includes bibliographical references and index.
    ISBN 0-9678130-4-2

    1. Stocks. 2. Investments. 3. Finance, Personal.
I. National Association of Investors Corporation.
II. Title.

HG4661.B53 2003   332.63'22
                             QBI03-200325

NAIC Registered Trademark Rights

NAIC Better Investing Book Series – policy statement:

NAIC Better Investing Book Series

The Better Investing Book Series is designed to provide information and tools to help individuals and investment clubs become successful long-term investors. By using the series, investors will follow a self-learning pathway, gaining knowledge and building experience to make informed investment decisions. The series provides information and resources for beginners, intermediate and experienced investors.
For more information contact NAIC:
1-877-275-6242, or visit the NAIC Web Site:
www.better-investing.org

Acknowledgements

NAIC Stock Selection **Handbook**

Author/Writer:	Bonnie Biafore
Executive Editor:	Jeffery Fox, CFA Director, Educational Development, NAIC
Editorial Consultant:	Barrie Borich
Index Consultant:	Kathleen Paparchontis
Educational Content Consultants:	Richard Holthaus, President & CEO, NAIC Kenneth Janke, Chairman, NAIC Thomas O'Hara, Chairman Emeritus, NAIC Robert O'Hara, Vice President, Business Development, NAIC Janet Rannenberg, Secretary & Director, NAIC CGAB Saul Seinberg, Director, NAIC CGAB
Creative Direction & Design:	Michael Bell
Design Consultants:	Ellada Azariah, Graphic Designer, NAIC Pamela Forton, Graphic Designer, NAIC Mary Treppa, Online Editor, NAIC
Production Coordinators:	Renee Ross, Childers Printing & Graphics, Inc. Jonathan Strong, Manager, Membership Development, NAIC
Technical Support:	Bradley Christensen, Information Technology, NAIC Christopher Ditri, Information Technology, NAIC Kenneth Smith, Information Technology, NAIC
Printing/ Production:	Childers Printing & Graphics, Inc. Printwell Acquisitions, Inc.

Table of Contents

Foreword

Following the NAIC investment principles has enabled many individual investors and investment clubs to be successful through the years. The first two – Invest Regularly and Reinvest Earnings – can be quite easy to follow. The third – Buy stocks that will grow more rapidly than the economy – is what this book is about. Learning how to find companies that are growing and selling at reasonable prices may seem like a difficult task, but when the proper tools are used, it becomes less daunting.

The NAIC Stock Selection Guide principles and analysis procedures were originally formulated by George A. Nicholson, Jr., who was chairman of NAIC's Board of Advisors. Through the years, contributions have been made for its improvement by Alex Carroll of Indianapolis along with Thomas E. O'Hara and Ralph L. Seger, Jr., both trustees of the association. While the refinements have been substantial, the basic form has remained the same for over a half century.

The form is really divided into two main parts. The first deals with the ability of management to make the company successful. Equally important is the section that emphasizes price. The finest growth company in the world can be purchased at the wrong price with the result being a poor investment. This book takes you through the steps to identify both.

It should be remembered that the NAIC Stock Selection Guide by itself does not guarantee success.

The form has always been an aid to good judgement and that judgement comes with time and experience.

It has often been said that, "Investing is an art, not a science." That may be so, but even artists have certain basics that they follow to produce a masterpiece. There are many judgement calls in preparing a study of a company and the stock. Don't be misled with the front of the guide. It is a chart, but not in the normal sense. It is really a picture of how the company has performed in the past and whether the management has been able to make the company grow.

The past is never a guarantee of the future. Past results do not mean the future will continue. Still, the picture can be an indication of what might happen in the next few years and gives a basis for future growth. It helps us organize the facts and then make judgement calls as to what we might expect.

Personally, I have used the NAIC Stock Selection Guide for more than 40 years and it has been an invaluable tool. It has enabled me to make my own investment decisions without relying on tips and stories.

I am confident it will also serve you well.

Kenneth S. Janke

CHAIRMAN
NATIONAL ASSOCIATION OF INVESTORS CORPORATION

Congratulations! You have made a wise decision to learn how to analyze stocks to build and manage your own investment portfolio.

If you don't realize it yet, you ARE the best person to manage your finances. You're investing your money for important reasons—a new home, your kids' college tuition, and retirement—so no one else will care about the results of your portfolio the way you will.

Some people turn to "risk-free" investments, thinking that they can't afford to lose their savings. Unfortunately, there is no such thing as a "risk-free" investment. Hiding money in a mattress still exposes the cash to the risk of the house burning down. Far more insidious—and almost certain to occur—is the risk of inflation. If you put your savings in a bank savings account, your savings are insured up to $100,000 by the Federal Deposit Insurance Corporation. But, inflation reduces the buying power of your money with each passing year. In fact, after 30 years of 3 percent inflation, $1 is worth only 40 cents. If you managed to squirrel away $1 million, that inflation would reduce your nest egg to only $400,000, 30 years later. Investing through mutual funds is one way to go. They are easy to start when your contributions are tiny. And, they don't require quite as much study as individual stocks, so they could be the answer for a person on the go. However, over longer periods of time, most actively managed mutual funds don't keep up with the major stock market indices. On the other hand, you can use low-cost index funds to earn a return that parallels returns for all or some portion of the stock market. If you want to learn more about investing in mutual funds, read the *NAIC Mutual Fund Handbook*.

If you choose to work with a financial advisor, you should make sure that the fee is worth the services you receive. However, even with a professional's help, you're better off being a knowledgeable consumer. Only then can you identify whether your advisor is suggesting investments that meet your objectives for return and risk. In addition, you can protect yourself from less scrupulous advisors who might try to sell you unsuitable investments or trade frequently in your account to increase the money they earn.

If you really want your portfolio to shine, there is nothing like investing in quality growth stocks. Over the past 76 years, the average compounded annual return on an investment in the stock market—with dividends reinvested—is about 11 percent. If you were to invest $10,000 one time only and achieve that 11 percent average return for 40 years, your nest egg would be worth over $650,000! Imagine how much you could collect if you contributed some money to your portfolio each month. Of course, some years are better than others. Stocks increased 54 percent in 1933, whereas in 1931 they plummeted 43 percent. The key to success—and one of NAIC's guiding principles—is to invest for the long term.

The National Association of Investors Corporation has taught thousands of people to invest successfully in individual stocks. Many of these investors, or the investment clubs to which many belong, earn returns that surpass the overall stock market indices — as well as the returns achieved by the majority of financial professionals. NAIC believes that your goal for average annual compound return should be 15 percent. By investing a mere $100 a month for 40 years and earning an average 15 percent, you would end up with a portfolio worth over $3 million. Even if you shoot for a lower return such as 12 percent to reduce your risk, you could still become a millionaire. All it takes is a little brain exercise and patience.

Investing in stocks is like reading a road map. You have to know where you want to go for the map to be helpful. So, take a quiet afternoon and define your objectives—whether it's sending your five kids to Ivy League colleges, retiring at 45, or traveling the world for a year. Don't forget to establish your tolerance for risk. The last thing you want is for your investments to make you nervous. Then, with these criteria in mind, you can start to build a financial plan that gets you where you want to go.

CHAPTER ONE:

The NAIC Approach

You're in Good Company

Do you have big plans for life, but aren't quite sure how to finance them? If you raised your hand, you're reading the right book. The NAIC approach to investing teaches you to take charge of your investments and make them work toward your goals.

Over the past 50 years, more than 5,000,000 people have learned to invest successfully the NAIC way.

These NAIC investors have discovered that investing doesn't have to be scary or difficult. By applying a few simple principles, any investor willing to dedicate a few hours and dollars each month can build a nest egg that would make anyone proud.

NAIC's Four Principles of Investing

Invest Regularly, Regardless of the Market Outlook

Reinvest all Earnings

Invest in Quality Growth Companies

Diversify to Reduce Risk

Works

NAIC's four principles of investing might seem so simple that they couldn't possibly work. On the contrary, simplicity is the beauty of the NAIC approach. The principles make so much sense that they are hard to forget—and are so easy that you can't find a good excuse for not using them.

1. Invest regularly, regardless of the market outlook

When you start investing, you might second-guess the stock that goes nowhere or worry about the market tanking right after you buy. For beginners, it's natural to focus on your mistakes and wonder if your successes will turn sour. Time, experience, and some evidence of long-term success help dispel your fears.

In the meantime, remind yourself that the value of stocks has increased an average of over 11 percent a year for the past 76 years despite cycles of boom, recession, depression and recovery. You win—and win big— over the long term simply by investing in the stock market. More often than not, it's a bad time to invest a big wad of money. Your kids need braces, your car needs new tires, there's always something more urgent. How about one dollar a day? That's no more than the pocket change you drop in a jar when you get home. But, after investing $1 a day in stocks from your 15th birthday until you retired at 65 (a total contribution of about $18,250) a respectable return of 10% would grow your savings to close to half a million dollars!

Investing small amounts regularly can calm beginners' jitters, not to mention improve your results. The technique, called dollar cost averaging, is simply investing a fixed amount of money on a regular schedule. When you do that, you automatically buy more shares when the price is lower and fewer when the price is higher. The result is a lower average purchase price and a higher overall return.

DON'T TRY TO TIME THE MARKET

Some people try to time the market, attempting to buy at the lowest lows and sell at the highest highs. They study and research and watch the market, often missing life in the process. What they also missed is that the return on money invested in the Standard & Poors (S&P) 500 for all trading days from 1986 through 1995 was 14.8%. Missing only the forty best days in those nine years, the return drops to 2.5%!

Dollars Invested	Share Price	Shares Purchased
$100	$10.00	10.00
$100	$12.50	8.33
$100	$8.00	12.50
$100	$12.00	8.33
$100	$15.00	6.66

Total Invested	$500
Shares Purchased	45.82
Average share price	$11.40

=($10 + $12 + $8 + $12 + $15)/5

Average purchased share price
= Total invested/Total shares
= $500 / 45.82 = $10.91

*How dollar
cost averaging works*

NAIC'S FOUR PRINCIPLES OF INVESTING

2. Reinvest all earnings

Companies have two ways to use their earnings. They can plow the money back into the company to help it grow or distribute some to owners of the company—the shareholders. This distribution of after tax profits is called a dividend. Just like the dollar a day you decided to invest after reading the first NAIC principle, the dividends that companies pay to their shareholders initially might seem like small potatoes. Don't make the mistake of squandering them. Reinvesting those tiny dividends turbo-charges your investment return.

Reinvesting the dividends that companies pay to you works similarly to the way rabbits multiply. When the offspring start to have babies of their own, the hutch gets crowded in a hurry. Well, when dividends start earning dividends, the dollars in your account start stacking up.

Earning dividends on your earnings is called compounding. It's hard to explain, but the results are simply magnificent. If you invested $100 in the S&P 500 index in 1926 and spent all the dividends you received, you would have amassed $10,350 by the end of 2000. If you reinvested those dividends, you'd be rolling in $258,652!

Check the account balances in the table below to see the difference that regular investing and dividend reinvestment can make in your investment results over time. This example uses a 10 percent return from price appreciation and 2 percent return from dividends.

3. Invest in quality growth companies

Quality growth companies make investing easy. They're easy to understand. Growth companies generally increase their revenues and earnings faster than the overall economy and inflation combined. The ones to buy also grow faster than a lot of their industry competitors.

Furthermore, what they've done in the past bodes well for more success in the future—and a more valuable share of stock five years in the future. As sales and earnings grow, each share of stock controls a more valuable slice of a company, so eventually people will pay more for that slice.

After you learn what to look for, growth companies are easy to spot. Then, you just have to check in each quarter to see whether their growth is continuing. By investing in growth companies, you can (mostly) ignore the state of the market or where a company is in the business cycle. Even better, with quality growth companies there is no need to worry about whether strategies to turn a company's problems around are successful.

Investment results over time

Years	ONE TIME $100 INVESTMENT		$100 A MONTH DIVIDENDS	
	Dividends Spent	Dividends Reinvested	Dividends Spent	Dividends Reinvested
5	$165	$182	$7,744	$8,167
10	$271	$330	$20,484	$23,004
15	$445	$600	$41,447	$49,958
20	$733	$1,089	$75,937	$98,926
25	$1,206	$1,979	$132,683	$187,885
30	$1,984	$3,595	$226,049	$349,496
40	$5,370	$11,865	$632,408	$1,176,477
50	$14,537	$39,158	$1,732,439	$3,905,834

Growth

Companies can grow sales in a variety of ways, including:

- *Expanding territory*
- *Increasing market share*
- *Building new stores*
- *Introducing new products or new applications for existing products*
- *Acquiring competitors*
- *Increasing prices*

But, there's a little more to it. Growth is a balancing act, perhaps closer to patting your head and rubbing your stomach at the same time. You can't increase prices or gain market share with lousy products. You had better make the best Freeblesnap in the world if you want to increase prices when competition is sniffing around. In high-tech industries or those that brave fickle consumer preference, management has to plan how to avoid getting stuck with obsolete products. They have to do all these things while keeping the cost of goods sold and overhead expenses as low as possible.

Companies can hit the lime-light with a popular product, then fade as quickly as the craze for Cabbage Patch dolls. (You remember them, right?) Other companies float along in the rising tides of their industry. But, for sustained performance, nothing beats great management—executives who can balance the pressures while navigating the company to higher ground.

Growth tends to slow as companies get bigger. It's like trying to turn an oil tanker or move a freight train. Nothing moves quickly in a big company. There's nothing slow about the explosive growth of a young company, but that growth sometimes includes a speedy stock price drop. The tortoise often outruns and out-invests the hare.

Unfortunately, some companies don't revitalize their products or adjust as the world changes. When a company's growth stalls or, even worse, starts to decline, it's time to get out and find another investment.

NAIC'S FOUR PRINCIPLES OF INVESTING

Quality

Quality is often difficult to quantify—the solid but soft thump of a closing car door or the ambiance of a restaurant. Some attributes of a quality company are qualitative measures, such as leadership in the industry and depth of management. Fortunately, other measures are easy to assess after you know how, such as financial strength, effective research and development, market strength, stability of earnings, above industry average pre-tax profit margins and return on equity. We won't get into details here, but read Chapter 11 on evaluating management and Chapters 22, 23, and 24 on financial reports for more on these measures.

Good value

A poor quality stock with dubious growth rates is a dog no matter how low the price. However, even the best quality growth stock can be a poor investment when it's overvalued. So, you ask, "What about regular investing and dollar cost averaging?" Those are two great tactics. But, when you decide to purchase a stock, you should make sure that it is a quality growth company at a reasonable price.

As you manage your portfolio, you might buy more shares of stocks that you own. Each time, you add your contributions to the stock that currently offers the best return with acceptable risk. It's dollar cost averaging with an extra kick. Sure, you dollar cost average just by investing your regular contributions. However, by directing your contribution to the stock with the brightest prospects, you boost your portfolio performance.

4. Diversify to reduce risk

If you could pick the one company that was destined for years of double-digit growth, you would make the most money by investing all your cash in that one investment. But, you can't pick the big kahuna. You can't even pick winners 100% of the time, even with diligent application of the NAIC tools. Be prepared for one out of every five stocks that you buy to be a loser. Then, you can sigh with relief when three do what you expect. But, don't forget to celebrate when one purchase exceeds your expectations.

The moral of the story is don't keep all your eggs in one basket or all your money in one stock (or industry.) Diversifying your investments reduces your risk. It prevents a mistake from wiping out a big chunk of your net worth. For example, a competitor's new product or consumers' changing tastes could wipe out a small company you were sure was a winner.

Diversifying by company size

Sales	Size	% of portfolio	Anticipated growth rate
Less than – $500 million	Small	25%	More than 15%
$500 million – $5 billion	Medium	50%	10% – 15%
More than – $5 billion	Large	25%	7% –10%

Large companies might grow more slowly, but usually have the wherewithal to ride out some storms. Even industries rise and wane.

Investors dumped the health care industry for fear of the affects of proposed health care reform in the early 1990s, whereas the chink in the computer industry façade finally appeared in the early 2000s.

When you choose the stocks for your portfolio from a variety of industries and company sizes, you can earn a market beating return without riding an investment roller coaster. True, if you're buying your first stock, there isn't a whole lot you can do to diversify that portfolio. But, you need only 15 to 25 companies of different sizes from at least 10 to 12 unrelated industries to reduce the risk in your portfolio.

Stick to the guidelines

You actually can diversify too much. When you start buying a little bit of everything, your investment return degenerates toward that of a stock market index, but with a lot more risk, not to mention brokers' commissions. Keep your stock portfolio simple. If you still crave one of every stock, put some cash in a low-cost index mutual fund.

That's all there is to it!

Set up an automatic transfer from your checking account to add money to your investment account regularly. Tell your broker to reinvest the dividends you receive. Many brokers offer the added bonus of reinvesting dividends without charging a commission. Find stocks that demonstrate strong and consistent growth and buy them at a good price. Purchase only as many stocks as you can follow (usually 15), but make sure they are of different sizes and from diverse industries.

CHAPTER TWO:

Fundamental Analysis

Getting to the Bottom of Studying Stocks

Fundamental (adj.) 1. of or forming a foundation or basis; basic; essential.

Fundamental analysis follows NAIC's stick-to-the-basics approach. By looking at the basic measures of a company, such as sales and earnings growth, profit margin, return on equity,

Price/Earnings ratio, and a few other financial measures, you can judge prospects of a company and estimate a value for its stock in the future. From there, it's an easy leap to compare the current stock price to the future value and see whether you've found a stock to buy.

Peter Lynch, the fund manager who piloted the Fidelity Magellan Fund to the Mutual Fund All-Stars Roster, and Warren Buffett, the brains behind Berkshire Hathaway, both use fundamental analysis to pick investments.

Fundamental analysis saves time over the long term

Your study of the fundamentals of a company meshes perfectly with the long-term view that NAIC investors take. In a high-caliber company, the basic drivers that make the company a good investment typically don't disappear overnight—although they can deteriorate over a few fiscal quarters. It might take some digging to see whether a company passes the fundamentals test. But, after it passes, you might hold that stock for years, even decades, with a quick checkup every three months to make sure it's still on track.

GROWTH VS. VALUE

Growth stocks have sales and earnings growth rates that outperform the economy and inflation—and, quite often, other stocks in the marketplace. Growth investors

buy these stocks because they expect the stock to increase in value as the earnings increase.

Stocks that appear to be on sale compared to their fair or intrinsic value are called value stocks. Intrinsic value means the perceived actual value of a stock, as compared to its market price. The companies are out of favor for some reason or could be trying to dig themselves out of some predicament. Value investors buy stocks that they hope are ready to turn around their tawdry past. The investors make their money when the market realizes that the sow's ear was really a silk purse.

In short, growth investors pay one dollar for a stock that will be worth two dollars in the future, whereas value investors pay one dollar for a stock that no one else realizes is worth two dollars today.

Growing sales and earnings are the most fundamental of fundamental measures. Higher sales and earnings increase the value of a company and eventually someone will pay more for something that has increased in value. Sales and earnings growth rates tend to be consistent in the quality companies that NAIC investors crave. You don't have to watch your investment day by day—checking that the basic measures still look good when the company issues a quarterly report is sufficient. In the graph below, Johnson and Johnson shows how price follows sales and earnings growth.

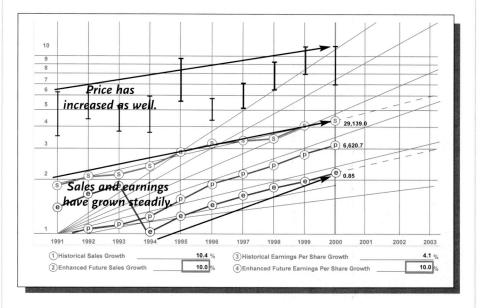

SPEAKING THE LANGUAGE

Miming that you want to buy sunglasses in Spain might work, but it's no great loss if you end up with sardines. On the other hand, misunderstanding profit margins or return on equity could cost you money. Keep reading to learn the basic vocabulary for studying stocks with fundamental analysis.

SHARES OF STOCK

Each share of stock is a share of ownership in a company. If you own 1,000 shares when there are 100,000 shares in a company, you own one percent of the company. One share of stock typically represents a tiny portion of ownership. However, that portion is yours and you get to cast your vote on issues at the annual meeting.

The owners of the company (also called stockholders or shareholders) like to know how the company has performed on a per share basis, so they can see what they get for their ownership. For example, two important measures that you will learn shortly are Earnings per share (EPS) and Dividends per share. Per share performance not only tells you about the value of your piece of the company, but also helps in comparing companies in the same industry to see which one delivers the best performance.

SALES (REVENUE)

Sales for a company are a lot like the salary you are paid for the work you do. Sales, also called revenue, are the dollars that flow into a company for the work it does, whether that is selling cars or consulting services, toys or telephone time.

COST OF GOODS SOLD AND EXPENSES

You might get nervous when you hear the term "cost of goods sold". It's unfamiliar and sounds like some arcane accounting phrase. But, it's easy. The cost of goods sold is simply the cost to the company of the things that it sells (the goods.) If the company sells widgets and they buy the widgets from a supplier for $2 each, that $2 is the cost of goods sold for the

widget. Expenses include other costs that the company incurs not directly related to the things that they sell, such as salaries for sales and administrative groups, research and development, costs for other functions, travel expenses, employee benefits, marketing, and training.

PROFIT OR EARNINGS

Pre-tax profit is the money left over from sales after subtracting costs and expenses.

Subtract taxes from the pre-tax profit and you get net profit or net earnings. Net profit is free and clear—management can reinvest that money into the business to fund future growth or distribute it to stockholders as dividends. Either choice is fine. However, you might prefer faster company growth to build your portfolio or dividends for income.

> ### NAIC uses pre-tax profit
> *Companies can take steps to reduce the taxes they pay. However, they have little control over whether tax rates increase or decrease. Studying the growth of pre-tax profit gives a better picture of a company's ability to perform.*

For faster growth, look at companies that reinvest their earnings. Companies

dependent on research and technological advances for growth, such as computer or pharmaceutical companies, often reinvest most earnings into research and development (R&D) or facility improvements. That reinvestment fuels their growth, which, in turn, helps the stock price increase.

However, if you are retired and want some income from your investments, look for companies that pay dividends. Ideally, dividends should increase over time as earnings grow. Even if a company pays a set percentage of their earnings as dividends, those dividends can increase if the company's earnings increase.

Some companies increase dividends by increasing the percentage of profits paid to shareholders. As a bigger slice of the profit pie goes to paying dividends, less is reinvested in the company. That eventually translates to slower or no growth.

PROFIT MARGINS

Company performance can stem from many things, such as the state of the economy, a particularly successful product, the rise or fall of competition, or changes in material costs. However, for consistent long-term performance, company management must be able to manage the many factors affecting a company through good economic times and bad. The pre-tax profit margin is the percentage of money that a company gets to keep, before taxes, from the revenue it produces. Profit margins vary by industry. Grocery stores do well to achieve a 5 percent pre-tax profit margin, whereas software companies are dogs if their pre-tax profit margin is only 40 percent. Regardless of the norm for the industry, above average and steadily increasing profit margins show that management can success-fully balance the strategies that increase sales and decrease or contain costs.

Management can increase sales by introducing new products, selling more products, building more stores, expand-ing territory, gaining market share from competitors, or increasing the price per unit of the product. However, management might also try to reduce the cost of goods sold by paying less for supplies or increasing the efficiency of production. Controlling overhead expenses is a constant priority for company executives, as bloating expenses are a sure drain on performance.

EARNINGS PER SHARE (EPS)

Earnings per share are the net profits of the company divided by the total number of shares outstanding—in short, the portion of earnings that you as the owner of one share of stock can covet. Analysts and investors watch EPS vigilantly, because, over time, stock price usually follow where EPS leads.

DIVIDENDS PER SHARE

Dividends per share are the money that the company pays to shareholders divided by the total number of shares out-standing. It's the money you receive out of the net profit for each share that you own.

PRICE

The price of a stock is what someone pays for a stock. The

bid price is what someone is bidding to buy a share, where whereas the ask price is the price at which someone is willing to sell their shares.

YIELD

The yield for a savings account is the interest rate that the bank pays you for the money in the account. The yield for stock is the percentage of the dividend per share to the price you paid for the stock. In effect, the dividends that you receive are like an interest rate paid on the money you invest-ed in the stock. For example, if you receive a $1 dividend on a share of stock that you paid $20 for, your yield is $1÷$20 or five percent (5%).

COMPOUNDED ANNUAL GROWTH RATE

In your savings account, the bank pays you interest on your money. The next time, they pay interest on your deposits as well as the interest you have received, compounding the interest. The compounded annual growth rate when you study a company follows the same principle. It shows the rate at which the company grows each year taking into account the growth from the year before.

Compound Growth Rates

Year	Sales	Dollar Increase	% Increase
Year 0	$1,000,000		
Year 1	$1,148,700	$148,700	14.9%
Year 2	$1,319,512	$170,812	14.9%
Year 3	$1,515,723	$196,211	14.9%
Year 4	$1,741,111	$225,388	14.9%
Year 5	$2,000,014	$258,903	14.9%

Average growth rate is total increase divided by the number of years

= 100 percent ÷ 5

= 20%

Compounded annual growth rate = 14.9%

For example, if a company increases sales from $1 million five years ago to $2 million in sales this year, *their sales increased by 100 percent over five years. However, you want to know the rate that you can apply each year to the ever-increasing sales that achieves that 100 percent increase. You don't just divide the 100 percent by five years. Look at the table to see how compounding works when calculating growth rates. The dollar increase in sales gets larger each year, while the increase is still the same percentage of the previous year's total sales.*

PRICE/EARNINGS RATIO (PE)

The Price/Earnings ratio (PE ratio or PE) is stock price divided by earnings per share. PE is one way to measure whether a stock is fairly valued. The PE ratio seems like a quantitative measure, but it actually says a lot about investor sentiment. The PE is the dollar amount that investors are willing to pay for each dollar of earnings that the company produces. The more optimistic they are about the company's future prospects, the more they might pay for each dollar of today's earnings.

As profitability increases, so does the return shareholders earn from their ownership in the company. Investors want to own that company, competing in an open market, bidding higher and higher to buy the stock, driving the price up. Have the earnings increased during this short feeding frenzy? No. So, the PE ratio increases as the price increases, showing the demand for the stock. Conversely, when a company's earnings per share drop, sellers try to sell their shares but fewer people want to buy the stock. The price drops until someone buys, lowering the PE at the same time.

Compare PEs to Dig Up Secrets

A lone PE ratio only says so much. However, comparing different types of PEs can divulge a world of information—good and bad. Some industries with rosy prospects command higher PEs, whereas industries with slower growth have lower PEs. Comparing the company's PE to the average PE for the industry can show whether the company is popular within the industry and tells whether the stock is "pricey" compared to its competitors.

Often, the PE for a company tends to stay within a given range, in part due to the prospects of the industry and in part from the company's quality and rate of growth. That doesn't mean that the PE won't jump above or below that range—just that it will return to that range from high or low extremes. The NAIC approach compares the current PE to its 5-year historical average PE ratio. The 5-year historical average is often, though not always, a good indication of the "normal" PE for a company. If the current PE is below the historical average, chances are good that the PE will rise to the historical average, giving the stock price a boost in the process. However, when the current PE is above the average, investors are paying a premium for the stock—and that can diminish the returns you receive.

Compare PEs to Dig Up Secrets

Sometimes investors are *overly* enthusiastic about a stock's future prospects. They might pay $40.00 for every $1.00 of earnings—a PE of 40. At other times, investors are pessimistic about a company and might pay only $8.00 for $1.00 of earnings—a PE of 8.

The PE ratio is price divided by earnings per share. But which price and what earnings? There are several PEs used frequently in financial circles. Here are the most popular:

Trailing PE (or current PE) is calculated by dividing the present price by the most recent four quarters of reported earnings. This PE is the most common PE ratio and gives a historical measure of PE.

Projected PE is the present price divided by the next four quarters of projected earnings. Of course, the projected PE is only as good as the earnings projections. However, the projected PE is like a peek into the future—what would the PE be if the company increased its earnings as projected?

RETURN ON EQUITY (PERCENT EARNED ON EQUITY)

Equity (also called shareholders' equity or book value) is like the net worth of a company—the amount you get when you subtract the total liabilities from the total assets. But, it also represents the dollars that shareholders have invested in the company, in addition to earnings retained in the business. Return on equity is the return that the company produces on that investment. Investors like to see that management can produce a steady and substantial return on equity.

GLOSSARIES
WHERE YOU CAN LEARN MORE

To become a true student of any subject, you must master the language. If you are interested in learning more about the vocabulary of investing, here are several sources to consider. *Wall Street Words: An Essential A To*

Z Guide for Today's Investor (Houghton Mifflin, 1997) written by David Logan Scott is a great book with easy-to-understand definitions for every financial term you might want to know.

If you are hooked on using the Internet, there are many online financial glossaries. The Yahoo! Finance glossary is thorough and easy to use. Campbell R. Harvey's glossary is probably the largest. If you don't like any of these glossaries, type "financial glossary" into your favorite search engine.

Yahoo! Finance
  biz.yahoo.com/f/g/g.html
Bloomberg Financial Glossary
  www.bloomberg.com/money/tools/bfglosa.html
Forbes Financial Glossary
  www.forbes.com/tools/glossary/index.jhtml
Campbell R. Harvey's Hypertextual Finance Glossary
  www.duke.edu/~charvey/Classes/wpg/glossary.htm
Investor Words
  www.investor words.com/
Financial Glossary.com
  www.financialglossary.com
Investopedia
  www.investopedia.com

CHAPTER THREE:

Getting To Know NAIC

You Know What You Want—But Not What It Looks Like

Your boss asks you to get a coatimundi for the company and disappears. After you learn that a coatimundi is a carnivorous animal, you have to figure out how to find one. But where do they live, what do they look like and what do they eat? Are they nocturnal—or more important, endangered?

Without a photograph, you might walk past one without knowing it.

The NAIC philosophy suggests investing in quality growth companies which are selling at reasonable prices. But, what does growth look like? Do low quality stocks smell bad? How do you know a reasonable price? The NAIC stock study forms transform company financial results, so you can easily see whether you've found what you're looking for, how to choose the best specimens and how to keep them healthy. This chapter introduces the forms that are available and what each one does.

What Are We Looking For?

Quick Profiles with the Stock Check List

Thorough Analysis Using the Stock Selection Guide

Choosing the Best Investment with the Stock Comparison Guide

Keeping Your Portfolio on Track with PMG & PERT

Summary

Stock Study Forms

What Are We Looking For?

Let's review the desirable characteristics of a stock described in detail in Chapter 1.

Growth: A growth company sports revenues and earnings that grow faster than the overall economy and inflation combined. Attractive growth companies also grow faster than most of their competitors and take steps to ensure that their futures are as prosperous as their past.

Growth Quality: Good quality companies are usually leaders in their industry. Their executives consistently produce impressive financial performance despite the setbacks that every company faces. The companies possess above-industry-average sales growth, earnings growth, pre-tax profit margins and return on equity.

Good Value: A poor quality stock can be a lemon no matter how low its price. On the other hand, even the best quality growth stock is a poor investment if you pay too much for it. Even when you use dollar-cost averaging, you will come out ahead if you use your regular contribution to purchase the stock in your portfolio that offers the best current return with acceptable risk.

Quick Profiles with the Stock Check List

The Stock Check List is an easy introduction to the NAIC stock study concepts. All it takes is a few pieces of data and answers to a couple of questions. Plus, the form doesn't take long to complete even if you're still getting comfortable finding financial data and feeling at one with your calculator. Chapter 6 includes detailed instructions for completing and using the Stock Check List.

The Stock Check List just begins to scratch the surface of analyzing whether a stock is a good investment. You should absorb the basics and the move on to the Stock Selection Guide (SSG) to perform more thorough stock studies as quickly as you can.

In the past, the Gross National Product (GNP) was the key measure of economic activity. The GNP represents the output of labor and property of U.S. residents regardless where the labor and property is located. However, it does not include income produced in the U.S. by foreign-owned businesses.

Beginning in 1991, gross domestic product or GDP became the most common measure of the health of the U.S. economy. The GDP is a better measure of domestic production—the output of products and services created in the United States whether the labor and property is owned by U.S. residents or foreign-owned. The GDP reflects both income and expenses and covers the durable and nondurable goods, structures, and services sectors of the market.

Measuring Economic Growth

NATIONAL ASSOCIATION OF INVESTORS CORPORATION

INVESTMENT EDUCATION FOR INDIVIDUALS AND CLUBS SINCE 1951

Stock Check List ®
for Beginning Investors

Company __Merck__

Prepared by __BJB__

Date __01/08/2003__

MRK

While Investors are learning to use NAIC's Stock Selection Guide, it is suggested the following Check List be used for each stock considered for investment.

1 PAST SALES RECORD

Sales for most recent year were	(1) $	47716.00
Sales for next most recent year were	(2) $	40363.00
Total of above (1+ 2)	(3) $	88079.00
Figure above divided by 2	(4) $	44039.50
Sales 5 years ago were	(5) $	19829.00
Sales 6 years ago were	(6) $	16681.00
Total of above (5 + 6)	(7) $	36510.00
Figure above divided by 2	(8) $	18255.00
Increase in sales in above period (8 from 4)	(9) $	25784.50
Percentage increase in sales (9 divided by 8)	(10)	141.2 %

CONVERSION TABLE

This % increase in Sales Gives	27	33	46	61	76	93	112	129	148	205	271
This % Compounded Annual Growth Rate	5	6	8	10	12	14	16	18	20	25	30

COMPOUND ANNUAL RATE OF SALES GROWTH WAS ___19.3%

Look for the percent increase that meets the objective you have set.

2 PAST EARNINGS PER SHARE RECORD

Earnings Per Share for most recent year were	(1) $	3.14
Earnings Per Share for next most recent year were	(2) $	2.90
Total of above (1+ 2)	(3) $	6.04
Figure above divided by 2	(4) $	3.02
Earnings Per Share 5 years ago were	(5)	1.60
Earnings Per Share 6 years ago were	(6)	1.35
Total of above (5 + 6)	(7)	2.95
Figure above divided by 2	(8) $	1.48
Increase in Earnings Per Share in above period (8 from 4)	(9) $	1.55
Percentage increase in Earnings Per Share (9 divided by 8)	(10)	104.75 %

See Conversion Table above to determine ➡️

Earnings Per Share have increased ___less___ than sales this period.
(more)   (less)

COMPOUND ANNUAL RATE OF EARNINGS PER SHARE GROWTH WAS ___15.4 %

Explain Apparent Reason for Difference in Sales and Earnings Per Share Growth: _____

_____

Figure 3-01: The Stock Check List for Merck from Investor's Toolkit

Discuss Possible Reasons for Past Growth:

A new product was successful _____✔_____

A cyclical business that experienced recovery _____

A research program has produced several new products or uses for older products _____✔_____

Purchase another company _____

Has taken larger share of business in its field _____

Skill of management _____✔_____

Will Factors Which Produced Past Growth Continue Effective

for the next five years ____✔__ yes, _____ yes, but less effective, _____ no.

3 PRICE RECORD OF THE STOCK

Present Price $___54.65___   Present Earnings Per Share ___3.14___

List Last 5 Years	High Price Each Year (A)	Low Price Each Year (B)	Earnings Per Share (C)	Price Earnings Ratio at High (A ~ C)	at Low (B ~ C)
1997	54.100	39.000	1.920	28.18	20.31
1998	80.900	50.700	2.150	37.63	23.58
1999	87.400	60.900	2.450	35.67	24.86
2000	96.700	52.000	2.900	33.34	17.93
2001	95.300	56.800	3.140	30.35	18.09
Totals	414.400	259.400	12.560	165.170	104.770
Averages	82.880	51.880	2.512	33.034	20.954

Average of High and Low Price Earnings Averages for the past five years.	26.994

Present Price is _____higher_____ than high price five years ago.
(higher)   (lower)

Present Price is __1.0%__ % higher that the high price 5 years ago. Compare this figure with the percent sales increase in 1 (10) and percent earnings per share increase in 2 (10).

The price change compares with sales growth and earnings per share growth _____favorably_____
(favorably or unfavorably)

This stock has sold as high as the current price in __4__ of the last 5 years.

In the past five years the stock ____has____ sold at unusually____high____ price earnings ratios.
(has)   (has not)   (high)   (low)

The Present price earnings ratio is____17.404____

In relation to past price earnings ratios the stock is currently

_____ selling at a higher ratio

_____ selling about the same

___✔___ selling lower

The average price earnings ratios of the past might be expected to continue_____
or should be adjusted to__25.00__ high, __15.00__ low.

4 CONCLUSION

1. The past sales growth rate _____does_____ meet our objective.
   (does)   (does not)

2. The past earnings per share growth rate _____does_____ meet our objective.
   (does)   (does not)

3. Our conclusion has been that possible earnings per share growth rate ____will____ meet our objective.
   (will)   (will not)
   in the coming five years.

4. The price of the stock is currently ____acceptable____
   (acceptable)   (too high)

This form is not meant to give you an adequate analysis of the stock, but is meant to help a beginner ask questions to indicate whether the company is likely to become more valuable and if it can be purchased reasonably. As Investors gain practice, a more thorough study of the stock is suggested using NAIC's Stock Select Guide and Report as a guide.

Growth on the Stock Check List

Analyzing growth is a simple affair on the Stock Check List. You determine how fast sales and earnings grew for the past five years and decide whether that growth rate meets your objective. If sales and earnings growth both pass your test, you move on to examining the price to earnings past record.

This handbook displays the computerized versions of the NAIC forms produced by the software programs NAIC Classic, Investor's Toolkit, and Stock Analyst Pro. They reproduce more clearly than paper forms, and, in most cases, look almost identical to their paper counterparts. When you start to study numerous stocks, analysis software will be at the top of your gift list.

The Check List only looks at sales and earnings at the beginning and end of the five-year period and it doesn't graph the company's growth. The form doesn't show whether a company's growth is consistent or if there are any losses in the recent past. You'll need to graduate to the SSG Section 1 graph to see just how consistent and fast a company has grown.

Quality on the Stock Check List

The Stock Check List asks a few questions about past growth. The answers on this list are good indicators of quality. Companies that use several strategies for growth can usually weather storms better than their one-trick-pony competition. Successful research programs, increasing market share, and skilled management all bode well for a company's future.

Consistently increasing sales and earnings are another sign of quality but they don't show up on the Stock Check List. You should inspect the sales and earnings number for the past 10 years to make sure that they are increasing consistently and don't show any recent losses.

Value

The Stock Check List doesn't actually present a buy price for a company based on your judgment. Instead, you check whether the price has increased at a similar rate to sales and earnings. If the price has skyrocketed compared to sales and earnings, the stock is usually overvalued. The Stock Check List also looks for Price Earnings ratios that are in line with those in earlier years.

Thorough Analysis Using the Stock Selection Guide

The Stock Selection Guide (SSG) is the foundation of NAIC stock analysis. Compared to the Stock Check List's rough sketch and quick synopsis, the SSG offers the tools to create a realistic portrait and detailed analysis of an investment. The SSG might go into more detail, but it still focuses on identifying quality growth companies with attractive stock prices. The SSG contains five sections: the first two focus on the growth of sales and earnings per share and the evaluation of management, the remaining three identify PE ratios, risk and reward, and five-year potential. Chapters 7 through 15 provide detailed explanations of the purpose of each section of the SSG, how to fill them out, how to apply judgment, and how to interpret the results of your stock study.

The Stock Selection Report is a valuable, but often overlooked, part of the NAIC stock study. This two-page form helps you organize your judgment and conclusions about a stock. You can review at a glance why you would or would not buy the stock, whether you are presenting it to your investment club for the first time or trying to decide whether to sell it.

SSG Section 1: Visual Analysis of Sales, Earnings & Price

Section 1 of the SSG provides a visual analysis of a stock by displaying a graph of data points for historical sales, earnings, pre-tax profit and price. Humans are quite adept at recognizing patterns, so you shouldn't be surprised by how quickly you learn to see growth and consistency in the lines for sales, earnings and pre-tax profit. The straight lines shown in figure 3-02 represent the average relationships of these data points. The lines are called trend lines. The upward angle of the historical trend lines shows the rate of growth, whereas nearly straight lines represent the consistent performance of an excellent management team.

The position of the price bars compared to the sales and earnings lines is a relative indicator of the PE ratio and hints at the valuation of the stock. When revenue or earnings grow faster than the share price and the price bars appear above the historical trend lines, the gap between the trend line and the top of the price bars grows smaller, just as the PE gets smaller when the earnings grow faster than the price. Larger gaps indicate higher PEs and, possibly, overvalued shares.

The rest of the SSG analysis hinges on your estimate of the company's future growth. After studying the historical trend lines on the graph and researching the company, you must estimate the future rate of sales and earnings growth. By drawing these forecast growth rates as projection lines on the graph, you can visually estimate figures for sales and earnings five years in the future.

Success*Tip!*

You can't simply plug in data on the SSG and pop out a reliable buy price for the stock. You must do your homework to understand what the company does and where it's going. Your judgment of the company's past and future performance adds realism to your stock study. Just as an artist might paint a flattering portrait when the client is paying big bucks, professional stock analysts often offer fetching pictures of stock prospects. Unfortunately, as an investor, you risk your hard-earned dollars if you try to make a stock look like a better investment than it really is.

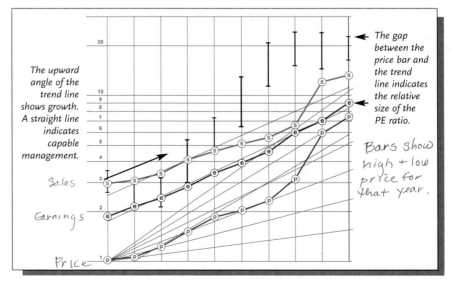

Figure 3-02: Viewing Sales, Earnings and Price on the SSG graph

SSG Section 2: Evaluating Management for Key Factors

Lottery winners know that anyone can get lucky. Making money consistently takes skill. Company management has to be knowledgeable and effective to produce the consistent performance that NAIC investors want. Pre-tax profit margins and percent earned on equity both test management's mettle.

BEATING INDUSTRY AVERAGES

Different industries have different typical rates for pre-tax profit margin and return on equity. For instance, in the food industry a 4 percent profit margin is good, but a computer software company had better beat 36 percent. A stable or increasing trend is not enough—the numbers in Section 2 should be above average for the industry. Chapter 5 tells you where to find these numbers and many others.

The pre-tax profit margin is the percentage that the company gets to keep (before taxes) of each dollar it makes in sales. Management has to be able to control costs under any condition to produce consistently increasing pre-tax profit margins. Percent earned on equity, also called return on equity, shows the return that management earns on the capital that shareholders have invested in the company.

Before moving to the "PE" and "Risk and Reward" sections of the SSG, scrutinize the key factors of the company carefully. The ability of management is a lasting force that drives the valuation of a company. If the consistency of profit margins and returns on equity aren't apparent, don't even think about looking for a good "buy" price for the stock. In fact, the risk and reward measures of a company often start to look better as its performance and quality deteriorate.

SSG Section 3, 4 & 5: Looking for Value

The next three sections of the SSG help determine whether the price makes the stock an attractive investment. The Price-Earnings history in Section 3 provides the data to evaluate the valuation of a stock as a potential investment. In Section 4, you use your forecast earnings and estimated high and low PEs to figure out whether the stock price can go high enough to offset the risk of the price dropping.

Section 5 is the coup de grace for a stock study. Even when the potential reward from price appreciation offsets the risk of the price falling, the total return of the investment must meet your objective for investment return. If it doesn't, you cut the stock from your list of potential investments.

THE PSYCHOLOGY OF PEs

A consistent PE means that investors have confidence in the stock. Rising PEs might indicate investor optimism, which can lead to healthy increases in the price. Then again, higher PEs could indicate unfounded exuberance, such as that shown by technology stock investors in 2000.

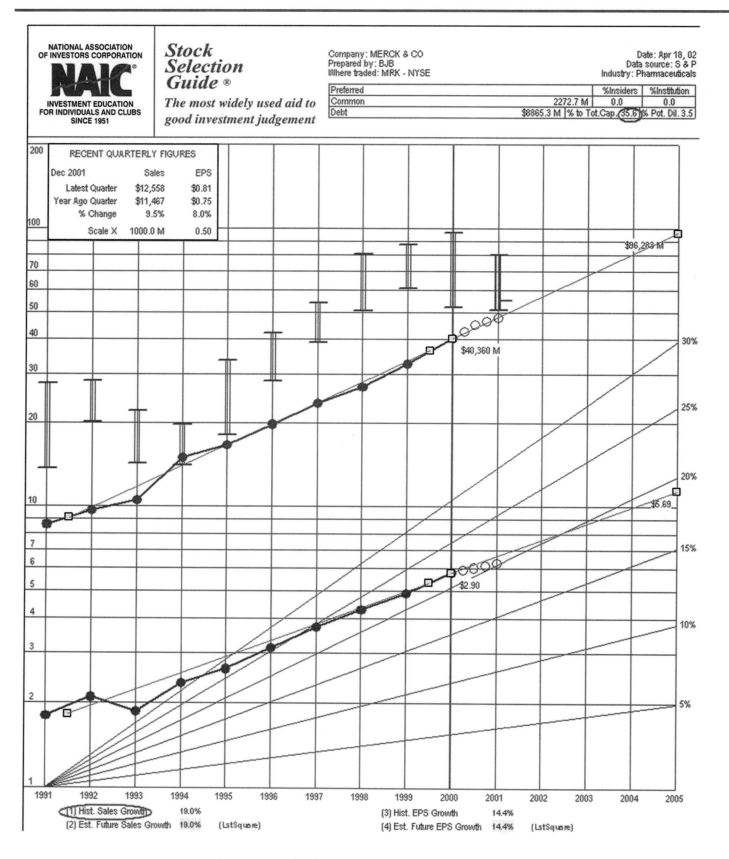

Figure 3-03: Stock Selection Guide of Merck from NAIC Classic

2 EVALUATING MANAGEMENT

MERCK & CO   Apr 18, 2002

	1991	1992	1993	1994	1995	1996	1997	1998	1999	2000	LAST 5 YEAR AVG.	TREND
A % Pre-tax Profit on Sales	37.1	37.2	30.0	30.1	29.3	28.7	27.9	30.8	27.0	25.1	27.9%	DOWN
B % Earned on Equity	43.2	48.9	21.6	26.9	28.4	32.4	36.6	41.0	44.5	46.0	40.1%	UP

3 PRICE-EARNINGS HISTORY as an indicator of the future

This shows how stock prices have fluctuated with earnings and dividends. It is a building block for translating earnings into future stock prices.

Current Price: $55.05   52 Wk High: $80.42   52 Wk Low: $51.00   Dividend: $1.40

	Year	A PRICE HIGH	B PRICE LOW	C Earnings Per Share	D Price Earnings Ratio HIGH (A÷C)	E Price Earnings Ratio LOW (B÷C)	F Dividend Per Share	G % Payout F÷C X 100	H % Hi. Yield F÷B X 100
1	1996	$42.13	$28.25	$1.57	26.9	18.1	$0.74	47.3%	2.6%
2	1997	$54.09	$39.00	$1.87	29.0	20.9	$0.87	46.6%	2.2%
3	1998	$80.88	$50.69	$2.14	37.7	23.6	$0.99	46.2%	2.0%
4	1999	$87.38	$60.94	$2.45	35.7	24.9	$1.12	45.7%	1.8%
5	2000	$96.69	$52.00	$2.90	33.3	17.9	$1.26	43.4%	2.4%
6	TOTAL		$230.88		162.6	105.4		229.2%	
7	AVG.		$46.18		32.5	21.1		45.8%	
8	AVERAGE PE			26.8	9 CURRENT PE				17.5

4 EVALUATING RISK and REWARD over the next 5 years

Assuming one recession and one business boom every 5 years, calculations are made of how high and how low the stock might sell. The upside-downside ratio is the key to evaluating risk and reward.

A HIGH PRICE - NEXT 5 YEARS
Avg. High PE ~~32.5~~ 20.0   X Est. High EPS $5.69   = Forecast Hi Pr $113.83

B LOW PRICE - NEXT 5 YEARS
(a) Avg Low PE ~~21.1~~ 15.0   X Est. Low EPS $2.90   = $43.50
(b) Avg Low Price of Last 5 Years = $46.18
(c) Recent Severe Market Low Price = $28.25
(d) Price Dividend Will Support = $53.45   Estimated Lo Pr $43.50

C ZONING
$113.83 High Frcst Price - $43.50 Low Frcst Price = $70.33 Range X 1/3 = $23.44

Buy Zone =	$43.50	to	$66.94
Hold Zone =	$66.94	to	$90.39
Sell Zone =	$90.39	to	$113.83

Present Market Price of $55.05 is in the   BUY zone.   Selected Zoning =   33/33/33

D UP-SIDE DOWN-SIDE RATIO (Potential Gain vs. Risk of Loss)
$$\frac{\text{High Price - Present Price}}{\text{Present Price - Low Price}} = 5.1 : 1$$

E PRICE TARGET (Price appreciation over the next five years in simple interest rates.)
$$\frac{\text{High Price}}{\text{Present Market Price}} \times 100 - 100 = 106.8\% \text{ Appreciation}$$

5 5-YEAR POTENTIAL

This combines price appreciation with dividend yield to get an estimate of total return. It provides a standard for comparing income and growth stocks.

A PRESENT YIELD
$$\frac{\text{Present Full Year's Dividend}}{\text{Present Price of Stock}} \times 100 = 2.5 \text{ Present Yield or \% Returned on Purchase Price}$$

B AVERAGE YIELD OVER NEXT 5 YEARS
$$\frac{\text{Avg. Earnings Per Share Next 5 Years } \times \text{ Avg. \% Payout}}{\text{Present Price of Stock}} = 3.4\%$$

C ESTIMATED AVERAGE ANNUAL RETURN OVER NEXT FIVE YEARS

		Simple		Compounded
Avg. 5 Year Appreciation Potential		21.4%		15.6%
Average Yield	+	3.4%	+	3.4%
Average Total Annual Return Over the Next 5 Years	=	24.7%	=	19.0%

Choosing the Better Investment with the Stock Comparison Guide

When you find a stock with all the right characteristics, the temptation to ring up your broker and yell "Buy!" is almost irresistible. But, resist you must. In growth industries, you might find that several stocks in that industry fit the profile—consistency, growth and an attractive price. Short-term cataclysm in the market can send several stocks from your watch list into the buy zone. When you can only buy one stock, how do you choose?

You want only the very best, but you rarely find a company that is a perfect 10. Instead, you must weigh the mixed bag of benefits and blemishes for each stock that you are considering for purchase. What's worse, the salient features for the companies reside in the stock studies covering your dining room table and spilling onto the floor. Using the Stock Comparison Guide (SCG), you can view stocks side-by-side for up to 30 criteria from your completed SSGs. With all the pertinent measures in one place, you can compare the criteria that you consider most important and decide which stock appears to be the better investment. Chapter 16 covers how to judge the criteria on the Stock Comparison Guide to pick the better stock to buy.

Keeping Your Portfolio on Track with PMG & PERT

Using the SSG and the Stock Comparison Guide diligently and with conservative judgment, you have an excellent chance of buying winners—at least four out of every five stocks you purchase—and doubling your money every five years. But, studying stocks doesn't end when you buy one. If you want to achieve the best return possible, you must manage your portfolio.

After you purchase stocks, you must follow their financial per-formance to watch for that fifth stock that turns out to be a dog. If a stock starts to show serious signs of missing your growth targets or deteriorates in other measures such as debt level or profit margins, you can sell it before the price drops too far.

Portfolio management also includes hunting for even better stocks than the ones you already own. You can improve your portfolio by replacing your existing stocks with ones that offer equal or better growth along with higher potential return.

		Abbott Lab ABT	JOHNSON & JNJ	Merck MRK	Pfizer PFE	Schering-P SGP
Stock Comparison Guide Prepared by _____ BJB, BJB, BJB, BJB, BJB Date 07/02/2002 See Chapter 15 of the *Investors Manual* for complete instructions. NAME OF COMPANY						
GROWTH COMPARISONS (From Section 1 of the NAIC Stock Selection Guide)						
X (1) Historical % of Sales Growth		7.9 %	10.5 %	19.4 %	18.1 %	11.9 %
X (2) Projected % of Sales Growth		9.0 %	10.0 %	10.0 %	11.0 %	7.0 %
(3) Historical % of Earnings Per Share Growth		11.5 %	14.0 %	13.8 %	19.0 %	16.5 %
(4) Projected % of Earnings Per Share Growth		9.0 %	11.0 %	8.0 %	13.0 %	7.0 %
MANAGEMENT COMPARISONS (From Section 2 of the NAIC Stock Selection Guide)						
(5) % Profit Margin Before Taxes (Average for last 5 Years)	(2A) Trend	25.8 DOWN	20.1 UP	26.0 DOWN	29.0 UP	30.2 UP
(6) % Earned on Equity (Average for last 5 Years)	(2B) Trend	35.9 DOWN	25.9 DOWN	41.7 UP	36.0 UP	41.4 DOWN
(7) % of Common Owned by Management		NONE	NONE	NONE	NONE	NONE

Figure 3-04: Comparing Criteria in the Stock Comparison Guide. Investor's Toolkit produced this one.

The Importance of Portfolio Management

As your portfolio grows larger, portfolio management becomes more important. In the beginning, your monthly contribution is a significant addition to your portfolio. A $50 monthly contribution is 10% of the value in a $500 portfolio. However, when your nest egg reaches $100,000, spend more time managing the $100,000 than deciding where you will add the .05% that your $50 represents.

The Portfolio Management Guide (PMG) and the reports within Portfolio Evaluation and Review Technique (PERT) help you track the performance of the stocks in your portfolio and make buy, sell and hold decisions. Chapter 19 goes into more detail on portfolio management. However, for the full treatment on NAIC's portfolio management tools, check out *NAIC's Using Portfolio Management Wisdom.*

The original purpose of NAIC's Portfolio Management Guide (PMG) was to highlight whether a stock was a buy, sell or hold at the current price. However, the PMG uses simple criteria for its recommendations—you shouldn't buy or sell on the advice of the PMG alone. But, you might want to update your stock study and give a stock the once-over to see if you agree with the PMG.

WATCHING PRICE & PE

You can also use the PMG graph to study the historical movements of the stock price and PE, and how they change in response to the company's performance and external influences.

If you use stock study software such as Stock Analyst PLUS or Investor's Toolkit Pro, *you don't have to look at the PMG for the buy, sell and hold recommendations. They appear on the Portfolio Summary and Portfolio Trend reports.*

The PERT Report

The PERT report presents a summary of SSGs in your portfolio that you can use to check for under-performing stocks or those that might warrant purchase of additional shares. The report shows the quarterly percentage change for sales, EPS, and pre-tax profit and the percentage change for the trailing 12-month EPS. If these numbers decrease significantly, you should watch that company carefully. If the deterioration continues, you can sell before the stock does too much damage to your portfolio.

The PERT Report Is Free!

You don't have to do any additional work to complete a PERT report, because all the values come from your completed SSGs. However, your SSGs have to be up-to-date for the PERT report to be useful. Other reports in the PERT collection do require additional data.

If company performance looks good, you can check valuation measures such as PE, relative value, PE as a percentage of growth rate (PEG) and percent compound annual rate of return on the PERT report. If the valuation measures look good, you might consider purchasing more of that stock with your monthly contribution.

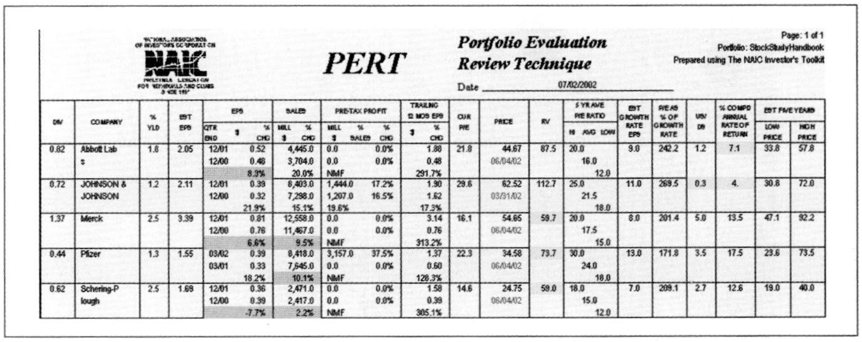

PERT — Portfolio Evaluation Review Technique
Page: 1 of 1
Portfolio: StockStudyHandbook
Prepared using The NAIC Investor's Toolkit
Date 07/02/2002

DIV	COMPANY	% YLD	EST EPS	EPS QTR END	EPS $	EPS % CHG	SALES MIL $	SALES % CHG	PRE-TAX PROFIT MIL $	PRE-TAX PROFIT % SALES	PRE-TAX PROFIT % CHG	TRAILING 12 MOS EPS $	TRAILING 12 MOS EPS % CHG	CUR P/E	PRICE	RV	5 YR AVE P/E RATIO HI AVG LOW	EST GROWTH RATE EPS	P/E AS % OF GROWTH RATE	U/D	% COMPD ANNUAL RATE OF RETURN	EST FIVE YEARS LOW PRICE	EST FIVE YEARS HIGH PRICE
0.82	Abbott Lab s	1.8	2.05	12/01 12/00	0.52 0.48	8.3%	4,445.0 3,704.0	20.0%	0.0 0.0	0.0% 0.0%	NMF	1.88 0.48	291.7%	21.8	44.67 06/04/02	87.5	20.0 16.0 12.0	9.0	242.2	1.2	7.1	33.8	57.8
0.72	JOHNSON & JOHNSON	1.2	2.11	12/01 12/00	0.39 0.32	21.9%	8,403.0 7,298.0	15.1%	1,444.0 1,207.0	17.2% 16.5%	19.6%	1.90 1.62	17.3%	29.6	62.52 03/31/02	112.7	25.0 21.5 18.0	11.0	269.5	0.3	4.	30.8	72.0
1.37	Merck	2.5	3.39	12/01 12/00	0.81 0.76	6.6%	12,558.0 11,467.0	9.5%	0.0 0.0	0.0% 0.0%	NMF	3.14 0.76	313.2%	16.1	54.65 06/04/02	59.7	20.0 17.5 15.0	8.0	201.4	5.0	13.5	47.1	92.2
0.44	Pfizer	1.3	1.55	03/02 03/01	0.39 0.33	18.2%	8,418.0 7,645.0	10.1%	3,157.0 0.0	37.5% 0.0%	NMF	1.37 0.60	128.3%	22.3	34.58 06/04/02	73.7	30.0 24.0 18.0	13.0	171.8	3.5	17.5	23.6	73.5
0.62	Schering-P lough	2.5	1.68	12/01 12/00	0.36 0.39	-7.7%	2,471.0 2,417.0	2.2%	0.0 0.0	0.0% 0.0%	NMF	1.58 0.39	305.1%	14.6	24.75 06/04/02	59.0	18.0 15.0 12.0	7.0	209.1	2.7	12.6	19.0	40.0

Figure 3-05: The PERT report summarizes your portfolio. Investor's Toolkit produced this one.

The Portfolio Trend Report

The PERT Portfolio Trend Report emphasizes bad news. It shows only the quarterly percentage changes, so they are easy to see. But, it also includes quarterly percentage changes for the previous quarter. If the company has two disappointing quarters, investigate immediately. If the deterioration looks like a long-term trend, find another company for your portfolio.

The Portfolio Trend Report also shows estimated total return if you purchased at the current price. However, the total return isn't the entire picture, so make sure to study your purchase candidates before picking one to buy. This report also shows the percentage that each company represents in your portfolio as well as the percentage of your portfolio in small, medium and large companies.

Portfolio Summary Report

The Portfolio Summary Report displays data from the Portfolio Management Guide such as: PE; relative value; the upside downside ratio; suggested buy and sell prices; and the buy, sell or hold recommendation. This report is convenient for investment club presentations. However, you should always dig a little deeper before deciding to buy or sell any stock.

INVESTOR'S TOOLKIT

Portfolio Trend Report

Page: 1 of 1
Portfolio: StockStudyHandbook
Prepared using The NAIC Investor's Toolkit

Date _____ 07/02/2002

TICKER	COMPANY	PERCENT CHANGE				EST. 5Y GROWTH	PROJECTED AVG. RET.	TOTAL RETURN	NUMBER OF SHARES	DOLLAR VALUE	% OF PORTFOLIO	PMGuide RECOM.
		QTR. SALES	QTR. PTP	QTR. EPS	12 Mo. EPS							
ABT	Abbott Labs	20.0%	NAN	8.33%	291.67%	9.0%	3.3%	7.8%	0	0.0	0.0%	
		NAN	NAN	NAN	NAN					44.67 06/04/02		
JNJ	JOHNSON & JOHNSON	15.1%	19.6%	21.88%	17.26%	11.0%	1.4%	5.3%	0	0.0	0.0%	
		10.8%	14.9%	16.26%	15.82%					62.52 03/31/02		
MRK	Merck	9.5%	NAN	6.58%	313.16%	8.0%	11.4%	14.3%	0	0.0	0.0%	Buy
		NAN	NAN	NAN	NAN					54.65 06/04/02		
PFE	Pfizer	10.1%	NAN	18.18%	128.33%	13.0%	13.8%	19.1%	0	0.0	0.0%	Buy
		11.4%	NAN	25.93%	385.19%					34.58 06/04/02		
SGP	Schering-Plough	2.2%	NAN	-7.69%	305.13%	7.0%	9.1%	13.1%	0	0.0	0.0%	
		NAN	NAN	NAN	NAN					24.75 06/04/02		

Figure 3-06: The PERT Trend Report previews company outlook.

PERT Worksheet A

The PERT Worksheet A (PERT-A) is a great tool for observing trends in performance—one company at a time. This worksheet shows data and percentage changes for quarterly and trailing 12-month sales, EPS and pre-tax profit. You get an early warning of deterioration. When pre-tax profit margins drop, EPS often follows. By watching these trends on PERT-A, you might be able to sell a stock before its declining performance appears in the stock price.

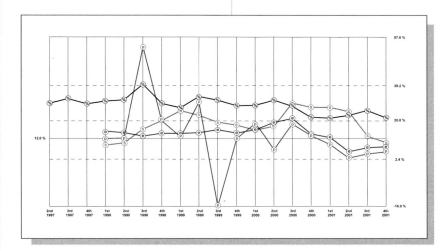

Figure 3-07: PERT-A shows quarterly trends. Investor's Toolkit produced this one.

USING PERT-A FOR BUYING

The graph in PERT-A is also useful for forecasting future growth rates for your SSG. Of course, you need lots of quarterly data before you even decide to buy the stock, but electronic data makes your data entry a breeze.

On the other hand, if a stock price drops or just sits in one place, you can check to see if the company's fundamentals are still good. If they are, you don't have to worry. In fact, that might be your signal to buy more.

PERT Worksheet B

The PERT Worksheet B (PERT-B) is a summary of fundamentals for a company, formatted much like Section 3 of the SSG. It shows prices, high and low PE ratios, five-year average PE ratios, dividends, percentage payout and high yield for the past ten years. This worksheet highlights trends in PEs; the five-year average PE column might hint at a "normalized" PE—the PE that the company returns to from its forays into high and low PE territory.

SUMMARY

The Stock Check List is the place to start studying stocks, but you should strive to graduate to the Stock Selection Guide for the best stock study results. The Stock Comparison Guide helps you choose between several candidate stocks.

The PERT reports help you decide which companies to sell or hold, and when to buy more. The PERT Worksheet A not only helps you manage your portfolio, but can point out growth trends that help you to better forecast growth rates for your SSGs.

CHAPTER FOUR:

The Math Isn't Hard

You Can Do This!

Math isn't hard. Numbers in a calculation behave the same way each time, which is more than you can say about teenagers or romantic partners. So, don't make excuses about being a creative type or how long it's been since you took math in school. Just read this chapter — and practice.

Just as an earthmoving truck might not seem extraordinary until you see it relative to a man whose head reaches halfway up its tire, financial numbers by themselves aren't that informative. But by comparing different financial figures for a company, or by comparing the same financials between different companies, you can determine whether the company is performing well or poorly.

Fractions

Playing Percentages

Averages

Rounding Numbers Is OK

How Compounding Works

Fractions

Fractions are as familiar as a slice of apple pie. You might cut a pie into eighths (1/8)—or quarters (1/4), if you like pie a lot. In the financial world, a fraction goes by the name of ratio. A ratio is a fraction—one number divided by another number. In investing, a ratio typically appears as a decimal number. Don't let that intimidate you; 1/2 is the same as .5.

The current ratio is one example of a ratio used to evaluate a company's financial strength.

It's a company's current assets divided by its current liabilities. The current ratio measures whether the company has the capability to meet short term financial obligations. If the current ratio is too low, the company may not be able to pay short term creditors, whereas a very high current ratio might mean that the company has too much money in accounts receivable and/or inventories.

To calculate a ratio, you simply divide one number by another. The formula for current ratio is:

$$\text{Current ratio} = \frac{\text{Current Assests}}{\text{Current Liabilities}}$$

If a company's current assets are $25 million and current liabilities are $14.75 million, the calculation for current ratio is:

$$\text{Current ratio} = \frac{25,000,000}{14,750,000} = 1.6949$$

what is the ideal ratio? Is it "1"?

The Price/Earnings (PE) ratio is probably the ratio you will use the most. It is the ratio of stock price divided by earnings per share. You will learn more than you ever thought you wanted to know about a PE ratio throughout this book. For now, it's good enough to understand how to calculate it. If a stock price is $28.75, and the company's EPS for the last four quarters is $1.25, you calculate the PE ratio as follows:

$$\text{PE ratio} = \frac{\$28.75}{\$1.25} = 23$$

You'll learn about other ratios such as the quick ratio, the acid test and inventory turnover as you read this handbook.

trailing PE = Current P/E
Research: Is there a difference?

Playing Percentages

The word percent originates from the Latin per centum, meaning "for one hundred." It represents how many items there are for every one hundred counted. A percentage is just a different way of displaying a ratio—with that pesky decimal point denoting parts of 100. For example, 25 percent means that 25 items out of every one hundred stand up to be counted. You can present that ratio in several ways:

As a fraction: $\dfrac{25}{100}$

As a decimal ratio: *.25*

As a percentage: *25%*

If the sales today are lower than the sales in the past, the dollar change will be negative. The calculation for the change in sales is the same whether sales are increasing or decreasing.

SHOWING INCREASES OR DECREASES AS A PERCENTAGE

If a company's sales increase by $100,000, is that good? Well, it's fabulous, if the company's sales were only $100,000 the year before, but it's cause for concern if the previous year's revenues were $35 billion. That's why so many financial measures appear as percentages. Ratios and percentages show the relative size of the numbers you're comparing. The Stock Check List calculates the percentage increase in sales over the past five years. As the example below shows, the dollar increase in sales over the past five years doesn't tell you much until you compare that increase to the amount of sales. There are a few things to remember when you calculate a percentage change in a company's financial numbers. At the root, you want to know how company financials have changed over time so you can forecast where the company is heading in the future. Let's calculate the percentage increase in sales, when sales five years ago were $12,594 million and sales today are $32,259.

1. To see the change since some point in the past, subtract the value in the past from the present value. *(See Success Tip to the left)*

Dollar change in Sales =	Present Sales - Sales five years ago	
	$32,259m - $12,594m =	$19,665m

2. Compare the dollar change to the sales in the past. Don't forget to multiply by 100 to calculate a percentage.

%Change in Sales =	$\dfrac{\text{Present Sales - Past Sales}}{\text{Past Sales}}$	=	$\dfrac{19.665}{12,594}$
=	19.665÷12,594	=	1.561
	1.561 X 100	=	156.1%

CALCULATING PERCENTAGES

If you already have a number that you want to turn into a percentage, just multiply it by 100. For example: .2562 X 100 = 25.62 %.

If you want to express a ratio as a percentage, calculate the ratio first, then multiply by 100. Profit margins usually show up as percentages. The net profit margin is the net profit of the company divided by sales. If a company's sales are $29,574 million and net profit is $6,495 million, the calculation is:

Net Profit Margin =	$\dfrac{\text{Net Profit}}{\text{Sales}}$	=	$\dfrac{6,495 \text{ million}}{29,574 \text{ million}}$	=	.2196 X 100	=	21.96%

Averages

Calculating the PEs for each month over the last five years might make your head hurt. But, the five-year average PE is one number that summarizes where the PE has been over the entire period. An average is halfway between the high and low values in the set.

Calculating an Average

To calculate an average, you add up the figures you have, and then divide the result by how many different figures you added.

For example, you can calculate the five-year average high PE using the high PE for each of the past five years.

Calculating a Weighted Average

There are times when some numbers are more important than others. For example, when you calculate an average PE, you might want to emphasize the PEs from more recent years, so that the average tends to reflect recent performance more than past performance. This method works whether the PEs are ascending or descending. When you use a weighted average to compute an average PE, make sure your weighting provides a conservative result.

You weight an average by multiplying each value in the average by a different weighting factor. The numbers multiplied by larger factors have more effect on the average.

Year	High PE	Calculation
1997	33.3	
1998	51.2	
1999	44.3	
2000	40.7	
2001	31.8	
Total PE =	201.3	Add up the values
Number of values	5	
Average	201.3 / 5	Divide the total by the number of values
Average	= 40.26	

Success Tip!

If you try dividing a weighted total by the number of values in the equation, your answer won't even be close to the numbers you're averaging. The weighting factors inflate the total Instead of dividing by the number of values in the average, you divide the total by the sum of the weighting factors.

Year	Average High PE	Weighting	Weighted High PE
1997	18	1	18
1998	20	2	40
1999	22	3	66
2000	23	4	92
2001	26	5	130
Total PE =	109	346	
Number of values	5	15	15
Average	109 / 5		346 / 15
	= 21.8		23

Rounding Numbers Is OK

Some people become enamored with the accuracy of computers beyond all reason or practicality. It's a bit like your friend with the calculator at a restaurant informing everyone at lunch that they owe 25 dollars and 27 and 1/2 cents. The amount might be accurate, but no one is going to fork over exactly that amount.

In stock studies, enthusiastic beginners forecast growth rates to tenths of a percent or press calculator buttons forever to figure a PE ratio to three decimal points. To be frank, the lazy beginner who stops at a whole number is better off. Whole numbers are easier to work with and your stock study won't suffer.

SPENDING TIME WHERE IT PAYS OFF

Spending time calculating ratios to science-like accuracy won't make you any more money in your investments. But, searching for new stocks to study, conducting research to support your judgment and managing your portfolio can dramatically improve your portfolio's performance.

Forecasting growth rates is difficult even when you do your homework. What makes you think that you can infallibly predict that Stanley Sprockets will grow at 12.2 percent? You can't. Sure, you might opt for 12.5 percent because 13 percent seems too high and 12 percent seems too low. Even then, why not apply an extra margin for error by rounding your growth estimate down to the next lowest whole number?

How Compounding Works

One of the fundamental NAIC principles is to reinvest all dividends, earnings and interest. Even though dividend amounts can look pretty small, they can boost your portfolio performance like nobody's business. When you buy more shares of stock with your dividends, you earn more money when stock prices go up. In addition, the next time the company issues a dividend, you receive more dividend dollars because you own more shares.

If you invested $100 in the S&P's 500-stock index in 1926 and spent all the dividends you received, your portfolio would have been worth $10,350 by the end of 2000. By reinvesting your dividends, you'd end up with $258,652! All this comes from reinvesting the few dollars of dividends you receive every quarter. Companies do the same sort of thing when they reinvest earnings into the company. If the company grows at 15 percent, reinvesting earnings provides even more fuel for growth.

The company can put previous years' assets and reinvested earnings to work, producing more earnings. The example below shows how earnings increase through compounding.

Year	EPS	Growth Rate	Additional EPS
0	$1.20	15%	$1.20 X .15 = $.18
1	$1.38	15%	$1.38 X .15 = $.21
2	$1.59	15%	$1.59 X .15 = $.24
3	$1.83	15%	$1.83 X .15 = $.27
4	$2.10	15%	$2.10 X .15 = $.31
5	$2.41		

COMPOUNDING RESULTS

CHAPTER FIVE

The More You Know a C

Doing Your Homework

As an NAIC investor, your relationship with a stock can last a long time. You want to know a stock's idiosyncrasies before you make that kind of commitment. Financial data might feed your NAIC stock study forms, but understanding the characteristics and outlook for a company fuels your forecasts for the future. You can dig up most of the information you need from home if you connect to the Internet. But, if you still aren't plugged in and wired up, data and analysts' reports are as close as your local library.

Getting to Know a Company

Where to Find Financial Data

Composition of a Value Line Sheet

Whether you attack your studies from the top down or the bottom up, stock analysis combines investigation into quantitative and qualitative attributes. You need qualitative information to understand the problems and potential that a company possesses. Only then can you tell whether past performance could continue in the future. But, you need a quantitative view of the financial numbers to really digest whether the past performance is enough to meet your objectives.

Getting to Know a Company

You can see some signs of consistency by looking at the NAIC stock study forms. Predictability in sales and EPS growth, as well as consistently increasing profit margins and return on equity indicate quality in a company—but they rely on quantitative analysis, the fundamental financial measures of a company. There's more to qualitative analysis—a company's strategies for growth, trends in the industry, brand strength and others. The more you learn about these not so quantifiable aspects, the better your forecasts for the future will be.

A Process for Qualitative Analysis

Novice investors might be confused, even frightened, by page after page of financial results. How do you make heads or tails of all those numbers? Fortunately, those numbers start to make sense when you understand the business strategies and operations that produce them.

A company's annual report and 10-K (a lengthy form filed with the Securities and Exchange Commission) are both good places to start to find out about its approach to business. See Chapter 22 to learn more about the sections of an annual report. The Value Line page for a company also includes a brief summary of elements that can influence a company's performance. You can also search for articles about a company in many locations— your local library probably has financial magazines such as *Business Week, Fortune, Barron's, Forbes, Smart Money, Kiplinger's Personal Finance* and others. If you use the Internet, you can search for analysts' reports, news stories and in-depth articles. Some of the material is available at no charge, whereas other reports might come with a price tag.

NAIC's Better Investing magazine profiles at least two stocks in each issue—one in the "Stock to Study", the second in the "Undervalued Feature". You can glean a wealth of information about a company or an industry from these monthly features.

Sources of Growth

How does a company produce its growth? Some strategies for growth can continue for decades, whereas others have their limits. Some companies grow by pumping out new products and services. When executed well, this strategy is the longest lived and could continue for years.

Companies can also grow by increasing profit margins, building more stores, selling more at each store (often called same store sales), increasing market share or acquiring other companies. Increasing profit margins is a desirable approach but it can only last so long. No matter how consistently a company increases its profit margins, a company can't exceed a 100 percent profit margin—it would keep more money than it makes! Similarly, a company can only build so many stores. After a point, a company's stores would merely compete with each other. Increasing sales at each store can last longer, as long as the company introduces more products or takes sales away from its competition.

Studying Strategies & Tactics

- Companies use many approaches to achieve their goals. Some work. Others don't. Use your research to identify the strategies and tactics a company uses, and to analyze the success of those gambits. Does it acquire other companies, assimilate them into the fold, and cut costs by combining duplicate functions?

- If a business unit or acquisition doesn't work out, does the company divest the unit to keep the company performance healthy?

- Is it struggling with increasing costs or has it found ways to reduce them, thereby improving profit margins?

- Does it sell to a broad and diversified base of customers or depend on one or two major clients?

- Does it possess strong brand recognition and aggressively fund R&D (research & development) to continually develop new products, or does it only have one or two in its stable?

- Are its products facing obsolescence or expiration of patent protection?

INTEREST RATES & STOCKS

Dropping interest rates tend to push stock prices higher in part because lower interest rates stimulate business. In addition, lower interest rates on bonds, certificates of deposit and other interest-paying investments make the higher returns of stocks more attractive.

The Big Picture

You should also review the influences from outside a company: the economy, competition, demographic trends, industry trends, interest rates, foreign exchange rates, technology, natural disasters and war. The economy and trends within an industry are powerful influences on a company. Companies can rise with the tide of a strong economy or sink when the economy inevitably wanes.

Demographic or industry trends can also rise and fall with the economic tide. As the population in the United States ages, the market for healthcare products and services grows, helping most companies in that industry. Tight family budgets caused by a bad economy slow sales of big-ticket items such as cars and increases sales of low-cost alternatives in almost every other industry. Families on the go might opt for convenience foods or fast-food restaurants instead of eating at an upscale gourmet restaurant.

The Value Line industry page and Standard and Poor's (S&P) Industry Surveys both briefly describe opportunities and threats faced by companies within an industry. If you use the Internet, you can search for an industry associationWeb site. For example, a search for pharmaceutical industry association returned over 300,000 possibilities, but one of the first ones listed is the Pharmaceutical America Association (www.phrma.org). One of the links on this site's home page connects you to a page where you can download the 2002 industry profile. This document includes discussion on research and development, intellectual property and patent issues, cost controls on pharmaceutical, and present and future technology.

Where to Find Financial Data

Companies that sell shares to the public must file financial reports with the Securities and Exchange Commission (SEC). And, from that filing, a torrent of financial data flows to financial analysis firms, mutual funds, publications, Web sites, as well as directly to individual investors. The organizations that provide data might pass it on to investors as is. Many provide added value by processing the data in some way to make the true picture of a company's performance stand out. This data manipulation leads to differences between the numbers in an annual or quarterly report and other data sources such as S&P, Value Line and others.

You can derive data from annual reports or 10-Ks. Although companies must report data in a standard way, there is enough variety in the categories used that you'll end up scratching your head. Consistently using data from one data provider, such as Value Line, S&P or Multex Investor, makes your job much simpler, because the data provider presents each company's figures in a more standardized way.

The Different Faces of Data

Data appears in a variety of forms and each of these forms has a name. "As reported" means data is just as the company reported it. "Restated" means that the data is modified to reflect performance if a company had operated in its current configuration. For example, when two companies merge, the restated data includes a combination of the historical data from both companies. "Standardized" data presents income and expenses in standard categories so that you can easily compare the performance of different companies. "Normalized" data excludes gains or losses from non-recurring events.

Value Line normalizes its data, and sometimes provides restated results. The footnotes at the bottom of the Value Line page include the description of changes it makes to the data. Multex Investor delivers restated data. S&P provides data in different formats, depending on the product. The S&P tear sheets—paper reports—generally present as reported data. However, S&P recently added its "core earning" data, a "normalized" approach. S&P Compustat electronic data files provide standardized data. S&P is the source of data for the download-able data available through NAIC's Online Premium Services (OPS).

Paper or Digital?

Most libraries have subscriptions to Value Line and S&P stock reports, and may have others such as Hoover's. If you are producing stock studies by hand, paper reports are your only answer. Of course, you can save a trip to the library by downloading these paper reports from a Web site. For a fee, you can subscribe to Value Line and download their reports, a convenient way to do it.

S&P (www.stockinfo.standard-poor.com/sr.htm) sells their reports online for a small fee. Some brokerages offer these reports at no charge. For example, Scott Trade provides S&P reports to all clients, whereas Schwab provides S&P, First Call, Market Guide and other reports at no charge to Schwab Signature service clients ($100,000 in assets or $10,000 in assets and 12 commissionable trades a year).

Importing Data

Downloading paper-based reports is fine, but if you use one of the NAIC computer programs, importing data directly into your software has many advantages. Electronic data is usually updated frequently, so there is less lag between your study date and the data you use. For example, OPS data is updated daily, so quarterly data appears as soon as it is available.

When you import data, you don't waste any time on data entry and you don't have to worry about typographical mistakes. You also avoid those painful calculator sessions. For example, pre-tax profit on sales, return on equity and quarterly performance all appear instantaneously. What's more, after you import the data, it's available to every NAIC form that is available in your software program: Stock Check List, Stock Selection Guide, Stock Comparison Guide, Portfolio Management Guide, and all the PERT reports and graphs.

(See Success Tip)

Composition of a Value Line Sheet

Many NAIC investors use Value Line for historical information and forecasts. Value Line normalizes its data, which means removing one-time events such as write-offs of large expenditures or additional income from selling a business unit. Value Line eliminates these non-recurring events because they affect performance, but probably won't reoccur.

(See Success Tip)

A Value Line page packs a lot of punch. One page includes most of the data you need to complete a Stock Check List or Stock Selection Guide and at the same time expresses some opinions about the company's outlook. The following pages describe the data and its location on the Value Line sheet. The number for each item corresponds to numbers in the margin on the Pfizer Value Line Sheet in this chapter.

As long as obtaining data is easy, make sure you use your data properly. Add the source and date for your data to the stock study form. If you study with others, use the same data sources for all your studies, so differences in stock studies are due only to differences in judgment. Don't combine data from different sources in a single stock study, unless you understand the numbers thoroughly and can make the necessary adjustments.

Most libraries have a subscription to Value Line in their reference section, although they might limit the amount of time that someone can use it during peak periods. Visit the library in off hours to do your research or make copies of the sheets for the companies you are studying to review at your leisure.

Across the Top

This section identifies the data available across the top of the Value Line sheet and within the price graph.

1. Company Name: Depending on its length, Value Line displays the full or abbreviated company name. Add the company name to identify each NAIC stock study form.

2. Stock Exchange: The stock exchange where the company stock is listed—NYSE for the New York stock exchange, NDQ for NASDAQ and ASE for the American Stock Exchange. Look for a company under this exchange listing if you look up prices in the newspaper.

3. Ticker Symbol: The ticker symbol is an abbreviation assigned to each company to uniquely identify them in the newspaper, on Web sites or on business news TV programs. Add the ticker to a stock study form as a reference when you want to look up a quote.

4. Recent Price and PE: The recent price is as of just before the publication of that issue of Value Line, so the price and PEs are not up to date. Look up the current price for the stock in the newspaper or on the Internet.

5. Price Range for the Past Ten Years: The high and low prices for each of the past 10 calendar years appear near the top of the sheet. The sheet shows

prices only for years that the company has been public (traded on an exchange) if less than 10 years. Value Line draws dashed horizontal lines on the right side of the price graph to indicate their projection price range for the next three to five years. Use the historical prices to complete the price table of the Stock Check List or Section 3 of the SSG.

6. Stock Splits: The price graph includes text with arrows to indicate when the company issued a stock split and the ratio for the split.

7. Value Line Rankings: Timeliness is Value Line's ranking for probable performance for the next 12 months relative to the

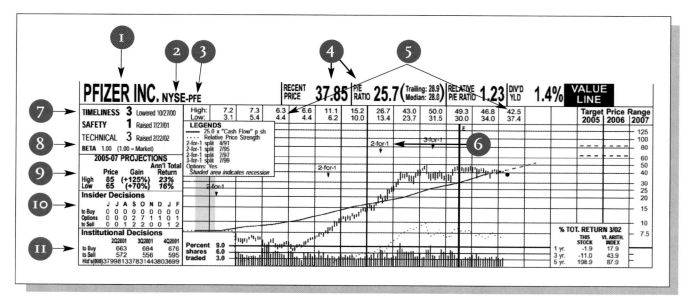

Figure 5-01: The top of the Value Line page

entire stock market (One is most timely, five least timely.) Safety is the potential risk associated with a stock, calculated by averaging the Price Stability Index and the Financial Strength Rating. One is the safest, whereas five is the riskiest. Technical is Value Line's ranking of the estimated stock price performance over the next three-to-six months (One is best, five is worst.) For long-term investors, Timeliness and Technical rankings aren't significant factors in your decisions, although you might use them in a decision to add to your holdings.

8. **Beta:** Beta is a measure of the affect of price fluctuations in the NYSE Composite Index on a company's stock price. A beta of 1.50 indicates that a stock might rise or fall 50 percent more than the NYSE Composite Index.

9. **2005-07 Projections:** These are Value Line's projections of the potential range of high prices for a stock. Value Line does not include a projection for worst-case prices. Don't use these prices for forecasts on your Stock Check List or SSG, although you could use them as a sanity check for your forecasted prices.

10. **Insider Decisions:** This table shows purchases, exercising options or selling of stock by company officers and directors for each month of the year. Buying usually indicates

confidence in the stock by the people who should know, whereas selling can result from many situations.

11. **Institutional Decisions:** This table shows purchases and sales by institutions such as pension plans or mutual funds. The number on the right in the last row shows the current number of shares owned by institutions in thousands. Use this number to calculate the percentage ownership by institutions on the SSG, as demonstrated in Chapter 7.

The Data Grid

The tabular section in the middle of the Value Line sheet provides data for the past 10 years for several financial numbers and for 16 years for others. It also includes forecasts for the next two years and for three-to-five years in the future. This section describes only a subset of the numbers in this section.

12. **Earnings per sh:** Earnings per share are net profit after taxes divided by the weighted average number of outstanding shares. Use these values to complete Section 2 of the Stock Check List and Sections 1 and 3 of the SSG.

13. **Div'ds Decl'd per sh:** This abbreviation represents dividends declared per share. The Board of Directors authorizes these dividends per common share to be paid during a company's fiscal year.

14. **Book Value per sh:** Book value per share is the shareholders' equity for a company divided by the number of shares outstanding.

15. **Commons Shs Outst'g:** Common shares outstanding represent the number of common shares owned by shareholders. Value Line shows the average number of shares outstanding during the year. If you prefer to use the most recent number of shares, you can obtain that number from company quarterly reports or Web sites.

16. **Sales:** Sales include all revenue from services or products sold by a company. Depending on the industry, Value Line might show other titles. For example, bank stocks might show Interest Income or Loan Income. Use sales to complete Section 1 of the Stock Check List or the SSG.

17. **Operating Margin:** Operating margin represents a profit percentage on sales, based on the difference between income from goods sold and the cost of making and selling those goods. It is not the same as the pre-tax profit on sales used in Section 2 of the SSG.

18. **Net Profit:** Net profit is income that remains after subtracting all expenses and taxes. Use net profit to calculate pre-tax profit manually for Section 2 of the SSG.

19. **Income Tax Rate:** The combined rate for federal, foreign and state income taxes reported to shareholders on pre-tax profit. Use this tax rate in your pre-tax profit calculation in Section 2 of the SSG.

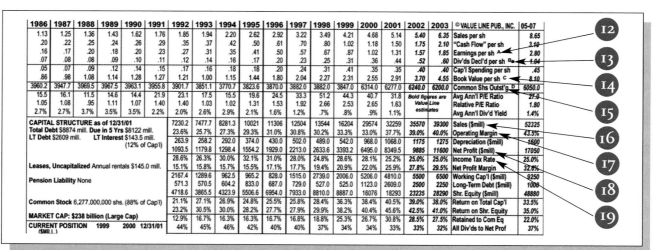

Figure 5-02: The data grid with annual values

The Text at the Bottom Edge of the Value Line Sheet

The lower right quadrant of the Value Line sheet includes a description of the business and an opinion from the Value Line analyst who covers the company.

20. **Business:** This section summarizes the business and any significant shareholders. It includes the company's address, telephone numbers and Web site. The percentage ownership by insiders (officers and directors) also appears toward the end of this section.

21. **Analyst's Opinion:** One analyst provides an opinion of the company's current situation and potential performance in the future. The date of the report appears at the bottom right. Remember, this is only one analyst's opinion. You should research the company to develop your own thoughts.

20

BUSINESS: Pfizer Inc. is a major producer of pharmaceuticals, hospital products, consumer products, and animal health lines. Important product names include, *Norvasc* (cardiovascular); *Zoloft* (antidepressant); *Zithromax* (antibiotic); *Lipitor* (cholesterol); *Aricept* (Alzheimer's); *Cardura* (cardiovascular); *Diflucan* (antifungal); *Zyrtec* (antihistamine); *Viagra* (impotence); *Celebrex* (rheumatoid arthritis and osteoarthritis). Int'l business, 38% of sales; R&D, 15.0%. '01 depreciation rate: 6.9%. Estimated plant age: 16 yrs. Has about 90,000 employees, 147,000 stockholders. Directors/Officers own less than 1% of stock (3/02 proxy). Chairman & Chief Executive Officer: Henry McKinnell. Inc.: Delaware. Address: 235 East 42nd Street, New York, NY 10017. Tel.: 212-573-2323.

Pfizer reported solid first-quarter results . . . Revenues advanced 11% (13% on a constant currency basis), year over year, driven by healthy gains in *Lipitor* (up 26%, to $1.9 billion), *Zoloft* (22%, $740 million), and *Neurontin* (50%, $568 million). U.S. pharmaceutical sales were up 15% (to $4.6 billion), while foreign sales increased 13%, in local currencies. Per-share profits, meantime, surged 18%, as operating margins continued to benefit from both the integration of Warner-Lambert (acquired in 2000) and an improving sales mix. **. . . but the company also lowered investors' expectations for the June period.** It indicated that earnings growth in the current quarter would be in the single digits, due both to difficult year-over-year expense comparisons and to heavy costs associated with new-product launches and R&D activities. Reflecting Wall Street's excessive (in our opinion) focus on the short term, Pfizer stock has retreated in the aftermath of the lowered guidance. **We still expect a 20% bottom-line gain for 2002 and for profits to compound at a 15%-plus rate in the subsequent 3 to 5 years.** Importantly, the huge drug-maker's key products continue to perform in line with expectations, and there are no signs that this is going to change anytime soon. Indeed, management is maintaining its $1.56-to-$1.60-a-share earnings guidance for the full year, indicating that second-half results would be very strong. We would note, however, that we have prudently trimmed three pennies from our estimate (to $1.57), moving closer to the low end of the range. Our initial share-net figure for 2003 is $1.85, which would represent an 18% year-to-year advance. Pfizer spends more than $5 billion annually on research and development, and will probably add about 15 new products to its already formidable drug portfolio by 2005-2007, including perhaps five this year. **This issue is one of our top drug-sector picks for the long haul.** Reflecting anxieties at the market, industry, and company-specific levels, Pfizer stock is now selling at valuations seldom seen in many years. Indeed, our view is that Wall Street's overreaction to one relatively poor quarter has provided investors with their best entry point in a long time.

George Rho   *April 26, 2002*

21

Figure 5-03: Seeing what an analyst has to say.

23 **22**

(A) Based on average shares outstanding. Excl. non-rec. gains (losses): '91, (10¢); '92, (14¢); '93, (27¢); '98, 18¢; '99, (5¢); '00, (38¢). Next eqs. report due late July. (B) Next div'd	meeting about June 21. Next ex date about May 5. Div'd payment dates: About Mar. 10, June 10, Sept. 10, Dec. 10.■ Div'd reinvestment plan available. (C) Incl. intangibles. In	'01: $1722 mill., 27¢/sh. (D) In mill., adj'd for stock splits. (E) Warner-Lambert, acquired 6/00, is included in historical data starting in 2000's first quarter.	Company's Financial Strength A++ Stock's Price Stability 75 Price Growth Persistence 95 Earnings Predictability 100

Figure 5-04: The bottom edge of the Value Line sheet.

22. **Value Line's Indexes:** Financial Strength is Value Line's measure of the strength of a company's financial position, ranging from a high of A++ to a low of C in nine steps. Stock's Price Stability is Value Line's rating of the stock's price volatility and sensitivity to the market. 100 indicates extremely stable, whereas 5 is extremely volatile. Price Growth Persistence is Value Line's rating of a stock's persistence in price growth compared to the average stock. Most persistent is 100 and least persistent is 5. Earnings Predictability rates the stability of historic year-to-year comparisons of earnings with most consistent equal to 100 and least consistent 5.

23. **Footnotes:** Footnotes explain details such as how earnings are reported, changes made in normalizing the data, or when dividends are paid at the end of the Fiscal Year.

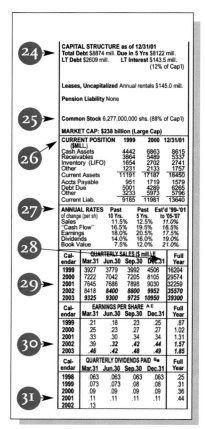

The Boxes on the Left Side

24. **Total Debt:** Total debt is the sum of long-term debt and debt due shown in the Current Position table. The percentage figure (% of Cap'l) represents the percentage of debt in the capital structure of the company.

25. **Common Stock:** Common Stock is the number of shares outstanding at the time of the Value Line report.

26. **Current Position:** This is a quick look at the company's current balance sheet assets and liabilities.

27. **Annual Rates:** The past five-year and 10-year growth rates, and the Value Line analyst's projected rates of growth for sales, cash flow, earnings, dividends and book value.

28. **Fiscal Year End:** This is the date on which a company's fiscal year ends. Companies often select a fiscal year that differs from the calendar year to better match the company's annual business cycle to its reporting periods.

29. **Quarterly Sales:** Quarterly sales are the sales for one fiscal quarter.

30. **Earnings Per Share:** Earnings per share are the quarterly earnings on a per share basis.

SuccessTip!

You can use the values from the last four quarters in this section instead of the EPS for the most recent fiscal year. If you study a stock late in its fiscal year or the company grows quickly, the last four quarters gives you a more realistic view of the company's earnings.

31. **Quarterly Dividends Paid:** The actual dividends paid quarterly. The annual dividend in this section might not equal the annual dividend in the data grid, because the quarterly dividends are for the fiscal year, whereas the data grid shows dividends for the calendar year.

Now that you know where to dig up data, it's time to start applying that information to stock studies. Turn to the next chapter if you want to start with the Stock Check List. If you want to jump right in to the Stock Selection Guide, go to Chapter 7.

CHAPTER SIX:

Jumping In with the

Your Stock Study Training Wheels

Do math, financial terms, research and reading the business section of the paper leave you a little breathless? Does the fear of losing money through investment mistakes make you swoon? You can take a deep breath. The Stock Check List is a gentle introduction to the techniques NAIC uses to select stocks. Its conservative approach helps you pick winners with analysis that a beginner can follow.

Simply look up a few financial numbers, make a few easy calculations, gather a little dirt on the company's business, and you're ready to decide whether the company is a prospect for purchase.

Calculating the Sales & Earning per Share Growth

Forecasting the Company's Future Growth

What About the Stock Price?

Stock Check List

The Stock Check List and the Stock Selection Guide are both stock study tools. Why two? NAIC teaches people how to invest and some folks like to ease into finances as they would a cold swimming pool. The Stock Check List doesn't go into as much detail as the Stock Selection Guide. There's less data to find, fewer calculations and less judgment to apply. You can begin investing while you learn the concepts at your own pace.

However, the Stock Check List is too simplistic to be your ultimate stock study tool of choice. The Stock Selection Guide offers a much more thorough analysis of a stock. You should press on to the Stock Selection Guide when you start to get comfortable with the Stock Check List. Or, if you're comfortable with math and learning new concepts, you might skip this chapter and start with the Stock Selection Guide.

Calculating the Sales & Earnings per Share Growth

Sales make things happen in a company. They pay for supplies, salaries and all the other expenses a company racks up. The money left over after covering costs can end up as dividends paid to shareholders or earnings reinvested in the

company to crank out even more growth. Either way, shareholders like to see sales and earnings per share increasing, because that bodes well for more growth, higher stock price and higher dividends.

The Stock Check List gauges how fast the company has grown over a recent five-year period. It uses the average of the most recent two years of sales compared to the average of sales five and six years earlier to smooth out dips or peaks, so your analysis doesn't paint an overly optimistic or pessimistic picture. The computations in Section 1 of the Stock Check List determine the percentage increase in sales over the five-year period. Then, you use the conversion table to find the compound annual sales growth rate.

Calculating Sales Growth

Calculations on the Stock Check List are reminiscent of tax returns. The directions on the form lead you through the steps. The big difference is that these calculations can make you money.

The instructions in this chapter are for completing a Stock Check List by hand. The example shown is the output from the Stock Check List in the Investor's Toolkit software package. The paper form and the software output look almost identical, so you can follow along in the chapter as you complete the steps on a paper Check List.

PFIZER INC. NYSE-PFE

RECENT PRICE	37.85	
P/E RATIO	25.7 (Trailing: 28.9 / Median: 28.0)	
RELATIVE P/E RATIO	1.23	
DIV'D YLD	1.4%	

VALUE LINE

TIMELINESS **3** Lowered 10/27/00
SAFETY **1** Raised 7/27/01
TECHNICAL **3** Raised 2/22/02
BETA 1.00 (1.00 = Market)

| High: | 7.2 | 7.3 | 6.3 | 6.6 | 11.1 | 15.2 | 26.7 | 43.0 | 50.0 | 49.3 | 46.8 | 42.5 |
| Low: | 3.1 | 5.4 | 4.4 | 4.4 | 6.2 | 10.0 | 13.4 | 23.7 | 31.5 | 30.0 | 34.0 | 37.4 |

Target Price Range 2005 2006 2007

LEGENDS
— 25.0 x"Cash Flow"p sh
.... Relative Price Strength
2-for-1 split 4/91
2-for-1 split 7/95
2-for-1 split 7/97
3-for-1 split 7/99
Options: Yes
Shaded area indicates recession

2005-07 PROJECTIONS

	Price	Gain	Ann'l Total Return
High	85	(+125%)	23%
Low	65	(+70%)	16%

Insider Decisions

	J	J	A	S	O	N	D	J	F
to Buy	0	0	0	0	0	0	0	0	0
Options	0	0	0	2	7	1	1	0	1
to Sell	0	0	1	2	2	0	0	1	2

Institutional Decisions

	2Q2001	3Q2001	4Q2001
to Buy	663	684	676
to Sell	572	556	595
Hld's(000)	3799813	3783144	3803699

| Percent shares traded | 9.0 / 6.0 / 3.0 |

% TOT. RETURN 3/02

	THIS STOCK	VL ARITH. INDEX
1 yr.	-1.9	17.9
3 yr.	-11.0	43.9
5 yr.	198.9	87.9

© VALUE LINE PUB., INC. 05-07

1986	1987	1988	1989	1990	1991	1992	1993	1994	1995	1996	1997	1998	1999	2000	2001	2002	2003		
1.13	1.25	1.36	1.43	1.62	1.76	1.85	1.94	2.20	2.62	2.92	3.22	3.49	4.21	4.68	5.14	5.40	6.35	Sales per sh	8.65
.20	.22	.25	.24	.26	.29	.35	.37	.42	.50	.61	.70	.80	1.02	1.18	1.50	1.75	2.10	"Cash Flow" per sh	3.10
.16	.17	.20	.18	.20	.23	.27	.31	.35	.41	.50	.57	.67	.87	1.02	1.31	1.57	1.85	Earnings per sh A	2.80
.07	.08	.08	.09	.10	.11	.12	.14	.16	.17	.20	.23	.25	.31	.36	.44	.52	.60	Div'ds Decl'd per sh B■	1.04
.05	.07	.09	.12	.14	.15	.17	.16	.18	.18	.20	.24	.31	.41	.35	.35	.40	.40	Cap'l Spending per sh	.45
.86	.98	1.08	1.14	1.28	1.27	1.21	1.00	1.15	1.44	1.80	2.04	2.27	2.31	2.55	2.91	3.70	4.55	Book Value per sh C	8.10
3960.2	3947.7	3969.5	3967.5	3963.1	3955.8	3901.7	3851.1	3770.7	3823.6	3870.0	3882.0	3882.0	3847.0	6314.0	6277.0	6240.0	6200.0	Common Shs Outst'g D	6050.0
15.5	16.1	11.5	14.6	14.4	21.9	23.1	17.5	15.5	19.6	24.5	33.3	51.2	44.3	40.7	31.8	Bold figures are Value Line estimates		Avg Ann'l P/E Ratio	27.0
1.05	1.08	.95	1.11	1.07	1.40	1.40	1.03	1.02	1.31	1.53	1.92	2.66	2.53	2.65	1.63			Relative P/E Ratio	1.80
2.7%	2.7%	3.7%	3.5%	3.5%	2.2%	2.0%	2.6%	2.9%	2.1%	1.6%	1.2%	.7%	.8%	.9%	1.1%			Avg Ann'l Div'd Yield	1.4%

CAPITAL STRUCTURE as of 12/31/01
Total Debt $8874 mill. Due in 5 Yrs $8122 mill.
LT Debt $2609 mill. LT Interest $143.5 mill.
(12% of Cap'l)

Leases, Uncapitalized Annual rentals $145.0 mill.

Pension Liability None

Common Stock 6,277,000,000 shs. (88% of Cap'l)

MARKET CAP: $238 billion (Large Cap)

	7230.2	7477.7	8281.3	10021	11306	12504	13544	16204	29574	32259	35570	39300	Sales ($mill)	52325
	23.6%	25.7%	27.3%	29.3%	31.0%	30.8%	30.2%	33.3%	33.0%	37.7%	39.0%	40.0%	Operating Margin	43.5%
	263.9	258.2	292.0	374.0	430.0	502.0	489.0	542.0	968.0	1068.0	1175	1275	Depreciation ($mill)	1600
	1093.5	1179.8	1298.4	1554.2	1929.0	2213.0	2633.6	3393.2	6495.0	8349.5	9885	11600	Net Profit ($mill)	17050
	28.6%	26.3%	30.0%	32.1%	31.0%	28.0%	24.8%	28.6%	28.1%	25.2%	25.0%	25.0%	Income Tax Rate	25.0%
	15.1%	15.8%	15.7%	15.5%	17.1%	17.7%	19.4%	20.9%	22.0%	25.9%	27.8%	29.5%	Net Profit Margin	32.6%
	2167.4	1289.6	962.5	965.2	828.0	1515.0	2739.0	2006.0	5206.0	4810.0	5500	6500	Working Cap'l ($mill)	9250
	571.3	570.5	604.2	833.0	687.0	729.0	527.0	525.0	1123.0	2609.0	2500	2250	Long-Term Debt ($mill)	1000
	4718.6	3865.5	4323.9	5506.6	6954.0	7933.0	8810.0	8887.0	16076	18293	23235	28290	Shr. Equity ($mill)	48880
	21.1%	27.1%	26.9%	24.8%	25.5%	25.8%	28.4%	36.3%	38.4%	40.5%	39.0%	38.0%	Return on Total Cap'l	33.5%
	23.2%	30.5%	30.0%	28.2%	27.7%	27.9%	29.9%	38.2%	40.4%	45.6%	42.5%	41.0%	Return on Shr. Equity	35.0%
	12.9%	16.7%	16.3%	16.3%	16.7%	16.8%	18.8%	25.3%	26.7%	30.8%	28.5%	27.5%	Retained to Com Eq	22.0%
	44%	45%	46%	42%	40%	40%	37%	34%	34%	33%	33%	32%	All Div'ds to Net Prof	37%

CURRENT POSITION ($MILL.)

	1999	2000	12/31/01
Cash Assets	4442	6863	8615
Receivables	3864	5489	5337
Inventory (LIFO)	1654	2702	2741
Other	1231	2133	1757
Current Assets	11191	17187	18450
Accts Payable	951	1719	1579
Debt Due	5001	4289	6265
Other	3233	5973	5796
Current Liab.	9185	11981	13640

ANNUAL RATES

of change (per sh)	Past 10 Yrs.	Past 5 Yrs.	Est'd '99-'01 to '05-'07
Sales	11.5%	12.5%	11.0%
"Cash Flow"	16.5%	19.5%	16.5%
Earnings	18.0%	20.5%	17.5%
Dividends	14.0%	16.0%	19.0%
Book Value	7.5%	12.0%	21.0%

BUSINESS: Pfizer Inc. is a major producer of pharmaceuticals, hospital products, consumer products, and animal health lines. Important product names include, *Norvasc* (cardiovascular); *Zoloft* (antidepressant); *Zithromax* (antibiotic); *Lipitor* (cholesterol); *Aricept* (Alzheimer's); *Cardura* (cardiovascular); *Diflucan* (antifungal); *Zyrtec* (antihistamine); *Viagra* (impotence); *Celebrex* (rheumatoid arthritis and osteoarthritis). Int'l business, 38% of sales; R&D, 15.0%. '01 depreciation rate: 6.9%. Estimated plant age: 16 yrs. Has about 90,000 employees, 147,000 stockholders. Directors/Officers own less than 1% of stock (3/02 proxy). Chairman & Chief Executive Officer: Henry McKinnell. Inc.: Delaware. Address: 235 East 42nd Street, New York, NY 10017. Tel.: 212-573-2323.

QUARTERLY SALES ($ mill.) E

Calendar	Mar.31	Jun.30	Sep.30	Dec.31	Full Year
1999	3927	3779	3992	4506	16204
2000	7222	7042	7205	8105	29574
2001	7645	7686	7898	9030	32259
2002	8418	8400	8800	9952	35570
2003	9325	9300	9725	10950	39300

EARNINGS PER SHARE A E

Calendar	Mar.31	Jun.30	Sep.30	Dec.31	Full Year
1999	.21	.18	.23	.25	.87
2000	.25	.23	.27	.27	1.02
2001	.33	.30	.34	.34	1.31
2002	.39	.32	.42	.44	1.57
2003	.46	.42	.48	.49	1.85

QUARTERLY DIVIDENDS PAID B■

Calendar	Mar.31	Jun.30	Sep.30	Dec.31	Full Year
1998	.063	.063	.063	.063	.25
1999	.073	.073	.08	.08	.31
2000	.09	.09	.09	.09	.36
2001	.11	.11	.11	.11	.44
2002	.13				

Pfizer reported solid first-quarter results . . . Revenues advanced 11% (13% on a constant currency basis), year over year, driven by healthy gains in Lipitor (up 26%, to $1.9 billion), Zoloft (22%, $740 million), and Neurontin (50%, $568 million). U.S. pharmaceutical sales were up 15% (to $4.6 billion), while foreign sales increased 13%, in local currencies. Per-share profits, meantime, surged 18%, as operating margins continued to benefit from both the integration of Warner-Lambert (acquired in 2000) and an improving sales mix.

. . . but the company also lowered investors' expectations for the June period. It indicated that earnings growth in the current quarter would be in the single digits, due to difficult year-over-year expense comparisons and to heavy costs associated with new-product launches and R&D activities. Reflecting Wall Street's excessive (in our opinion) focus on the short term, Pfizer stock has retreated in the aftermath of the lowered guidance. We still expect a 20% bottom-line gain for 2002 and for profits to compound at a 15%-plus rate in the subsequent 3 to 5 years. Importantly, the huge drug-maker's key products continue to perform in line with expectations, and there are no signs that this is going to change anytime soon. Indeed, management is maintaining its $1.56-to-$1.60-a-share earnings guidance for the full year, indicating that second-half results would be very strong. We would note, however, that we have prudently trimmed three pennies from our estimate (to $1.57), moving closer to the low end of the range. Our initial share-net figure for 2003 is $1.85, which would represent an 18% year-to-year advance. Pfizer spends more than $5 billion annually on research and development, and will probably add about 15 new products to its already formidable drug portfolio by 2005-2007, including perhaps five this year. This issue is one of our top drug-sector picks for the long haul. Reflecting anxieties at the market, industry, and company-specific levels, Pfizer stock is now selling at valuations seldom seen in many years. Indeed, our view is that Wall Street's overreaction to one relatively poor quarter has provided investors with their best entry point in a long time.

George Rho   April 26, 2002

(A) Based on average shares outstanding. Excl. non-rec. gains (losses): '91, (10¢); '92, (14¢); '93, (27¢); '98, 18¢; '99, (5¢); '00, (13¢). Next eqs. report due late July. (B) Next div'd meeting about June 21. Next ex date about May 5. Div'd payment dates: About Mar. 10, June 10, Sept. 10, Dec. 10.■ Div'd reinvestment plan available. (C) Incl. intangibles. In 2000's first quarter. '01: $1722 mill., 27¢/sh. (D) In mill., adj'd for stock splits. (E) Warner-Lambert, acquired 6/00, is included in historical data starting in 2000's first quarter.

Company's Financial Strength	A++
Stock's Price Stability	75
Price Growth Persistence	95
Earnings Predictability	100

To subscribe call 1-800-833-0

Figure 6-01: The Pfizer Value Line sheet.
Reprinted by permission of Value Line Publishing, Inc.

The first four steps in Section 1 of the Stock Check List calculate the average of the most recent two years of sales. The next four steps figure the average for the years 5 and 6 years ago. Steps 9 and 10 find the percentage that sales have increased over the 5 years.

 1. Locate the value for "Sales ($mil)" for the most recent full year, on the middle right hand side of the Pfizer Value Line sheet. Enter this number on line (1). In this study, the most recent full year is 2001 and the number for sales is 32259 (over $32 billion.)

Success Tip!

Make sure you use the most recent full year of data on the Value Line sheet, which is the column in the table of data just to the left of the numbers in bold print. Those bolded numbers are Value Line's forecasts for the future.

 2. On line (2), enter the value for "Sales ($mil)" for the <u>next</u> most recent year, the year 2000 in this study.

 3. Add the amounts entered on lines (1) and (2), and enter the sum on line (3).

 4. To calculate the average sales for the last two years, divide the value on line (3) by two, and enter the result on line (4).

5. On the Value Line sheet, count back five years from the most recent year (1996 in this study), and enter the value for Sales on line (5).

6. Enter the value for Sales one year earlier than the year used on line (6), 1994 in this example.

7. Add the amounts entered on lines (5) and (6), and enter the sum on line (7).

8. To calculate the average sales, divide the value on line (7) by two, and enter the result on line (8).

 9. To compute the dollar amount that sales increased over the five-year period, subtract the amount on line (8) from the amount entered on (4). Enter the result on line (9). For Pfizer, 30916.5–10663.5 = 20253.

10. The percentage increase in sales is the increase in sales divided by the sales from five years ago. Divide the increase in sales from line (9) by the sales five years ago on line (8). Then multiply the decimal result by 100 to produce a percentage, and enter the result on line (10). For Pfizer, divide 20253 by 10663.5, and then multiply by 100.

49

NATIONAL ASSOCIATION OF INVESTORS CORPORATION

NAIC®

INVESTMENT EDUCATION FOR INDIVIDUALS AND CLUBS SINCE 1951

Stock Check List ® for Beginning Investors

Company <u>Pfizer</u>

Prepared by <u>BJB</u>

Date <u>06/07/2002</u>

PFE

While Investors are learning to use NAIC's Stock Selection Guide, it is suggested the following Check List be used for each stock considered for investment.

1 PAST SALES RECORD

Sales for most recent year were	(1) $	32259.00
Sales for next most recent year were	(2) $	29574.00
Total of above (1+ 2)	(3) $	61833.00
Figure above divided by 2	(4) $	30916.50
Sales 5 years ago were	(5) $	11306.00
Sales 6 years ago were	(6) $	10021.00
Total of above (5 + 6)	(7) $	21327.00
Figure above divided by 2	(8) $	10663.50
Increase in sales in above period (8 from 4)	(9) $	20253.00
Percentage increase in sales (9 divided by 8)	(10)	189.9 %

CONVERSION TABLE

This % increase in Sales Gives	27	33	46	61	76	93	112	129	148	205	271
This % Compounded Annual Growth Rate	5	6	8	10	12	14	16	18	20	25	30

Look for the percent increase that meets the objective you have set.

COMPOUND ANNUAL RATE OF SALES GROWTH WAS _____ 24.0%

2 PAST EARNINGS PER SHARE RECORD

Earnings Per Share for most recent year were	(1) $	1.31
Earnings Per Share for next most recent year were	(2) $	1.02
Total of above (1+ 2)	(3) $	2.33
Figure above divided by 2	(4) $	1.17
Earnings Per Share 5 years ago were	(5)	.50
Earnings Per Share 6 years ago were	(6)	.41
Total of above (5 + 6)	(7)	.91
Figure above divided by 2	(8) $	.46
Increase in Earnings Per Share in above period (8 from 4)	(9) $	.71
Percentage increase in Earnings Per Share (9 divided by 8)	(10)	156.04 %

See Conversion Table above to determine ➡

Earnings Per Share have increased <u>less</u> than sales this period.
(more)   (less)

COMPOUND ANNUAL RATE OF EARNINGS PER SHARE GROWTH WAS _____ 21.0 %

Explain Apparent Reason for Difference in Sales and Earnings Per Share Growth: <u>nothing unusual</u>

Figure 6-02: The Stock Check List for Pfizer from Investor's Toolkit.

Discuss Possible Reasons for Past Growth:

A new product was successful _____✓_____

A cyclical business that experienced recovery_____

A research program has produced several new products or uses for older products_____

Purchase another company_____✓_____

Has taken larger share of business in its field_____

Skill of management_____✓_____

Will Factors Which Produced Past Growth Continue Effective

for the next five years _____✓_____ yes, _____ yes, but less effective, _____ no.

3 PRICE RECORD OF THE STOCK

Present Price $ ___34.58___   Present Earnings Per Share ___1.31___

List Last 5 Years	High Price Each Year (A)	Low Price Each Year (B)	Earnings Per Share (C)	Price Earnings Ratio	
				at High (A ÷ C)	at Low (B ÷ C)
1997	26.700	13.400	.570	46.84	23.51
1998	43.000	23.700	.670	64.18	35.37
1999	50.000	31.500	.870	57.47	36.21
2000	49.300	30.000	1.020	48.33	29.41
2001	46.800	34.000	1.310	35.73	25.95
Totals	215.800	132.600	4.440	252.550	150.450
Averages	43.160	26.520	0.888	50.510	30.090
Average of High and Low Price Earnings Averages for the past five years.				40.300	

Present Price is _____higher_____ than high price five years ago.
 (higher) (lower)

Present Price is ___29.5 %___ % higher that the high price 5 years ago. Compare this figure with the percent sales increase in 1 (10) and percent earnings per share increase in 2 (10).

The price change compares with sales growth and earnings per share growth _____unfavorably_____
 (favorably or unfavorably)

This stock has sold as high as the current price in ___4___ of the last 5 years.

In the past five years the stock _____has_____ sold at unusually_____high_____ price earnings ratios.
 (has) (has not)   (high) (low)

The Present price earnings ratio is ___26.397___

In relation to past price earnings ratios the stock is currently

_____ selling at a higher ratio

_____ selling about the same

___✓___ selling lower

The average price earnings ratios of the past might be expected to continue_____
 or should be adjusted to___26.40___ high, ___18.00___ low.

4 CONCLUSION

1. The past sales growth rate _____does_____ meet our objective.
   (does) (does not)

2. The past earnings per share growth rate _____does_____ meet our objective.
   (does) (does not)

3. Our conclusion has been that possible earnings per share growth rate _____will_____ meet our objective.
   (will) (will not)
   in the coming five years.

4. The price of the stock is currently _____too high_____
   (acceptable) (too high)

This form is not meant to give you an adequate analysis of the stock, but is meant to help a beginner ask questions to indicate whether the company is likely to become more valuable and if it can be purchased reasonably. As Investors gain practice, a more thorough study of the stock is suggested using NAIC's Stock Select Guide and Report as a guide.

The Conversion Table at the end of Section 1 lines up values for percentage increase in sales on the top row with values for compound annual rate of sales growth in the bottom row. Find the number on the top line that is closest to the percentage increase in sales on line (10). In this study, 189.93% is closest to 205.

Locate the number in the cell below the percentage increase in the top row, 25% in this study. Enter this number on the line for Compound Annual Rate of Sales Growth. Because 189.93% is lower than the 205, you can also choose to reduce the number to 24% as your best estimate. This growth rate should meet or exceed the minimum growth rate for a company of the candidate's size. For example, Pfizer is a large company, so we should expect a sales growth rate of 7% or more. Pfizer's 24% is outstanding.

CALCULATING EARNINGS PER SHARE GROWTH

Determining the Earnings per Share (EPS) growth (Section 2 of the Check List) for the company isn't any different than calculating the sales growth. Simply use the numbers in the "Earnings per sh" line of the Value Line sheet instead of Sales.

1. Locate the value for "Earnings per sh" for the most recent full year from the Pfizer Value Line sheet. Enter this number in Section 2, on line (1). In this study, the most recent full year is 2001 and the number for EPS is $1.31.

2. On line (2), enter the value for EPS for the next most recent year, 2000 in this study.

3. Add the amounts entered on lines (1) and (2), and enter the sum on line (3).

4. To calculate the average EPS for the last two years, divide the value on line (3) by two, and enter the result on line (4).

5. On the Value Line sheet, count back five years from the most recent year (1996 in our study), and enter the value for EPS on line (5).

6. Enter the value for EPS one year earlier than the year used on line (5), 1994 in this example.

7. Add the amounts entered on lines (5) and (6), and enter the sum on line (7).

8. To calculate the average EPS, divide the value on line (7) by two, and enter the result on line (8).

9. To compute the dollar amount that EPS increased over the five-year period, subtract the amount on line (8) from the amount entered on (4), and enter the result on line (9). For Pfizer, 1.17–.46 = .71

10. You calculate the percentage increase in EPS by dividing the increase in EPS by the EPS from five years ago. Divide the increase in EPS from line (9) by the EPS five years ago, line (8). Then multiply the decimal result by 100 to produce a percentage, and enter the result on line (10).

Use the Conversion Table at the end of Section 1 to find the compound annual growth rate for the percentage increase in EPS. In this study, 156.04% is closest to 148, representing a Compound Annual Rate of Earnings Per Share Growth of 20%. As 156.04% is a little above 148, we'll estimate the compound growth rate at 21%

to reflect this difference. This growth rate should meet or exceed the minimum growth rate for a company of the candidate's size. Pfizer's EPS growth isn't as high as its sales growth, but 21% is still exceptional for a large company.

The Difference Between Sales & EPS Growth

A company's sales and earnings usually don't grow at the same rate— buying back shares, reducing costs or focusing on more profitable products/services can increase earnings faster than sales. Earnings might grow slower than sales if competition is hampering the company's profit margins or costs have run out of control.

• Compare the Compound Annual Rate of Sales Growth in Section 1 to the Compound Annual Rate of Earnings Per Share Growth in Section 2. If the Earnings per Share growth is slower than sales growth, as is the case wih Pfizer, enter "Less" in Section 2 of the Check List. If the Earnings per Share growth is faster, enter "More."

BUT WILL IT LAST?

EPS might grow faster than sales for a time, but that can't last forever. Companies can only buy back so many shares, cut costs so low, or increase its profit margins so high. Eventually, EPS growth will meet or slide below the rate of sales growth.

• *Find out why EPS grow faster or slower than sales. You can search the annual report or ask the company's investor relations department. Their phone number appears in the Business section in the middle of the Value Line sheet.*

Forecasting the Company's Future Growth

It's hard to tell what a company might do in the future if you don't understand what it did in the past. Factors that contribute to growth can appear and disappear while you're not looking. Page two of the Stock Check List provides six possible reasons for past growth. Search for the answers by reading news articles, the summary on the Value Line sheet, the company's annual and quarterly reports, or other financial sources. You can also ask the investor relations department.

For example, a new drug that stops gray hair could fuel growth for years as the aging baby boomers face harsh reality. However, companies whose success relies on a single product (or a single large client) are risky. If people's gray hair goes away, but their heads are injured, the lawsuits would sink the company and your investment. Look for a diversified business strategy: numerous products, a wide geographical area or a broad base of clients.

After you understand the company's strategies, check off each reason that applies for the company's growth. You can even write in a reason if the Stock Check List doesn't list it. When a company employs several strategies for growth, you can feel more confident about checking "Yes" on the "Will Factors Which Produced Past Growth Continue Effective for the Next Five Years" line. As the skill of management is the desirable reason for growth, you can have more confidence growth will continue. You might decide to check "Yes, but less effective," if the company's strategies are running into obstacles. For example, competition is increasing, or the company's market share borders on monopolistic. Of course, if those gray heads are still being injured, you'll probably check "No."

What About the Stock Price?

The Price Record of the Stock in Section 3 of the Check List compares the price and earnings per share over the past five years to determine whether this suggests that the stock is a good value at its current price.

Up-to-Date Price & EPS

Enter the present price for the stock on the Present Price line. Daily newspapers, Web sites brokers and many other sources provide price quotes. Pfizer's price on June 4, 2002 was $34.58.

Do not use the price on the Value Line page. That is the price nine days prior to the date of the Value Line report, which is ancient history.

The Price Record Table

The Price Record table in Section 3 of the Check List displays prices and price earnings ratios for the last five years. This table makes it easy to see whether the earnings and the stock price have increased consistently. In addition, the PE ratios can indicate whether the stock price is a good value or overvalued. The best way to fill in the years in the first column is starting at the bottom. In the cell just above "Totals," enter the last full year of data. This is the

Keeping EPS Up-to-Date

Using the last four quarters of EPS keeps your study in line with a company's current growth. Using last year's data, particularly near the end of the fiscal year, can underestimate the company's merit.

There are two ways to obtain the number you need to fill in the Present Earnings Per Share line of the Check List. You can add up the earnings for the last four quarters in the Earnings per Share box on the lower left of Value Line sheet. In this stock study, add up the EPS from the second quarter of 2001 to the first quarter of 2002 (.30 + .34 + .34 + .39) = $1.37. You can also use the Earnings per Share for the most recent full year of data in the table of annual data on the Value Line sheet. "Earnings per sh" is the third line down from the top of the table. In this study, the most recent full year of data is 2001 and the EPS is $1.31.

same year used for Sales on line (1) in Section 1. Enter the previous year on each line until you reach the top of the chart. For our example, enter 2001 in the bottom row, followed by 2000, 1999, 1998 and 1997.

• Enter the high price for each year in the second column. The label at the top of this column is High Price Each Year (A). You can find the high and low prices across the top of the Value Line sheet, just above the chart of the stock price.

• Enter the low price for each year in the third column, Low Price Each Year (B). Low prices appear on the Value Line sheet just below the high price above the stock price chart.

• Enter the EPS for each year from the "Earnings Per Sh" line on the Value Line sheet in the Earnings per Share column (C).

A deficit, shown by a negative number for EPS, means that the company LOST money. (Value Line denotes a deficit by a small letter d before the number, as in d1.22.) A deficit is a red flag. Call the company and find out why. Better yet, look for another company to study.

• To calculate a high PE, divide the high price in the High Price column by the EPS in the Earnings Per Share column. Enter the result in the Price Earnings Ratio at High column. If you forget how to calculate the PE ratio, just look for the formula in the column heading: (A ÷C).

• For each year, divide the low price by the earnings per share. To calculate a low PE, divide the low price in the Low Price column by the EPS (B÷C). Enter the result in the Price Earnings Ratio at Low column.

Calculating Average Price Earnings Ratios

Stock prices jump around all the time for all sorts of reasons even with rock solid company performance. PEs bounce right along with the stock price. But, usually the PE will move back up or down to the average PE. PEs are affected by the overall market conditions, as well as by the company. In a bad market, all PEs go down. After several years of a good market, PEs go up again.

To calculate a five-year average, you add up the numbers for all five years in each column of the Check List Price Record and then divide the sum of that column by five. For example:

 I. Add up all numbers in the High Price column, and enter the total in the cell below the most recent high price.

 2. Divide the total by five and enter the average high price in the bottom cell of the High Price column.

Repeat these two steps using the numbers in the Low Price column (B) to calculate the average low price, the numbers for Price Earnings ratio at the High for the average high PE column (A÷C), and the Price Earnings ratio at the Low for the average low PE column (B÷C).

To calculate the five-year average, add the average high price earnings ratio and the average low price earnings ratio (from the lower right hand columns of the table), and divide the result by 2. Enter the result at the bottom right of the Price Record table. For Pfizer, the average high PE is 50.5; the average low PE is 30.1. The five-year average calculation is (50.5 + 30.1) ÷ 2 = 40.3

Analyzing Price & PE

The Price Record section includes observations and questions that identify whether the stock is selling at a good price. The questions are simple, but sometimes the correct answers aren't obvious. Just keep two things in mind. First, the price of a quality growth stock should increase along with the company's earnings. Second, PE ratios that are a little on the low side can boost share price as the PE moves to the average or high PE. Whereas high PEs dropping back to the average or lower can drive the stock price down. The following subheadings discuss each point of analysis.

> **PRESENT PRICE IS (HIGHER/LOWER) THAN HIGH PRICE FIVE YEARS AGO**

Compare the present price at the top of the Price Record table to the high price for the earliest year in the "High Price" column. If the present price is higher than the price five years ago, enter "higher."

The price of a quality growth stock tends to increase, so "higher" is the answer you want to see. If the answer is "lower," investors have little faith in the stock.

PRESENT PRICE IS ____ % HIGHER THAN THE HIGH PRICE FIVE YEARS AGO

Calculate the percentage change between present price and the high price five years ago.

 1. Subtract the high price of five years ago from the present price. In this study, $34.58 – $26.70 = 7.88.

 2. Divide the result by the high price of five years ago, and multiply by 100. For Pfizer, the percentage change in price is $7.88 ÷ $26.7 X 100 = 29.5%.

THE PRICE CHANGE COMPARES WITH THE SALES GROWTH AND EARNINGS PER SHARE GROWTH (FAVORABLY/UNFAVORABLY)

Compare the percentage change in stock price to the percentage change in sales (Section 1 of the Check List) and earnings (Section 2 of the Check List). If the price change percentage is close to the change in sales and EPS, enter "favorably." A slightly higher price growth is favorable because it shows that investors are confident in the stock and will reward it for continuing its growth. A slightly lower price growth is also favorable because it means that the price doesn't yet reflect the company's good performance. However, if the price change is much higher than sales and EPS growth, the stock is probably overvalued. If the price change is much lower, it could indicate problems. If it is much lower or much higher, enter "unfavorably."

Pfizer's price changed 29.5 percent while the EPS increased by over 156%. This disparity is a red flag. In fact, the company recently announced that their next quarter's performance wouldn't be up to par.

The stock has sold as high as the current price in ____ of the last five years.

Compare the present price to each price listed in the "High Price" column. Enter the number of years where the high price is as high as or higher than the Present Price. The stock price should increase along with sales and EPS growth. Therefore, a growth stock's price ideally should reach new highs every year. The fewer years with the same high price the better. Pfizer's price has reached the present price in four of the last five years—another red flag.

PE ratios depend on many things including the industry that the company is in, the growth rate of the company and the general state of the overall stock market. You can determine whether the company's PE ratios are typical or unusual by comparing them to the industry average PE on the Value Line industry sheet or the company's five-year average PE. If the PE ratios vary significantly from these other PEs, select the word "has."

A stock that sells at unusual PE ratios is risky. PEs on the high side threaten to plunge back to earth. But, PEs that drop through the floor might indicate fundamental problems in the company, erratic performance or even the fickleness of mutual funds that own shares. It's preferable to have the PE ratios that are close to the average or lower PE.

Calculate the present price earnings ratio by dividing the present price by the present earnings per share. For Pfizer, the present PE ratio is $34.58 \div \$1.31 = 26.4$.

Compare the present PE ratio to past PEs and the five-year average PE in the Price Record. If the present PE is higher than past PEs, check "selling at a higher ratio." Pfizer's PE is below the five-year average, so you should check "selling lower."

Look for a stock where the PE is at or below past PE ratios. There's no point in paying a premium for a company. Of course, a PE significantly below past PEs is a red flag. Pfizer's present PE of 26.4 compared to the five-year average of 40.3 is not a problem.

Comparing PEs to Test for Value

Comparing a PE to the average PEs in the Price Record as well as to the industry average PE indicates whether a company's price is reasonable. High PEs don't last, and when they drop, the stock price drops as well. Low PEs are only temporary if the company continues to perform well and the market is in a "bull" mode. Plus, the stock price gets a real boost when the PE increases as well as the earnings per share. To complete the next Stock Check List questions, study the company's PEs as follows:

• Are the PEs excessively high and/or low? High averages indicate an overvalued stock, but excessively low PEs could mean unpleasant news lurking somewhere.

• What do the numbers tell you about possible future PEs? Dropping PEs might drop still further, which can drag a stock price down even when earnings stay steady. PEs on the way up might continue to expand, but you shouldn't count on that. You should make a judgement as to the overall state of the market in estimating future PEs.

• Do you think that investors will sustain these PEs?

Remember the siren call of the average or normal PE. It can drag an elevated PE back to earth, but it can sometimes boost a low PE.

• How do the PEs compare to the industry average PE? If a PE is higher than the industry average, make sure that the company's growth warrants that optimism. If a company with great growth has a PE lower than the industry average, check for bad news. If there isn't any, you may have found a real winner.

THE AVERAGE PRICE EARNINGS RATIOS OF THE PAST MIGHT BE EXPECTED TO CONTINUE _____

If the PE ratios in the Price Record table and the present PE ratio don't fluctuate much, you might expect the present PE ratio to continue. If PEs seem high, the PE might drop. If PEs are low, but the company is performing well, the PE might increase in the future.

OR SHOULD BE ADJUSTED TO _____ HIGH, _____ LOW

If the present PE is significantly different from the average PE, you might decide to adjust the average high PE and average low PEs. Be very conservative. If the present PE is very high, bring it down closer to the five-year average PE. If the PEs have been decreasing steadily, they might continue to drop. Therefore, it's a good idea to lower your average PEs. Try to judge the current conditions of the market. If the market has been bettering irrational new highs or new lows for several years, a reversal in direction is likely to take place in our five year time frame.

With Pfizer's present PE lower than any of the comparative PEs, it would be wise to adjust the high and low PE ratios. For example, you could use the present PE of 26.4 as the high PE, and then choose a low PE, such as 18.

Success Tip!

You can use the high and low PE ratios to determine a reasonable price range for a stock by multiplying the PE ratios by the present Earnings per Share.

To Buy or Not to Buy

There are no hard and fast rules to deciding whether a stock is a good investment. Investors can fall in love with a company's story and ignore the fundamental numbers. Be as objective as you can when you answer these concluding questions.

THE PAST SALES GROWTH RATE (DOES/DOES NOT) MEET OUR OBJECTIVE

To double your money in five years, a stock must provide a return of approximately 15% a year. However, larger companies carry less risk and often pay dividends, so you might buy a large company with a 7% growth rate.

Compare the compound annual sales growth rate in Section 1 with the growth rate objective for the company's size (see Chapter 1). If the compound annual growth rate is in or above the range, enter "does." If the growth rate is below the range, enter "does not."

PFIZER PE COMPARISONS

Type of PE	Value	Comparison
Present PE	26.4	
Average High PE	50.5	Lower
Average Low PE	30.1	Lower
Five-year average PE	40.3	Lower
Industry Average PE	33.4	Lower

THE PAST EARNINGS PER SHARE GROWTH RATE (DOES/DOES NOT) MEET OUR OBJECTIVE

Compare the compound annual rate of earning per share growth in Section 2 to the growth rate objective for the company's size (see Chapter 1). If the compound growth rate is in or above the range, enter "does." If the growth rate is below the range, enter "does not."

Pfizer's sales and earnings growth rates have been exceptional for a company of its size. However, the red flags from the Price Record section prompt caution in answering the rest of the questions.

OUR CONCLUSION HAS BEEN THAT POSSIBLE EARNINGS PER SHARE GROWTH RATE (WILL/WILL NOT) MEET OUR OBJECTIVE IN THE COMING FIVE YEARS

Look at the earnings per share numbers in the table in Section 3 of the Check List. If the numbers are consistently increasing from year to year, chances are good that they will continue to increase. If the earnings growth is slowing, decreasing or fluctuating, future growth might not meet your objective. Evaluate everything that you have read or researched about this company. Do not base your judgment strictly on the numbers on the Stock Check List.

THE PRICE OF THE STOCK IS CURRENTLY (ACCEPTABLE/TOO HIGH)

You need a potential price range for the next five years to judge the current stock price. If the current price is closer to the low end of the range, the price is probably acceptable. You can use the present earnings per share and the average high and low PEs from Section 3 to calculate the price range.

Earnings x (Price/Earnings) = Price.

• To calculate the high end of the five-year price range, multiply the Present Earnings per Share from the Price Record by the average high PE. If you adjusted the average high PE, use your adjusted value.

• To calculate the low end of the five-year price range, multiply the Present Earnings per Share from the Price Record by the average low PE. If you adjusted the average low PE, use your adjusted value.

If the present price is nearer the low end, the price is acceptable. If the present price is above the middle of the range, wait until the stock price has dropped before purchasing. If you have decided that you would like to own this company but the price is too high, place it on a watch list and update the Stock Check List at least once a quarter to track it. If the price drops lower in the range, buy.

To calculate the potential high price for Pfizer, multiply the present EPS by the high PE. Earlier, we chose to adjust Pfizer's high PE to a lower number—the present PE ratio to 26.4. To calculate the potential low price for Pfizer, multiply the present EPS by the low PE. We also chose to adjust Pfizer's low PE to a lower number, 18 in this example.

Potential Pfizer High Price = 1.31 x 26.4 = $34.58

Potential Pfizer Low Price = 1.31 x 18 = $23.58

Pfizer's present price is at the high end of Pfizer's potential price range. The company announced a disappointing quarter. You might decide to watch Pfizer and buy it if the price drops. Of course, when a stock price drops significantly, you should do some research to find out why before purchasing the stock. Others might opt for more aggressive PE ratios and see a long-standing strong competitor in pharmaceutical beaten down for one lousy quarter. The savvy beginner thinks about moving on to the Stock Selection Guide to study the stock in more detail.

CHAPTER SEVEN:

Graduating to the Sto

You're in the Big Time

The NAIC investment approach is a beguiling combination of simplicity and sophistication. No, this isn't a wine review. But you can start studying stocks after understanding just a few concepts. Using conservative judgment with the Stock Check List, you can invest successfully even as a beginner. At the other end of the spectrum, investors who have used the NAIC methodology for years still use the Stock Selection Guide, but append their own strategies for research and analysis. Experience has shown the SSG to be an excellent tool, explaining a large percentage of stock valuation theory.

How the Stock Selection Guide Works

Entering the SSG Header Information

There's More to Capitalization than You Might Think

Although you can get started with a few concepts and add to your arsenal of analysis techniques over time, some repetition of concepts is helpful when you begin. As you will remember, Chapters 1 and 2 discussed what to look for in a stock, whereas Chapter 3 introduced the NAIC stock study forms and how they help us find good investments. This chapter explains how the Stock Selection Guide (SSG) distinguishes good and bad investments and reviews the attributes of desirable investments. We'll also cover how to complete the header and capitalization sections of the SSG. Chapters 8 through 15 guide you through the entire SSG.

How the Stock Selection Guide Works

The first two sections of the SSG focus on growth rates and management performance, whereas the remaining three sections help to identify a stock's value.

Success Tip!

You can't just plug data into the SSG and pop out a reliable buy price for a stock. The judgment you apply, based on your research of the company, can make the difference between achieving your investment objectives and losing money. You'll improve your returns more by recognizing a company's weaknesses than by trying to make it look better than it really is.

SSG Section 1: Visual Analysis of Sales, Earnings & Price

Growth companies increase revenues and earnings faster than the general economy and inflation combined, as well as most competitors in the same industry. These companies work hard to produce consistent results for their shareholders. Market conditions, fluctuations in the business cycle and successful turnarounds don't matter as much when you invest in growth companies for the long term.

Section 1 of the SSG displays a graph of historical sales, earnings, pre-tax profit and prices. You will be amazed at how quickly you learn to recognize

growth and quality patterns in these trend lines for sales, earnings and pre-tax profit. The upward angle of the historical trend lines shows the rate of growth, whereas nearly straight lines represent the consistent performance of a quality management team.

Your SSG results hinge on your estimate of the company's future growth. After studying the historical trend lines on the graph and researching the company, you must conservatively estimate the future rate of sales and earnings growth. By drawing these forecast growth rates as projection lines on the graph, you can visually estimate sales and earnings five years in the future.

SSG Section 2: Evaluating Management

Good growing companies become leaders in their industry with substantial financial strength. This doesn't mean that small companies don't offer excellent growth. They are often leaders in a niche within the industry; substantial strength has nothing to do with the amount of annual sales. Growth can come from effective research and development (R&D), market strength, and competent management. Effective R&D, market strength or market share, and consistent growth are easy to see. A pipeline of new products or a high percentage of revenue from newly introduced products indicates an effective R&D program. You can find numbers for market share in many stock reports or the company's annual report. As you will soon see, strong consistent growth is the focus of Section 1 of the SSG.

But, how can you tell if management is competent? Many things can affect a company's performance: the economy, an incredibly successful product, the absence or appearance of competition, and rising and falling costs. Good management produces consistent perform-ance by taking advantage of the opportunities and mitigating the hazards. Steadily increasing pre-tax profit margins and return on equity indicate management that is on the ball. Sections 1 and 2 of the SSG help you test management's skills.

PRE-TAX PROFIT MARGIN

The pre-tax profit margin is the percentage that the company gets to keep, before taxes, of each dollar it makes in sales. Increasing sales or reducing costs leads to high profit margins. Steadily increasing pre-tax profit margins shows that management can balance the strategies that increase sales and decrease or contain

Pre-tax profit margin =	$\dfrac{\text{Sales} - \text{Cost of Goods Sold} - \text{Overhead}}{\text{Sales}}$

costs. Management can increase sales in many ways: expanding territory, persistent innovation, taking market share from competitors, or increasing the price per unit of the product.

To increase prices or gain market share, products must be of superior quality with little competition—a rarity these days.

Management can decrease the cost of goods sold by paying less for supplies or increasing the efficiency of production. In high-tech industries or companies that hinge on fickle consumer preference, management must plan produc-tion to reduce the amount of unsellable inventory. Management also must control or reduce overhead, which includes salaries, travel expenses, benefits, marketing, training, rent, advertising and utilities.

PERCENT EARNED ON EQUITY

"Percent earned on equity" is the return that management achieves on investors' money (including earnings retained in the business). Steadily increasing percent earned on equity means that the company is receiving a better return each year on the money it has invested.

Percent earned on equity =	$\dfrac{EPS}{Book\ Value\ per\ share}$

"Book value" is another term which is the same as "equity" or shareholder equity. It represents the net amount of company dollars after subtracting total liabilities from total assets. The term "book" is derived from the "accounting records or accounting book". Thus, book value is an accounting measure using historical costs. Percent earned on equity is an indicator of how well management is utilizing the company's resources contributed by shareholders' money and reinvested earnings.

GROWTH & CONSISTENCY ARE REQUIRED

If growth and consistency aren't quickly apparent, you don't need to explore the stock further. Ironically, a company sometimes looks better as its performance and quality deteriorate. For example, as performance declines, the price often plummets. As the price drops, so does the PE ratio, which then reduces the relative value (the current PE divided by the five-year average PE.) All of a sudden, the relative value makes it look good—but it's because sales or earnings growth has dropped off.

Before you get too excited about a 20% profit margin or return on equity, remember to compare the values to the averages for the industry. As mentioned in an earlier chapter, different industries have different typical rates for these two measures. Four percent profit margin in the grocery industry is good, but lousy in computer software where 36% is common.

Good Value

Even with the best quality growth stock, you make your money when you buy at a reasonable price. Paying too much can turn an excellent growth stock into a mediocre investment. True, long-term investing can eventually overcome a high purchase price, but discriminating selection when you buy maximizes your portfolio performance. On the other hand, a poor quality growth stock is a lemon no matter how low its price. Make sure that a company offers growth and consistency before looking at whether its current price is a reasonable value.

SSG Section 3: Price-Earnings History

Section 3 sets up data necessary for evaluating the price-earnings ratios of an investment. High and low prices along with earnings feed the calculations for high and low PE ratios. The PE ratios contribute to the calculations for average high and low PEs as well as the five-year average PE. And, the PE ratios help to forecast future high and low prices. Finally, you can determine yield from dividends using the earnings and dividends.

SSG Section 4: Evaluating Risk & Reward

Section 4 provides what you've waited for—information on whether the stock is a candidate for purchase. This section uses the estimated values from SSG sections 1, 2 and 3 to forecast potential future stock prices. The relative value uses the PEs in Section 3, whereas the upside-downside ratio determines value from the forecast high and low prices.

ESTIMATED HIGH & LOW PRICES

You calculate the forecast high price by multiplying the projected high PE investors might pay for the company by the highest earnings that the company might generate in the next five years. Similarly, the estimated potential low price for a growth company is the projected low PE multiplied by the lowest earnings the company might generate

(next five years). Chapter 12 goes into the details about how to pick the PEs and EPS to forecast high and low prices five years out.

PRICE ZONES

One way to choose a good buy price is to divide the range between the forecast high and low prices into three zones: buy, maybe (hold) and sell. If the current price is near the bottom of the buy range, most of the potential price movement is up, so the potential reward is great compared to the potential loss.

The top of the buy zone represents the highest reasonable purchase price. In many cases, premier companies in an industry are out of the buy range. However, you will learn that stock prices often go up and down for many reasons other than the company's performance. You can establish a watch list and wait for the stock to drop into the buy zone. Of course, you should check to make sure that the price drop wasn't due to problems that arose in the company.

JUDGMENT IS KEY

It may seem odd that judgment in Section 3 would be so important. It's just a bunch of numbers and a few simple calculations. However, the rest of the stock study, including the forecast high and low price, the upside-downside ratio and the total return, all rely on the projected PEs you choose. You'll learn all about judgment on the SSG throughout the next few chapters.

UPSIDE-DOWNSIDE RATIO

The upside-downside ratio compares the amount of potential stock price increase to potential stock price decrease. NAIC considers a company a good value if the potential gain is at least three times the potential loss, an upside-downside ratio of 3:1. *(4:1)* The upside-downside ratio is purely a measure of the potential increase or decrease in stock price—not the probability that the stock price will reach those levels.

Upside-downside ratio =	Estimated high price – Current price
	Current price – Estimated low price

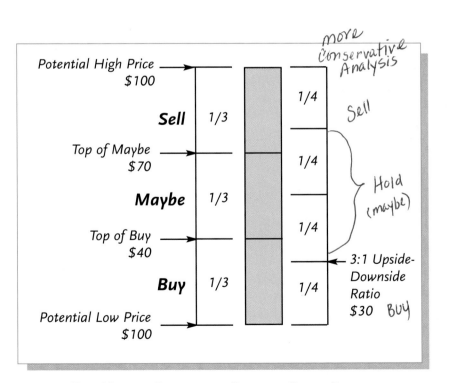

more Conservative Analysis

Sell

Hold (maybe)

THE UPSIDE-DOWNSIDE RATIO & PRICE RANGES

RELATIVE VALUE

Relative value is the ratio of the current PE to the average adjusted PE for the last five years. You pay a premium when you buy stock when its PE is above the five-year average. Because high PEs tend to drop back to more reasonable levels, you risk the price dropping after you purchase. One school of thought says that a relative value somewhere between .85 and 1.10 indicates a good value for your investment. Relative value over 1.10 might indicate that the stock is overvalued, whereas relative value under .85 could be a red flag for problems of which you are unaware.

projected relative value?

SSG Section 5: Five-Year Potential

Your ultimate goal is the total return that you receive by buying the stock. The total return is the return from both price appreciation and dividend yield. Your total return goal should be to average approximately 15% per year, thus doubling your investment every five years.

Section 5 evaluates the total return (from both price appreciation and dividends) for an investment if you purchase the stock at its current price. NAIC strives for a portfolio return of

15% per year. However, not every company in your portfolio must achieve that return. Small companies might provide a total return greater than 15 percent due to their faster growth rates. Small companies usually don't pay dividends, so their total return is often from price appreciation alone. Large companies grow slower, which leads to less return from price appreciation. However, when you add in the return from dividends, you might still end up with a total return greater than 15 percent.

Success Tip!

The Stock Check List only looks at return from price appreciation, but the SSG shows the total return.

Entering the SSG Header Information

The SSG header identifies some basic information about the stock study.

• **Company:** This is the name of the company you are studying.

• **Date:** Data changes constantly, so you want to base buy or sell decisions on a study with a recent date. Enter the date you perform the study (and then use the stock price for that date later in the form.)

• **Prepared By:** This space is for the name or initials of the person preparing the SSG.

• **Data Source:** Data sources massage the data in different ways. Value Line normalizes the data, whereas S&P Stock Reports present "as reported" data. These data difference can change the results of a stock study, so you should only compare studies that use the same data source. NAIC's On-Line Premium Service (OPS) uses the normalized S&P data.

• **Where Traded:** This is the stock exchange where the stock trades. This information appears to the right of the company name at the top of the Value Line page.

• **Industry:** Different data sources assign companies to industries differently. Use the category as assigned by the data source (such as Value Line) that you use for the stock study. Get industry averages from the same data source. For example, if you use the paper Value Line reports, flip forward in the book until you see the industry page and use that industry.

Success Tip!

If you have trouble finding any data on the Value Line page, refer to Chapter 5 for a refresher.

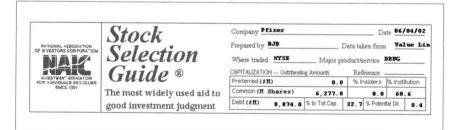

Figure 7-01: The SSG Header for Pfizer using Investor's Toolkit.

There's More to Capitalization than You Might Think

The capitalization section identifies the level of risk for a company. Volatility, debt and dilution present risk to shareholders. Everyone's tolerance for risk is different, so you must make sure a company isn't too risky for your taste.

Volatility

If you don't like roller coaster rides, volatility in stock price can hurt your portfolio performance and jangle your nerves. 'The number of shares outstanding affects the volatility of a stock's price. Companies with fewer shares tend to be more volatile than those with lots of outstanding shares.

When a company announces good news, investors like to buy the shares. And in the face of bad news, shareholders are like rats leaving a sinking ship. If a company has a small number of shares outstanding, there might not be enough to go around when the news is good—the share price shoots up as people clamor to buy. Unfortunately, when the news is bad, finding buyers is tough.

• **Preferred:** Preferred shares usually entitle shareholders to specific dividend rates. But, preferred stock holders have "first rights" to distribution of assets if the company closes its doors. If a company offers preferred

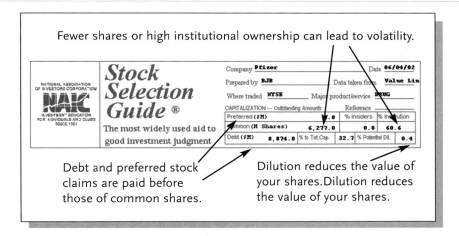

Fewer shares or high institutional ownership can lead to volatility.

Debt and preferred stock claims are paid before those of common shares.

Dilution reduces the value of your shares. Dilution reduces the value of your shares.

Figure 7-02: Checking capitalization and risk in the SSG header.

shares, your common shares could become worthless if the company goes out of business. The preferred shares, if they exist, appear in the Capitalization section on the Value Line page. Pfizer does not have any preferred shares, so Preferred doesn't appear at all.

• **Common:** The common shares outstanding appear as Common Stock in the Capital Structure section of the Value Line sheet. Pfizer has over six billion shares, which is quite a few. Volatility might appear when a company has only a few million shares.

• **% Insiders:** When the people running the company are invested in the company, their interests are the same as yours—to increase the share price and to hold for the long term. For a small company,

WHEN INSIDERS OWN TOO MUCH

If insiders own too much of a stock, shares might not trade as much, leading to increased volatility. In addition, companies held mainly by a small group of people, such as a family, might be impacted by decisions contrary to shareholders' interests.

insider ownership might be 30%, whereas insiders might own 1% or less in a large company, as is the case with Pfizer. The insider ownership appears as Directors/Officers ownership in the Business section in the middle of the Value Line page.

See page 48

• **% Institution:** Institutions, particularly mutual funds, have a short-term view—they trade frequently and get out at the least sign of a problem, no matter how short-lived. High institutional ownership can make a stock price very volatile. To calculate the percent of institutional ownership, divide the shares owned by institutions by the common shares outstanding (multiply by 100 to convert to a percentage.) The calculation below shows the numbers for Pfizer. The number of shares owned by institutions is the last number in the last line of the Institutional Decisions section near the top right of the Value Line page.

% Institution =	Institutional shares x 1000 / Common Shares Outstanding	3,803,699 x 1000 / 6,277,000,000	= .606 = 60.6%

Success Tip!

The heading in the last line of the Institutional Decisions section is Hld's (000.) This means that the number of shares shown is in thousands, so you must multiply that number by 1000 to see the actual number of institutional shares.

When Business Goes Bad

High levels of debt are risky for a company, because it has to pay its debt obligations whether it's doing well or not. If the company runs short of money during a recession, the debt obligations could force the company to go out of business. Debt compounds the risk to shareholders because the company must pay claims from debt and preferred stockholders before common shareholders receive anything.

Some industries such as banks, financial institutions, and utilities typically operate using higher levels of debt. Some successful companies in other industries have proven that they can carry high debt over many years. In general, debt percentage greater than 35 percent is risky. But, you should compare a company's debt percentage to the industry average before you decide. The percentage figure (% of Cap'l) directly below LT Interest in the Capital Structure section of the Value Line report indicates long term debt divided by total capitalization.

• **Debt:** Use the Total Debt shown in millions from the Capital Structure section of the Value Line page.

• **% To Total Cap:** Total Capitalization is the sum of a company's debt and the equity held by shareholders. Shareholders equity appears as Shr. Equity ($mill) four lines below the Income Tax Rate in the data table on the Value Line page. Make sure to use the number for the most recent full year of data. For Pfizer, % to Total Cap is:

% To Total Cap =	Total Debt / Total Debt + Shareholders' Equity	
=	8,874 million / 8,874 million + 18,293 million	= .3266 = 32.66%

The Danger of Dilution

When a company issues more shares, such as granting options to employees and officers of the company or issuing convertible bonds, those shares cut into the current shareholders' ownership of the company. The new shares dilute the shareholders' portion of earnings and assets. For example, if a company has $10 million in earnings and 1 million shares outstanding, each shareholder "owns" $10.00 in earnings. If the company granted 100,000 shares through options, the pool of shares grows to 1,100,000 shares, and each share gets $9.09 in earnings. If the employees exercise their options, the EPS drops to $9.09, which could lead to a drop in share price.

Success Tip!

Some data sources, such as Multex Investor and S&P tear sheets, report diluted earnings, whereas others report basic earnings. Value Line usually reports diluted earnings, but not always. The footnotes at the bottom of the page tell you which years use diluted earnings. Use the number of diluted shares to calculate EPS for your study to make sure that a buy is really a buy.

• **% Potential Dilution:** If the data source reports basic earnings, as Value Line does for this Pfizer report, you can find the number of basic and diluted shares in the company's most recent Income Statement. Your data source might show a different number of basic shares than those in the quarterly report, as is the case with Pfizer. In this case, you can use the shares outstanding from your data source (Value Line's 6277 million shares) with the diluted shares from the quarterly report (6305.9 million), as demonstrated in the calculation below.

```
Weighted average shares used to calculate earnings per common share amounts:
   Basic                                                                    6,205.5
                                                                            =======
   Diluted                                                                  6,305.9
                                                                            =======
```

Figure 7-03: Quarterly Reports (10-Q) show basic and diluted shares.
[handwritten: Company's]
[handwritten: Annual Report]

In the calculation below, the basic shares are those reported by Value Line for Pfizer. Value Line's number of shares for Pfizer is closer to the number of diluted shares, which provides a conservative view of the impact of dilution. At .46%, dilution is not an issue.

Before you continue with graphing sales and earnings in Section 1, review the risks identified in the capitalization section. Make sure that volatility, debt levels and potential dilution are acceptable.

% Potential Dilution =	$\dfrac{\text{Diluted Shares} - \text{Basic Shares}}{\text{Basic Shares}}$	$\dfrac{6305.9 - 6277}{6277}$	= .0046 = .46%

CHAPTER EIGHT

SSG Section 1 - A Pict

A Picture Is Worth a Thousand Numbers

You can scour S&P reports and Value Line pages until you need quadrifocal glasses, but those tables of numbers might continue to confuse. There are thousands of companies you can buy. Only some are good investments. You need a snapshot that shows whether you've found a divine investment or a financial fiasco. The first section of the SSG provides the illustration you need to see whether you want to get to know the company further.

A Picture of
Financial Health

Diagnosing
Fiscal Heartburn
or Serious Disease

Plotting the
Picture of Past Growth

What's Next?

A Picture of Financial Health

Section 1 of the SSG contains a graph of historical sales, EPS, pre-tax profit and prices for a stock. Numbers growing at a constant rate appear as a straight line on the graph, which makes it easy to spot a consistent growth company. Lines for historical sales, EPS and pre-tax profit that climb the graph like railroad tracks—nice and straight and parallel to each other—represent the consistent performance produced by a skilled management team. The angle of these lines shows whether the company's growth is strong enough to meet your investment objectives.

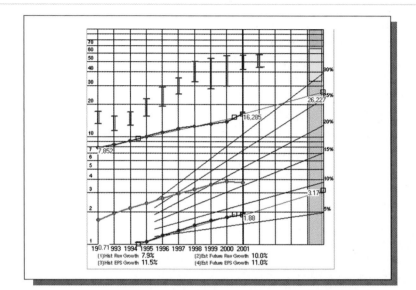

Figure 8-01: Railroad tracks heading up the SSG graph in Stock Analyst PLUS!

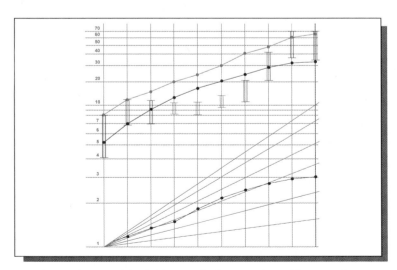

Figure 8-02: This SSG graph from NAIC Classic *shows slowing growth. Note how the middle line, which is EPS, is a curve that continues to flatten out.*

Diagnosing Fiscal Heartburn or Serious Disease

A good-looking graph doesn't make a company a sure thing, but it indicates that the company is worth more study. An ugly graph is a sign of problems. As a beginner, you're better off leaving companies with unsightly graphs to the experts.

Problem performance comes in several guises. Section 1 of the SSG makes slowing growth, erratic growth, years with losses, and slumps in growth readily apparent. For very young companies, accelerating growth rates are soon followed by slower and slower growth rates.

Slowing growth is to be expected and you must learn to recognize a normal rate of slowing. Companies that grow at 50 percent or more a year simply can't continue at that pace. But, it's important to recognize slowing growth rates, so you can estimate sales, EPS and price conservatively. When a large company's growth slows below that of the economy and inflation, your chances of meeting your investment objectives are slim. Erratic growth poses two problems. First, it wears on your nerves to watch a stock price gyrate along with sales and EPS numbers. More importantly, inconsistent growth is a sign that management is struggling. That struggle could bode badly for future performance.

When a company loses money, it's hard to ignore on the SSG Section 1 graph. There's no place to plot a negative number so the year ends up blank on the graph. If you use NAIC software, such as *NAIC Classic*, the historical lines drop off the bottom of the page, foreshadowing what the stock price could do if the company stumbles again.

Slumps show up as bowl-shaped "droops" in the historical lines for sales and EPS. They appear frequently in the Section 1 graph for cyclical companies. Cyclical companies do well when the economy is

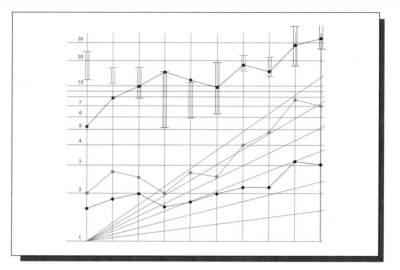

Figure 8-03: Erratic growth looks like saw teeth.

strong and slow when the economy is bad; the growthlines on the graph sharpen and flatten in tandem with the economy. Cyclical companies can make great investments when you buy at the right price. But, analyzing them takes a little more work, so you should hold off until you gain more experience.

Plotting the Picture of Past Growth

As a company grows, the numbers for its sales and EPS grow exponentially. If you plot these numbers on a regular graph, the growth line would be a curve that changes continually. That makes it hard to identify the company's growth rate. But, by plotting the company's

financials on the special graph in the SSG, a steady growth rate appears as a straight line. This special graph is known as a semi-logarithmic graph.

Success Tip!

When you plot numbers on an SSG by hand, be careful that you count the divisions and plot your numbers correctly as you move up the axis. If you use NAIC software, there are no intermediate lines between the horizontal guide lines, because the software plots the numbers for you.

THE GRIDLINES ON THE GRAPH LOOK A LITTLE ODD

If you use NAIC software to create SSGs, you don't have to worry about how to plot numbers on the Section 1 graph. But, when you complete SSGs by hand, plotting numbers is easier if you understand a few things about the graph.

• Numbers that grow at a constant rate appear as a straight line on the SSG graph. That's due to math that you probably don't want to try to understand at this point in your learning.

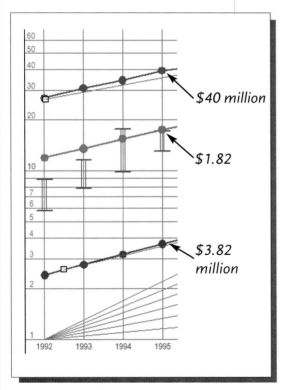

Figure 8-04: The spacing of the horizontal lines change and the numbers on the scale can represent any factor of ten.

• The numbers on the left side of the graph can represent any factor of ten—cents, dollars, or millions of dollars. You can plot sales in millions of dollars right next to EPS in cents.

• On a paper SSG form, the number of spaces between the numbers change. There are 10 spaces between the numbers 1, 2, 3 and 4, but only 5 spaces between 4, 5, 6, 7, 8, 9 and 10. Each division between 1 and 4 represents 1/10th of the range. For example, the third line between 1 and 2 denotes 1.3. If you choose millions for the units, this line represents $1,300,000. The third line between 6 and 7 stands for 6.6 because each line signifies 1/5 (or 2/10th) of the range.

• Next to the first horizontal line on the graph is number one. There is no horizontal line for zero and negative numbers are nowhere to be seen. When a company loses money, its losses, in effect, drop off the page.

ADDING THE YEARS TO THE HORIZONTAL AXIS

Before you can plot any financials on the graph, you must add the years across the bottom of the graph. There are ten positions for years in the past, and five for years into the future. The tenth line from the left side of the graph is thicker than the others and represents the last full year of data. To add years to the graph, follow these steps:

1. Enter the year for the last full year of data from your data source under the thick line on the graph.

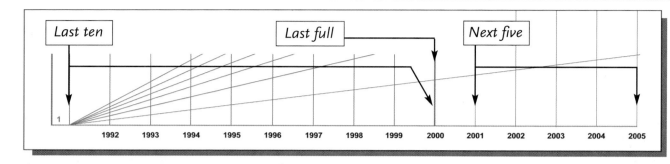

Figure 08-05 The first ten spots are for the past ten years, whereas the five spots after the thick vertical line are for the next five years.

2. Work backwards, adding the years into the past until you reach the left margin.

3. Add the five years into the future until you reach the right margin.

GUIDELINES FOR PLOTTING

• Start plotting as low on the graph as you can. Remember that you have to leave room at the top of the graph for plotting sales and EPS for five years into the future. You can note in the left margin whether the point represents cents, dollars or millions.

• For companies that grow rapidly, you might have to skip the values for the early years to fit the values for future years on the graph.

• Don't worry about precision. You can eyeball the location for a point on the graph. When you look for trends, the difference between $2.81 and $2.80 won't make a difference.

• Draw sales, EPS and pre-tax profit in different colors or symbols so you can differentiate the lines.

PRE-TAX PROFIT IN SECTION 1

If you use NAIC software, you can easily see pre-tax profit in SSG Section 1. If you complete an SSG by hand, you have to calculate pre-tax profit before you plot it. Section 1 graphs the dollar amount of pre-tax profit. Section 2, Evaluating Management, includes pre-tax profit margins, which represent pre-tax profit divided by sales.

If you complete SSGs by hand, you can postpone plotting pre-tax profit until you're interested enough in the company to study further. However, when your interest in a stock is piqued, computing pre-tax profit is incredibly valuable, because drops in profit and profit margins can presage problems before they appear in the EPS and stock price.

The Plot Thickens

This section uses numbers from the Pfizer Value Line sheet in Chapter 5 for plotting sales and EPS numbers on the SSG graph.

ADDING THE YEARS FOR PFIZER

On the Pfizer Value Line page, the numbers for the year 2002 appear in boldface on the data table. The boldface numbers are estimates of the future. This means that the year 2001 is the most recent full year of actual data. Add 2001 underneath the thick vertical line at the bottom of the SSG graph.

• Fill in the years until you reach ten years in the past. For Pfizer, the first year on the left side of the graph should be 1992.

• Add five years into the future, in this example 2002 through 2006.

PLOTTING SALES FOR PFIZER

Pfizer's 1992 sales of $7,230 million and 2001 sales of $32,259 million fit easily when you start plotting at the bottom of the graph.

• 1992 Sales were $7,230 million. Place a point on the first vertical line in the graph just above the horizontal line labeled 7.

• 1993 Sales were $7,477 million. Place a point on the second vertical line in the graph (above the year 1993) about halfway between the horizontal lines for 7 and 8.

• 1994 Sales were $8,281 million. Place this point on the third vertical line in the graph.

The point should lie on the first horizontal divider above the line labeled 8. Remember, on the paper SSG form there are only five spaces between the numbers 8 and 9, so one divider represents 2/10ths.

• Continue plotting sales until you complete all the past years of data through 2001.

PLOTTING EPS FOR PFIZER

Pfizer's EPS are in dollars, so the numbers in the left margin represent dollars. Remember to plot EPS in a different color. If you are color blind, you can draw symbols at each point—such as little dollar signs for sales or a piggy bank for EPS.

• 1992 EPS were $.27. Place a point on the first vertical line in the graph on the seventh horizontal divider above the line labeled 2. Remember, there are ten spaces between the numbers 2 and 3 so one divider represents 1/10th.

• 1993 EPS were $.31. Place a point on the second vertical line in the graph on the first horizontal divider above the line labeled 3.

• 1994 EPS were $.35. Place this point on the third vertical line in the graph on the fifth horizontal divider above the line labeled 3.

• Continue plotting until you have added EPS for each past year of data.

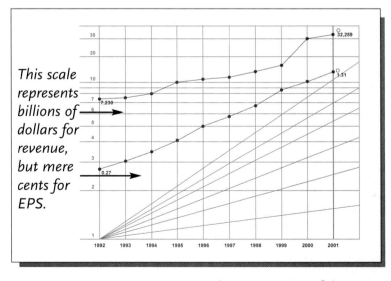

Figure 08-06: You can use the same section of the SSG scale to represent cents or billions of dollars. Stock Analyst PLUS! produced this graph.

WHAT'S NEXT?

Now that you have sales and EPS plotted on the Section 1 graph, it's time to transform those plotted points into historical trend lines. Selecting a historical trend line is your first opportunity to apply your judgment to a stock study. Turn the page to Chapter 9 to learn how to draw a historical trend line and determine a company's historical growth rates.

CHAPTER NINE

SSG Section 1 - Trend

Getting to the Point

Just as the painter Seurat could create images of parks and people from small colored dots, you can start to sketch a picture of a company's growth when you connect the dots for sales, EPS and pre-tax profit, on the graph in Section 1 of the SSG. You can even draw lines between points in a rich palette of colors—U.S. Grant green being a steady favorite. When you track the data points in Section 1 you will uncover a company's historical growth trends.

Constructing
  Historical Trend Lines

  Finding
    Historical Growth Rates

  Entering
    Recent Quarterly Data

Spotting

Before you can forecast where a company is going, you have to figure out where it's been. Any company's fortunes can change for better or worse. But a company with a wild past might have a hard time settling down, whereas a company dedicated to growth often seems to crank out performance through thick and thin. When you finish plotting the data points in Section 1, you can connect the dots on the graph to see whether the company produces those railroad tracks that NAIC investors like to see or presents a less desirable graph, as described in the section "Diagnosing Fiscal Heartburn or Serious Disease" in Chapter 8.

Constructing Historical Trend Lines

In Chapter 8, you added the points to the graph in Section 1. Before drawing trend lines, you have to connect the points on the graph so you can see how growth varied or remained steady over time. To differentiate between the different growth lines, use different colored pencils for sales, EPS and pre-tax profit. If you have trouble picking out colors for your home projects, you can use the same colors as *NAIC Classic*

software: sales in blue, EPS in maroon, and pre-tax profit in green. *Investor's Toolkit* shows sales in green, EPS in blue, and pre-tax profit in magenta.

If you complete SSGs by hand, there are several ways to draw trend lines through the historical data points. You don't need a precise trend line—your stock study will do the job whether you determine that growth is 10 percent or 10.1276 percent. For this reason, the easiest approaches, such as the inspection and mid-point methods, are the most popular. However, if you use NAIC software to study stocks, you'll find that those packages usually use a statistical technique called the Least Squares method. And that's just fine as long as the computer is doing the legwork.

The Inspection Method

Just about everybody spent a good part of preschool trying to pound square pegs into round holes. At some point, kids figure out how to match shapes, and from then on recognizing patterns is second nature. The inspection method relies on your ability to see a pattern in data points. You simply draw a line that best represents the pattern of points on your graph.

For example, Abbott Labs (figure 9-01) growth has been steady. The trend line practically draws itself. The historical trend line passes through the data points for sales and EPS like a hot knife through butter. Even the pre-tax profit points define a straight line.

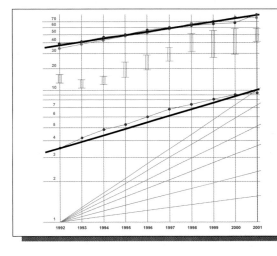

FIGURE 9-01: THIS FIGURE, ILLUSTRATING ABBOTT LABS SALES GROWTH, SHOWS A HISTORICAL TREND DRAWN BY EYE-BALLING THE LINE THROUGH THE DATA POINTS OF AN NAIC CLASSIC GRAPH.

Drawing a trend line for Pfizer offers a slight complication. Pfizer's growth was rock steady from 1992 through 1999. Just like Abbott Labs, the trend line draws itself, as shown in figure 9-02. However, sales and EPS jumped up in 2000. In 2001, they resumed their previous angles. It turns out that Pfizer acquired Warner-Lambert in 2000, so the total value for sales and EPS jumped up to reflect both Pfizer's and Warner-Lambert's sales. After the acquisition, the company's sales and EPS are growing at the same rate as before.

How do you draw a trend line for this? The purpose of the trend line is to identify the company's growth rate, not the value of sales or EPS. So, in Pfizer's case, the trend line drawn through 2000 and 2001 is parallel to the trend line for years 1992 through 1999. In this case, you can extend the 2000/2001 trend line back as far as you want.

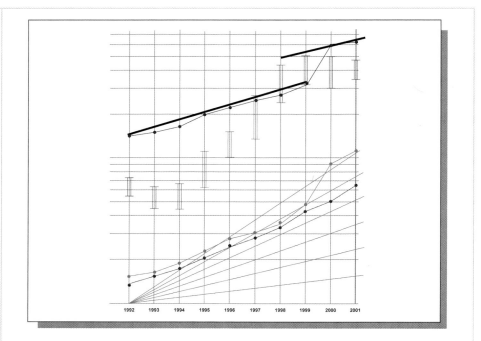

1992	1993	1994	1995	1996	1997	1998	1999	2000	2001

Figure 9-02: Pfizer's historical sales jumped up between 1999 and 2000 because of a merger with Warner-Lambert.

The Mid-Point Method

The mid-point method throws some simple math into the mix. It uses the average of the first and second five-year periods in ten years of history. Draw the trend line through these two average values. You can use the mid-point method on sales, EPS and pre-tax profit.

To draw a trend line using the mid-point method, follow these steps:

1. Calculate the average value for the first five-year period.

2. Plot the average for the first five years on the middle year of the five-year period (year 3).

3. Calculate the average value for the second five-year period.

4. Plot the average for the second five years on the middle year of the five-year period (year 8).

5. Draw the trend line through the averages at years 3 and 8 and extend the line in both directions.

Pfizer First Five-Year Average			Pfizer Second Five-Year Average		
Year 1	7230		Year 6	12504	
Year 2	7477		Year 7	13544	
Year 3	8281		Year 8	16204	
Year 4	10021		Year 9	29574	
Year 5	11306		Year 10	32259	
Total	44315		Total	104085	
Divide by 5	1st five-year average	**8863**	Divide by 5	2nd five-year average	**20817**

ARE CALCULATED TRENDS BETTER?

In studying stocks, your judgment far outweighs the results of some calculations. For instance, the trend line produced by the inspection method is closer to the truth than the one computed by the mid-point method. The mid-point method can't differentiate between true sales growth and that produced by the acquisition in 2000. If you look at the historical trend line and the line between sales for 2000 and 2001, you can see that the trend line has overestimated historical growth.

The Peak Method

The peak method is best suited for cyclical companies (i.e. firms that closely follow the economic business cycle). The sales and EPS for cyclical companies drift up and down along with the economy. Even though a cyclical company's fundamentals change, the peaks usually reach higher and higher. You can forecast the peak in the next business cycle by drawing a historical trend line between the peaks on the graph.

Success Tip!

Novices should avoid cyclical companies. They require stock analysis techniques that are a little confusing at first. You should be comfortable with investing in growth companies before adding cyclicals to your portfolio.

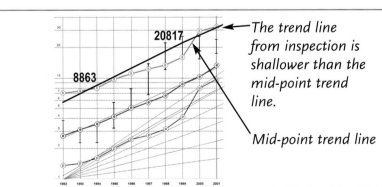

20817

8863

The trend line from inspection is shallower than the mid-point trend line.

Mid-point trend line

Figure 9-03: The mid-point method draws a trend line through two points representing the average values for the first five years and second five years of history.

The Area Method

With this method, you draw the trend line so that the area above the trend line equals the area below the line. You can try shading the areas above and below. In practice, this is similar to the inspection method.

Applying Judgment to the Historical Trend Line

You might wonder how you can add judgment to historical trend lines. After all, you can't change past performance of a company. However, historical trend lines are supposed to show the trend of the past performance. For example, if a company's growth rate was slowing, you would draw a trend line using the data from more recent years, so you don't overestimate historical growth. In fact, years in which company performance differs significantly from other years occur often enough that they have a name: "outliers".

Outliers are data that you might eliminate because they aren't representative or relevant to a company's performance. You might eliminate data for some years for several reasons:

• For novice investors, severe dips in the most recent five years are unacceptable—the company has had problems and you might not know enough to figure out if they are out of the woods. Don't even continue your stock study. Look for a company with steady upward historical trend lines.

• For more experienced investors, recent dips are red flags. Research the company further to see if they have taken steps to resolve their issues.

• Deficits or severe dips in the first five years on the graph might be outliers if they don't reoccur. You can forgive a young company for a tough year or two early on. A company might run into trouble but correct the problem. Always research the cause of the deficit or dip to ensure it won't happen again.

• When the plotted points create a curve like one half of a rainbow, the early years had higher growth than the recent past. When growth is slowing, eliminate the early years in the graph when you construct the historical trend line. The company's growth will probably never be as high as it was in the past.

For the best results, draw the historical trend lines conservatively. Spectacular performance doesn't seem to last, whereas poor performance often sticks around. With outliers, eliminate data only if its removal reduces the historical growth rate to create a more conservative SSG.

Finding the Historical Growth Rates

Ultimately, you want to figure out the company's growth rate over the past ten years. To do this, you can compare the trend line drawn through the historical points to the template growth lines (i.e. percent guidelines) in Section 1. These template growth lines all originate from the origin of the graph—the number "1" in the bottom left margin. Each template appears at a slightly steeper angle, representing a higher growth rate.

If you attend a NAIC-sponsored SSG class, you might receive a transparency printed with the template growth lines. If you have a transparency like this, place the origin of the transparency at the point where the historical trend line intersects the left margin. With the horizontal lines on both charts aligned, just find the line on the transparency closest to the historical trend line. Look at the growth rate for that line in the right margin and you have your historical growth rate. If you use the NAIC software, historical growth rates are automatically calculated for you.

If you don't have a transparency, you can use two pieces of paper to get the same effect.

1. Line up a piece of paper along the right half of the historical trend line (see Figure 9-04.) The paper should extend an inch or two to the left of the most recent year.

2. Line up a second piece of paper to the left of the first.

3. Slide the second piece of paper down until the lower edge intersects the origin of the graph in Section 1.

4. Now, the lower edge of the paper represents the angle of the growth line. Draw a line along the bottom edge of the paper all the way to the right margin. You can read the growth rate from the percentages that appear in the right margin.

In this example, the sales growth line is just above the 10 percent template line— right around 11 percent.

• Repeat this process to find the EPS growth rate.

• After you find the growth rate line for sales and EPS, enter the historical growth rate for sales on the line for Historical Sales Growth at the bottom of Section 1. Add the historical growth rate for EPS on the line for Historical Earnings per Share Growth.

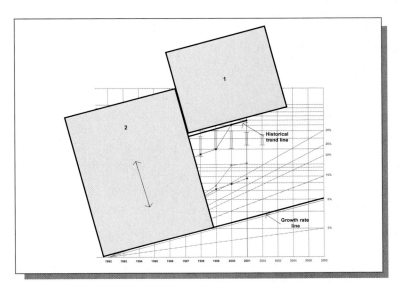

Figure 9-04: Finding the growth rate from the historical trend line.

Entering Recent Quarterly Data

The last data to add to Section 1 is the sales and EPS for the most recent quarter and the quarter one year ago. With these numbers, you calculate the percentage change in sales and EPS over the year to make sure the company's most recent growth is good enough to continue the stock study. Quarterly sales and EPS appear in boxes at the bottom left corner of the Value Line sheet. As in the data table for annual figures, quarterly data forecasted for future periods appear in bold.

Success Tip!

Many companies perform better at certain times of the year. For example, toy stores do most of their business right before Christmas, whereas home improvement stores are busiest in the spring and summer. By comparing the most recent quarter to the same quarter a year ago, you compare quarters with similar business activity.

Calculating Quarterly Sales

 1. Find the sales number for the most recent quarter (the last number that isn't printed in boldface on the Value Line page.) Pfizer's most recent quarter is the first quarter of 2002, which ends on March 31.

 2. Write the quarter and date in the Recent Quarterly Figures box in the Section 1 graph. For example, for Pfizer, enter "2002 Q1, ends 3/31/2002."

 3. Write in the sales number on the line for sales for the most recent quarter. Pfizer's most recent sales were $8,418 million.

4. Write in the sales for the first quarter of 2001 (one year ago) to the line for sales for the year ago quarter. Pfizer's sales one year ago were $7,645 million.

5. Finally, calculate the change in sales over the year.

Percentage Change in Sales =	Present Sales − Past Sales / Past Sales	=	$8,418 m − $7,645 m / $7,645 m
=	$773 m / $7,645 m	=	10.1%

Calculating Quarterly EPS

1. Write in the quarterly EPS for the most recent quarter. Pfizer's most recent quarterly EPS were $.39.

2. Write in the EPS for the quarter one year ago. Pfizer's EPS for the first quarter of 2001 were $.33.

3. Finally, calculate the change in EPS over the year.

Percentage Change in EPS =	$\dfrac{\text{Present EPS} - \text{Past EPS}}{\text{Past EPS}}$	=	$\dfrac{\$.39 - \$.33}{\$.33}$
=	$\dfrac{\$.06}{\$.33}$	=	18.2%

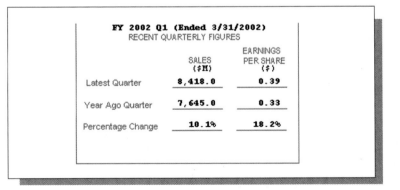

Figure 09-05: Calculating growth for the most recent quarter. This figure uses the recent quarterly figures from Investor's Toolkit.

Success*Tip!*

For a refresher on calculating percentage change, see "Showing Increases or Decreases as a Percentage" in Chapter 4.

THE NEXT STEP IN A STOCK STUDY IS TO FORE-CAST FUTURE GROWTH RATES FOR THE COMPANY BASED ON HISTORICAL GROWTH RATES AND YOUR RESEARCH.

CHAPTER TEN:

SSG Section 1 - Forec

Fiscal Fortune Telling

When fortune tellers tell you the story of your future they use astute observation and adroit conversation to extract those uncanny personal tidbits that make you wonder how a stranger could know so much about you. If you pay attention, you'll notice that prognosticators don't actually do a whole lot of prognostication.

Here in the SSG you'll play fiscal fortuneteller— astutely observing a company's performance and financials, studying reports, and engaging its investor relations folks in conversation. Unlike your soothsayer-for-hire, you are well equipped to forecast the future of the company.

Researching Potential Growth

Estimating Future Growth Rates

Drawing Projection Lines for Sales & EPS

asting Growth

A company's future growth is a pivotal point in a stock study. The estimated future growth rate drives potential sales and earnings five years into the future and determines whether a growth company is selling at a good price. The SSG doesn't spit out a future growth rate. Forecasting a future growth rate requires your judgment. Judgment requires knowledge. Chapter 5 discusses some sources of information about companies. If you use the Internet, you can learn about Web sites that provide background and analysis on companies in the NAIC Computerized Investing & Internet Handbook. In this chapter, you'll identify the first places to check for company information and how to use that information to determine how fast a company might grow in the future.

Researching Potential Growth

There's no excuse for not doing your homework. Your local library probably has at least half a dozen sources for company information, such as Value Line, Standard & Poor's, and Hoover's. In addition, Web sites abound with financial data and reports, news, and stock analysis. You could easily become overwhelmed by information overload. But, you can create good stock studies using just a few sources of information.

Value Line

Each Value Line sheet includes a brief summary of a company's performance, potential or present problems, productive steps, and opportunities for the company. The summary usually concludes with the analyst's forecast for the future. The Value Line company summary is a good place to start to find out what you should investigate. However, you should take the analyst's forecast with a grain of salt. Analysts tend to

---

READING BETWEEN THE LINES

The Value Line drug industry page says that it now costs $800 million to discover and develop a new drug, compared to $300 million in the early 1990s. Drug companies have to commit big money to research and development to keep their pipeline filled. For drug companies, look for above-industry average contributions to R&D. What happens when a company spends all that money on drugs that don't make it to market? You might also check the percentage of a company's drugs that are successful.

The Value Line industry page appears in front of the Value Line sheets for the companies in the industry. It provides composite statistics for the entire industry such as net profit margin, return on shareholders' equity and average annual PE ratio. You can compare a company's measures to these industry composites to see if their performance is above or below average. The Value Line industry page discusses problems or prospects facing the industry as a whole. Armed with this information, you can examine how a company is handling these industry issues.

be optimistic, so glowing reports might not turn out to be as bright as you might hope. On the other hand, if the analyst is all gloom and doom, that is indeed a cause for concern.

For example, Pfizer's Value Line summary mentions that their key products continue to meet sales expectations and that the company will release 15 new products over the next three years. It takes years and millions of dollars to produce a drug. Drug companies must get everything they can out of each drug they market and keep the pipeline filled with drugs at every stage of development. The success of Pfizer's current products and their pipeline of products bode well for their future.

News & Current Company Events

Recent events are important to every stock study. Annual reports come out, well, once a year. Quarterly reports appear each quarter—every three months give or take a day. Value Line company reports appear every 13 weeks. Big things (good or bad) can happen in the time between these reports.

For example, in early June 2002, *CBS MarketWatch* ran a story announcing FDA approval of a new label for one of Pfizer's successful drugs, Celebrex, affirming its safety. This meant there was less chance of the stock price dropping due to a safety concern. Pfizer's price rose a little on this news.

Good news can boost a stock's price. However, bad news usually has a faster, and often more pronounced, effect on price. If a stock that you're studying or watching drops in price, turn to the news to see if it's bad (lower sales, EPS, or profit margins, or other declining fundamentals). You might find that the news is noise; the market has overreacted. In this case you've found a great opportunity to buy a great stock at a low price.

For up to the minute news, you can't beat the Internet. Web sites such as *www.multexinvestor.com*, *www.thestreet.com*, and *www.quicken.com* offer news from many sources. In addition, you can instruct some sites to send you e-mail with late-breaking news on any company that interests you. You can also read the *Wall Street Journal*, the business section of newspapers, or financial magazines, such as *Fortune*, to keep current on your stocks and watch lists.

Annual & Quarterly Reports

The annual reports that companies produce often include enough fluff to make some nice pillows. But, these reports also offer a look at past performance, what the company is doing, and what company management thinks about the future. The 10-K SEC Form is also an annual report, but the SEC defines the format and contents of the 10-K, which can make it more difficult to gloss over issues. Quarterly reports and the SEC quarterly 10-Q provide more succinct information about events during the most recent quarter.

Some sections of the annual reports offer more fodder for your growth forecasts than others do. The "Letter to Shareholders" is the CEO's message to the people who own the company. Certainly, CEOs aren't always forthcoming about problems. But, the tone and content of the "Letter to Shareholders" says a lot. If the company has problems, the CEO should address them and explain what the company is doing to resolve them. If everything is peachy, the CEO might talk about the plans for producing results that are more splendiferous in the future. Some CEOs predict the company's future growth rate. Of course, they aren't always right. But, a CEO's estimate is an insider's perspective.

Pfizer's 2002 Letter to Shareholders reports that 94 new compounds are in development, 68 projects are in place to expand the use of existing products, and 15 new medicines will be available over the next 5 years. The Pfizer pipeline seems full. The letter also mentions that Pfizer has teamed with IBM and Microsoft on Amicore, software and services to reduce physicians' paperwork so they can focus on providing care. Some investors might view expansion as a hedge against issues like healthcare reform and managed pharmacy benefits. Other investors might feel that Pfizer is moving away from its core competency. There isn't one answer. You have to decide for yourself. The annual report usually contains another section with more explanations from management. This section has many names: Management Analysis, Management Discussion, Review of Operations. No matter the name, this section includes details about how the company produced its performance and, sometimes, what you can expect in the future.

Pfizer's review of operations reported 10% revenue growth, 28% net income growth, 34% operating margins and R&D spending of $4.8 billion (10% of revenues). This section also forecast double-digit growth for the next three years. They expect profit margins to improve due to productivity initiatives and cost savings from the merger with Warner-Lambert. In addition, Pfizer plans to spend 10% of revenues on R&D in 2003— over $5 billion dollars.

Estimating Future Growth Rates

You can't pick future growth rates simply based on history. You have to get to know the company.

Estimating Sales Growth

Find out what contributed to their growth in the past: products, good management or acquisitions. Decide whether the company is likely to continue their growth, slow down or, in some cases, grow faster. Threats such as competition or expiring patents might dampen growth in the future, whereas growing market share, productive R&D or cost cutting initiatives can boost growth.

As you learn more, you'll add more questions to your list. Use the sources described in the previous section to find your answers.

• How much does the company spend on research and development? Is that amount above or below the industry average?

• How much revenue comes from recent products or services?

• Does the company have patents about to expire?

• Is the management that produced growth still in place? How close are they to retirement?

• How much competition does the company have? Should they expect more or less in the future?

• Has the company increased its market share?

• Has it purchased one or more other companies?

• Does the company face any significant lawsuits?

Pfizer's recent sales growth has been 11 percent, although recent quarterly rates are a little lower. However, Pfizer produces several successful drugs, such as Lipitor and Zoloft. In addition, their pipeline is solid for the next five years, which means the company should be able to continue their current growth. News stories in early July 2002 reported that Pfizer can now sell the Adams confectionary business (Trident, Chiclet and Dentyne brands) and Schick-Wilkinson shaving products business, which they acquired from the purchase of Warner-Lambert. By selling these non-healthcare businesses, Pfizer can continue to grow as they did before the Warner-Lambert addition.

Making Adjustments

Steady growth: When a company grows steadily over 10 years (see figure 9-01 for Abbott Lab's growth graph), you can usually assume that the trend will continue. Simply use the historical growth rate for the estimated future growth rate, with perhaps a slight downward adjustment to reflect anticipated slowing.

Irregular growth: If sales and EPS skitter above and below the trend line, you might want to reduce your estimated growth rate by one or more percentage points to buffer against a company's unpredictability. If growth is too irregular, look for another company to study.

Slowing growth: If growth is slowing, don't use the 10-year average growth for your estimated future growth rate. Check the growth rate for the past three years. To be conservative, choose a growth rate even lower than the three-year growth rate. Also, look at the growth rate in the recent quarterly figures box in Section 1. If the growth rate has slowed further, be even more conservative with your estimate. For example, if a company's growth has slowed from 25 percent over 10 years to 15 percent for the past three years, and 12 percent in the most recent quarter from

the year-ago quarter, you might want to estimate future growth at 10 percent or below.

Don't estimate sales and EPS growth above 20%. That level of growth is difficult to sustain over a long period of time, particularly as a company gets larger.

After you decide on a future growth rate for the company, add your estimate to the Estimated Future Sales Growth line at the bottom of the Section 1 graph. Before you proceed to estimating future EPS growth, consider whether the estimated future sales growth rate is sufficient for a company of its size. For example, Pfizer's $32 billion in sales puts the company in the large company category. The 11 percent forecast growth rate is above the 7 percent growth we generally expect from a giant company.

Estimating Future EPS Growth

In many cases, you can estimate EPS growth rate similarly to sales. However, EPS growth can differ from sales because of rising or decreasing expenses, share buy backs or dilution, and changes in tax rates. Reducing costs means that the company makes more profit. That profit ends up as more earnings for each share in the company. In conjunction with estimating future EPS, you should fill in Section 2 of the SSG (see Chapter 11). Also, you should consider that if a company buys back shares, there are fewer shares over which to divide the earnings of the company—the likely result, higher earnings per share.

Add your estimate for EPS to the Estimated Future Earnings Per Share Growth line at the

In general, don't estimate EPS growth at a rate faster than sales growth. Even though a company can grow EPS faster than sales by cutting costs or buying back shares, these activities cannot continue forever. Eventually, EPS growth will drop to the same or lower rate than sales. If you do forecast EPS faster than sales, ensure that the factors that contribute to EPS growth will continue for at least five more years.

bottom of the Section 1 graph. As you did with sales growth, consider whether the estimated future EPS growth rate meets your goal for a company of its size.

Pfizer appears to have grown EPS steadily at 18 percent over the past 10 years. In Chapter 9, the historical trend line and recent quarterly figures pointed to sales growth of 11 percent. Pfizer has a few factors that point to EPS growing faster than sales—at 14%—for at least the next five years.

Pfizer's profit margins (SSG Section 2 in next chapter) have increased steadily over the past ten years. Their profit margins should continue to improve as the company reduces costs by continuing to integrate Warner-Lambert into the business. Eliminating the low margin candy, gum and razor businesses will increase profit margins even more as more of sales come from higher margin pharmaceuticals. Increasing profit margins mean that the company keeps more of the money it makes, which leads to EPS growing higher than sales. Pfizer also announced a $10 billion stock buyback. As the company buys back shares, the earnings of the company are divided by fewer shares, which leads to higher EPS growth.

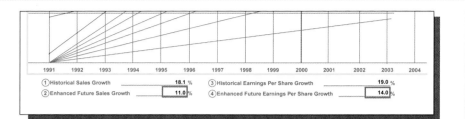

Figure 10-01: Add your estimate of future sales and EPS growth rates. This figure shows the historical and estimated growth rate boxes from Investor's Toolkit.

Drawing Projection Lines for Sales & EPS

Projection lines represent the estimated future sales and EPS growth. The historical trend lines indicate the direction of sales and EPS over the past 10 years. The projection lines indicate potential sales and EPS five years into the future. The future EPS contribute to calculating an estimated future high price, which is one factor in whether the stock is selling at a good price.

You can use the same two pieces of paper from figure 9-04 to draw the projection lines.

I. Line up a piece of paper with the template growth line for the estimated future growth rate you chose (see Figure 10-02.) The right

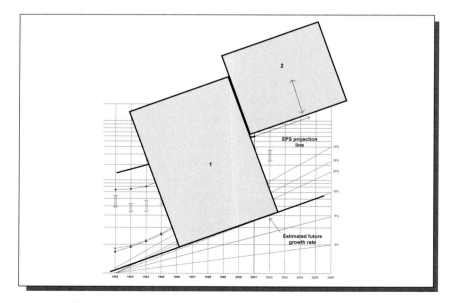

Figure 10-02: Drawing a projection line for EPS growth.

edge of the paper should also line up with the data point for the most recent year.

2. Line up a second piece of paper to the right of the first.

3. Slide the second piece of paper up or down until the lower edge intersects the data point for the most recent year.

4. Now, the lower edge of the paper represents the projection line for growth for the next five years. Draw a line along the bottom edge of the paper all the way to the right margin.

After you draw the projection lines over to the right margin, you can determine the sales and EPS figures five years into the future. To do this:

1. Mark the point where the projection line crosses the right margin.

2. Use a straight edge to draw a horizontal line from the right margin to the left margin.

3. Mark the point where the horizontal line crosses the left margin.

4. Use the numbers on the scale in the left margin to determine the value of sales and EPS five years in the future.

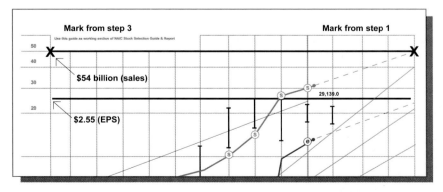

Mark from step 3   **Mark from step 1**

$54 billion (sales)

$2.55 (EPS)

29,139.0

Figure 10-03: You can find future sales and EPS by reading numbers from the SSG graph.

CHAPTER ELEVEN

SSG Section 2 - Evalu

Getting to Know Good Management

Good corporate leaders set up strategies far in advance to defend against competitive attacks, while developing business opportunities where none existed before. Regardless of the strategies and tactics that these executives employ, you can assess their results with a few key measures.

Identifying
  Good Management

    Analyzing
      Management with
      Pre-Tax Profit Margin

    Getting Your
      Money's Worth

    Using the
      Preferred Procedure

ating Management

Pre-tax profit margins and percent earned on equity tell a lot about the ability of a company's management. Chapter 2 introduces these measures, whereas Chapter 3 explains how they help us find good investments. This chapter covers pre-tax profit margin and percent earned on equity in more detail and explains how to calculate them.

Identifying Good Management

Similar to sales and EPS, pre-tax profit margins and percent earned on equity should both be above the industry average and trend upward. Above average figures indicate strong management. Upward trends indicate that management not only keeps things running, but also makes improvements as a matter of course.

Analyzing Management with Pre-Tax Profit Margin

$$\text{Pre-tax profit margin} = \frac{\text{Sales} - \text{Cost of Goods Sold} - \text{Overhead}}{\text{Sales}}$$

Pre-tax profit margins represent how much of each sales dollar a company keeps before taxes. Increasing sales brings in more dollars, whereas decreasing costs reduces how many dollars are spent. Either approach increases the profit margin, but both can also lead to lower quality, poorer service, customer dissatisfaction or ineffective operations if implemented poorly. If sales drop, cutting costs can change from cutting fat to removing vital organs, and a company can quickly become a patient in critical condition. Good management achieves long term growth by balancing sales initiatives and cost controls.

The Value Line industry page and the Multex Investor Web site (www.multexinvestor.com) both provide industry averages. You can calculate the average pre-tax profit margin for an industry by using industry average net profit and tax rate on the Value Line industry page and applying the calculations for pre-tax profit margin in this chapter. Compare return on equity for the company to the Return on Shareholders' Equity on the Value Line industry page.

Finding Industry Averages

The SSG focuses on pre-tax profit margin rather than net profit margin. The government can and does change tax rates and there is only so much that businesses can do to control the taxes they pay. Pre-tax profit margins eliminate taxes from the equation.

Management can increase sales by expanding territory, taking market share from competitors, or increasing the price of a product. Companies must develop products of extraordinary quality to increase prices without losing market share to competition.

On the other hand, paying less for supplies or increasing production efficiency can reduce costs. Management must control or reduce overhead expenses, such as salaries and benefits, travel expenses, marketing and advertising, rent, and utilities. In many industries, such as computers or women's fashion, management has the added burden of planning for and minimizing obsolete inventory.

Calculating Pre-Tax Profit on Sales

Some sources of data provide the numbers for pre-tax profit, whereas others such as Value Line present net profit. However, you can calculate pre-tax profit using net profit and the tax rate. From there, you can compute the pre-tax profit margin.

There are several steps to manipulating net profit into the pre-tax profit margin. However, if you take one step at a time, you can complete this calculation without venturing farther than adding, subtracting, multiplying and dividing.

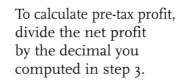

Each item in the first column of the table below has a letter prefix. Calculation formulas appear in parentheses and reference the letter prefix for the items to use in the equation.

Value Line provides 10 years of net profit, tax rates and sales in the data table on each company Value Line sheet.

1. Enter the last 10 years in the first row of the table with the earliest year in the first column on the left.

2. Enter the value for net profit from Value Line in the cell in the first row of the table. This value often represents millions of dollars.

3. Value Line includes the tax rate as a percentage. Divide the percentage tax rate from Value Line by 100 to create a decimal number.

4. To add the taxes back into the profit, you need the decimal that represents what remains after taxes. To compute this decimal, subtract the tax rate from "1."

For example, if a company's tax rate is 30% (as in year 1994 below), the amount that remains of profit after taxes is 70%. Since the decimal for the tax rate is .30, the amount that remains is 1 − .30, or .70.

5. To calculate pre-tax profit, divide the net profit by the decimal you computed in step 3.

6. Enter the values for sales in the row for sales. These are the same numbers that you graphed in Section 1.

7. Pre-tax profit margin is the pre-tax profit divided by sales. Multiply the decimal number for the pre-tax profit margin by 100 to present the margin as a percentage.

8. Repeat these steps until you have calculated pre-tax profit margins for the last 10 years.

The first year in the following table shows each step in the pre-tax profit margin calculation. The subsequent years include blanks so you can practice more and more of the calculation. You can check your calculations against the numbers in Figure 11-01.

a. Year	1992	1993	1994	1995...
b. Net profit	1093	1179	1298	
c. Tax rate as a decimal	.28	.26	.30	
d. 1 – Tax rate	.72	.74	.70	
e. Pre-tax profit (b/d)	1518	1593		
f. Sales	7230	7477	8281	
g. Pre-tax profit on sales (e/f)	.21			
h. Percent pre-tax profit margin (x 100)	21%			

Stepping Through the Pre-Tax Profit Margin Calculation

Pfizer's recent pre-tax profit margins are above average for the industry. The drug industry margin for 2001 is 26 percent, calculated using numbers from the Value Line Drug industry page: net profit of $35,895 million, a 28.5% tax rate and $193,325 million in sales. Pfizer's pre-tax profit margins have also increased steadily for the past 10 years. In addition, Pfizer's margins have grown rapidly from 24.6% to 34.6% in the last five years. Although these profit margins are quite good, Pfizer stands an excellent chance of improving profit margins even more over the next five years by selling the candy, gum and razor businesses it obtained from Warner-Lambert and increasing the percentage of high-margin drugs.

Looking for Consistency

If you use a table like the one above, enter the years from the first row of your table in the heading row of Section 2 of the SSG. Then, enter the pre-tax profit margins from the bottom row of your calculation table into the first row of Section 2.

You can find a blank pre-tax profit margin worksheet in the back of this book.

• Look for a steady upward trend that is also above average for the industry.

• Be skeptical of above-average profit margins that make a big jump. The company might have taken actions that provide short-term improvements at the expense of long-term performance.

• Numbers that stay the same over the years might mean that a company has cost control down to an art with little room for improvement. However, don't rush to applaud management. Flat numbers can easily represent stagnation.

2 EVALUATING MANAGEMENT		Company Pfizer (PFE)											06/04/02		
		1992	1993	1994	1995	1996	1997	1998	1999	2000	2001	LAST 5 YEAR AVG.	TREND UP	TREND DOWN
A	% Pre-tax Profit on Sales (Net Before Taxes ÷ Sales)	21.2	21.4	22.4	22.8	24.7	24.6	25.9	29.3	30.5	34.6	29.0	UP	

Figure 11-01: Adding pre-tax profit margin values to Section 2.

When profit margins start to drop, the company keeps less money from each dollar of sales, which eventually reduces earnings. If you think that profit margins could drop in the future, go back and scrutinize your estimated future EPS growth rate in Section 1. That growth rate should not be higher than your estimated sales growth rate. When profit margins are poised to fall, the EPS growth rate should probably be lower than that of sales.

Getting Your Money's Worth

Percent earned on equity is the return that management achieves on stock investors' money (including earnings retained in the business for future growth). More correctly, the term stock investors' money is usually called equity, shareholders' equity, or book value. It represents the net amount of company dollars after subtracting total liabilities from total assets. The term "book" is derived from the "accounting records or accounting book". Thus, book value is an accounting measure using historical costs. Percent earned on equity is an indicator of how well management is utilizing the company's resources contributed by shareholders' money and reinvested earnings.

Percent earned on equity =	$\dfrac{EPS}{Book\ value\ per\ share}$

Calculating the Return on Investors' Money

Calculating percent earned on equity is easier than computing the pre-tax profit margin. However, a table simplifies your calculations for the 10 years you need for Section 2. A blank worksheet for percent earned on equity appears in the back of this book.

 1. Enter the last 10 years in the first row of the table with the earliest year in the leftmost column.

2. Enter the values for EPS from Value Line in the first row of the table.

 3. Enter the book value per share from Value Line in the second row of the table.

4. To calculate percent earned on equity, divide EPS by book value per share. Multiply the decimal by 100 to present the return on equity as a percentage.

5. Repeat these steps until you have calculated percent earned on equity for the last ten years.

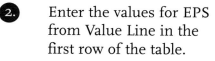

a. Year	1992	1993	1994	1995...
b. EPS	.27	.31	.35	
c. Book value per share	1.21	1.00	1.15	
d. Percent earned on equity (b/c) x 100	22.3	31		

Determining Percent Earned on Equity

Demanding a Good Return

If you use a table like the prior one, enter the years from the first row of your table in the heading of Section 2 of the SSG. Then, enter the percent earned on equity from the bottom row of your table into the second row of Section 2. Look for a steady upward trend that is also above average for the industry.

Pfizer's percent earned on equity (also called return on equity or ROE) numbers are above average for the industry. The drug industry average is 29 percent for year 2001 from the Value Line industry page. Percent earned on equity almost doubled over the past 10 years and the ROE growth has accelerated during the past five years. Value Line forecasts that Pfizer's ROE (in the Return on Shareholder Equity row of the data table) will drop to 35 percent in the next three to five years. This number is still above the industry average and bears watching.

Determining the Trends in Section 2

The trends in Pfizer's case are easy to spot. However, when a company's Section 2 numbers bobble around, you can test for an upward trend by comparing the most recent year's values to the averages for the last five years. Of course, that means that you're about to calculate a five-year average.

Success Tip!

For a quick review of the steps to calculate a five-year average, revisit Chapter 4.

1. Enter the five-year average for pre-tax profit margin in the Last Five-Year Avg. cell in the first row of SSG.

2. Enter the five-year average for percent earned on equity in the same column.

3. If the most recent year's numbers are higher than the average, add a checkmark or the word UP in the trend box. If the most recent year's numbers are lower than the average, add the word DOWN in the trend box.

2 EVALUATING MANAGEMENT		Company **Pfizer** (PFE)												06/04/02
		1992	1993	1994	1995	1996	1997	1998	1999	2000	2001	LAST 5 YEAR AVG.	TREND UP	DOWN
A	% Pre-tax Profit on Sales (Net Before Taxes ÷ Sales)	21.2	21.4	22.4	22.8	24.7	24.6	25.9	29.3	30.5	34.6	29.0	UP	
B	% Earned on Equity (E/S ÷ Book Value)	22.3	31.0	30.4	28.5	27.8	27.9	29.5	37.7	40.0	45.0	36.0	UP	

Figure 11-02: Adding percent earned on equity to Section 2.

Calculating Five-Year Averages for Section 2		
	Pre-tax profit margin	% earned on equity
1997	24.6	27.9
1998	25.9	29.5
1999	29.3	37.7
2000	30.5	40.0
2001	34.6	45.0
Five-year total	144.9	179.2
Average (Total ÷ 5)	29.0	35.8

1997	1998	1999	2000	2001	LAST 5 YEAR AVG.	TREND	
						UP	DOWN
24.6	25.9	29.3	30.5	34.6	29.0	UP	
27.9	29.5	37.7	40.0	45.0	36.0	UP	

Figure 11-03: Compare the figures from the most recent year to the five-year average to determine the trend.

Using the Preferred Procedure to Check EPS Growth

After you calculate the pre-tax profit margin in Section 2, you can corroborate your estimate of EPS five years out using the NAIC Preferred Procedure. The Preferred Procedure is a method for calculating EPS from sales, which are easier to predict. You can apply estimates for a company's future profit margins, taxes, dividends from preferred shares, and the number of common shares outstanding to determine the EPS in the future.

You can apply judgment to each step of the Preferred Procedure to hone in on future EPS. For example, if the pre-tax profit on sales percentage has been dropping steadily, you can use a lower value to calculate the pre-tax profit. If the tax rate or number of shares has been increasing, you can adjust those numbers to calculate net profit or EPS.

1. You start with the estimated future sales—the sales figure that you added where the sales trend line crosses the right margin of the Section 1 graph. Pfizer's projected sales from the graph in Section 1 = $54,227 million.

2. Pre-tax profit equals sales five years out multiplied by a pre-tax profit margin. Because Pfizer's pre-tax profit margins should continue to increase over the next five years, this example uses the current pre-tax profit margin of 34.6 percent to be conservative.

3. Net profit is the profit that remains after paying taxes. It equals pre-tax profit multiplied by (1 – Tax Rate). There's no apparent reason to expect tax rates to change in the future, so we use Value Line's forecasted tax rate of 25 percent.

4. Estimated EPS equals net profit divided by the number of shares out-standing. The company just announced a $10 billion stock buyback, so the number of shares should continue to drop. Value Line forecasts the shares at 6,050 million over the next three to five years. Fewer shares result in higher EPS.

The eyeball method of reading the EPS from the right margin of Section 1 of the SSG results in EPS of $2.55. The Preferred Procedure EPS are $2.32, which tells you that the Section 1 estimate is in the right ballpark. If you want to be extra conservative, you can use the Preferred Procedure EPS when they are lower than your estimate from Section 1. This example continues to use the EPS forecast with 14% growth from Section 1 of the SSG.

One Final Check

Before you move on to Section 3, review what you've found in Sections 1 and 2.

• Is the company growing sales and EPS at a consistent pace?

• Are sales and EPS growing fast enough for a company of that size?

• Are pre-tax profit margins above the average for the industry and increasing steadily?

• Is the return on equity above the industry average and increasing steadily?

If you don't get the answers you want for these questions, stop the study right here and look for another stock to analyze.

Pre-tax profit =	Sales x Pre-tax profit margin	
	$54,227 million x 34.6% =	$18,762 million

Net profit =	Pre-tax profit x (1 – tax rate) =	
	$18,762 million (1 – .25) =	$14,071 million

EPS =	Net profit	=	$14,071 million	$2.32
	# of shares		6,050 million	

History Repeats Itself

Price earnings ratios, like fashions, seem to go full circle if you wait long enough. In the heat of a bull market, PEs go through the roof. They fall back to earth when reason, or even despair, takes hold. However, over time each company sports a PE ratio which reflects its prospects for future growth.

By studying the history of PE ratios in Section 3 of the SSG, you can separate fad from timeless fashion. You might not know whether hemlines are headed up or down, but you can forecast the direction of a company's PEs.

Adding Data to the Table

Calculating
PE Ratios & Yield

Calculating
Averages in the
Price-Earnings History

Deciding When to
Throw Numbers Out

You might think that price-earnings history is just a container for some numbers and simple calculations. However, Section 3 of the SSG displays these numbers so you can assess the value of a potential investment. Earnings affect prices. Dividends contribute to total return. PEs fidget around. However, you can analyze the patterns in Section 3—eliminating fleeting results, using dependable numbers and judging the endurance of trends—to determine the value your investment holds.

Adding Data to the Table

The price-earnings history captures the most recent five years of high and low prices and EPS in order to calculate PE ratios. It also tracks dividend per share in order to calculate the yield that the stock offers (both the percent payout and percent high yield). And, present price appears for the calculation of the current PE for the stock.

To fill out Section 3, you need the following data:

• **Years:** Enter the last five years for which a company has actual data in the first column of the price-earnings history. For example, the most recent year of data for Pfizer is 2001,

so 2001 appears in the bottom row in Section 3. The first row counts five years back, to 1997 in Pfizer's case.

• **Present Price:** Get a quote from today's newspaper or surf almost any Web site to get the most recent price quote. Section 3 calculates the present PE by dividing the present price by the EPS for the most recent full year of data. Enter the present price on the present price line at the top of Section 3. Pfizer's price as of June 4, 2002, used in our example, is a quote from *www.quicken.com*.

• **High This Year:** Get the 52-week high price from a newspaper or the Internet. Enter the 52-week high price on the High This Year line at the top of Section 3.

• **Low This Year:** Get the 52-week low price from a newspaper or the Internet. Enter the 52-week low price on the Low This Year line at the top of Section 3.

• **High prices:** Value Line shows the high prices for the last 10 years across the top of each company sheet. Transfer the

high prices for the past five years into this column starting with the earliest year and continuing to the most recent year of full data.

• **Low prices:** Value Line shows the low prices for the last 10 years just below the high prices. Enter the low prices for the past five years into this column from the earliest to the most recent year of full data.

• **EPS:** EPS for the last 16 years appears in the table on the Value Line sheet. Enter EPS for the past five years in this column.

• **Dividend per Share:** Value Line displays the Div'ds Decl'd per sh just below EPS on the company sheet. Enter the dividends per share in this column.

Success Tip!

If you use NAIC software such as Investor's Toolkit, Stock Analyst PLUS! *or* NAIC Classic, *you can save data entry time by downloading data directly into your software package. You can learn more about sources of data from the* NAIC Computerized Investing & the Internet Handbook *or the user manual that comes with your software package. You can also obtain the present price from numerous* Web *sites on the* Internet. *In some cases, these prices are up to date as of the time you requested the price quote.*

Calculating PE Ratios, Payout & Yield

You do nothing more than divide some numbers by others to calculate the measures in Section 3. These measures help identify whether a stock is worth purchasing or a target to sell. Each column in Section 3 of the SSG has a letter to identify it. The header for each calculated column shows the formula for the calculation using those letter identifiers. For example, the high PE ratio column includes a formula, A÷C, where A is high price and C is EPS.

3 PRICE-EARNINGS HISTORY as an indicator of the future

This shows how stock prices have fluctuated with earnings and dividends. It is a building block for translating earnings into future stock prices.

PRESENT PRICE 34.580 HIGH THIS YEAR 45.000 LOW THIS YEAR 33.290

	Year	A PRICE HIGH	B PRICE LOW	C Earnings Per Share	D Price Earnings Ratio HIGH A÷C	E Price Earnings Ratio LOW B÷C	F Dividend Per Share	G % Payout F÷C X 100	H % High Yield F÷B X 100
1	1997	26.7	13.4	0.57	46.8	23.5	0.230	40.4	1.7
2	1998	43.0	23.7	0.67	64.2	35.4	0.250	37.3	1.1
3	1999	50.0	31.5	0.87	57.5	36.2	0.310	35.6	1.0
4	2000	49.3	30.0	1.02	48.3	29.4	0.360	35.3	1.2
5	2001	46.8	34.0	1.31	35.7	26.0	0.440	33.6	1.3
6	TOTAL		132.6		252.5	150.5		182.2	
7	AVERAGE		26.5		50.5	30.1		36.4	
8	AVERAGE PRICE EARNINGS RATIO	40.3		9	CURRENT PRICE EARNINGS RATIO	26.4			

Figure 12-01: Adding the data to the price-earnings history

Calculating the High PE Ratio

The high PE is really a fabrication. It is the highest price for the stock during the year divided by the EPS for that year. But, the stock reached its highest price before the company ever achieved the EPS you use. Over the five years of price-earnings history, the high PE indicates how much investors were willing to pay for earnings that the company produced. For 1997, Pfizer's high PE was:

$$\text{High PE (D)} = \frac{\text{High Price (A)}}{\text{EPS (C)}} = \frac{26.7}{.57} = 46.8$$

Calculate the high PE for each year and enter the result in the high PE column.

Calculating the Low PE Ratio

The low PE is the lowest price for the stock during the year divided by the EPS for that year. It too is fiction. The stock reached its lowest price before the company attained the EPS for the year. The low PE signifies how little investors were willing to pay for earnings that the company produced. For 1997, Pfizer's low PE was:

$$\text{Low PE (E)} = \frac{\text{Low Price (B)}}{\text{EPS (C)}} = \frac{13.4}{.57} = 23.5$$

Calculate the low PE for each year and enter the result in the low PE column.

Percent Payout

The percent payout (% payout) is the percentage of profit that the company pays to share-holders as dividends. If you're

$$\% \text{ payout (G)} = \frac{\text{Dividend per share (F)}}{\text{EPS (C)}} = \frac{.23}{.57} = .40 = 40\%$$

looking for steady income to pay bills during your retire-ment, you might get excited about dividends. For investors who prefer to watch the stock price go up, a higher payout might not be so welcome. Distributing a large portion of earnings as dividends could be a signal that re-investing

earnings into the company just isn't worth it. High payouts appear frequently in mature companies or industries where growth is slower.

Calculate the percent payout for each year and enter the result in the % payout column.

Some industries such as utilities traditionally pay out high dividends. Fast growing companies or industries where research and development are critical often keep profits in the company to fuel growth.

Success Tip!

A dramatically increasing payout ratio might be a red flag that a company is trying to hang on to shareholders by pumping up dividends. However, increasing dividends could jeop-ardize research and development and future growth. As a general rule look for dividend increases that are the same percentages as EPS increases.

Calculating Averages in the Price-Earnings History

Section 3 shows averages for the low price, the high PE, the low PE and the percent payout. Section 4 of the SSG uses the averages for low price, low PE and percent payout to determine potential low prices for the next five years. The average high PE contributes to the estimate for a potential high price over the next five years.

Percent High Yield

The percent high yield (% high yield) represents the yield from dividends that the company pays. The SSG determines the high yield in order to determine a low price in Section 4 for stocks that pay large dividends. The high yield comes from dividing the dividend per share by the low price.

Calculate the percent high yield for each year and enter the result in the % high yield col-umn. In a declining stock mar-ket, a dividend helps support the price of the stock.
A sizeable number of investors value dividends and step in during a declining market to buy stocks that reach a yield they consider favorable.

$$\% \text{ High Yield (H)} = \frac{\text{Dividend per share (F)}}{\text{Low price (B)}} = \frac{.23}{13.4} = .017 = 1.7\%$$

Calculating Five-Year Averages

Calculating these average values over five years should be familiar by now. But, here's a quick review of the steps:

 1. Add up the numbers in the column. For example, for Pfizer's low price, add up the low prices for the last five years and enter the total in the Total cell in the low price column.

 2. To calculate the average, divide the total by 5.

Repeat this calculation for the high and low PEs and the percent payout. Enter the average values in the second to last row in the price-earnings history.

Calculating the Five-Year Average PE Ratio

You obtain the average PE ratio for the last five years using the average high PE and the average low PE. Because there are only two values in this average, you only divide the total by 2. The average PE over the last five years often acts as a barometer for the PE of a company. However, this is true only if the trend of PEs remains the same as it was when the five year average was calculated. For example, with a bull market that ran for over 10 years, many companies have 5 years of elevated PEs. Read the next section in this chapter to learn how to handle Section 3 values that don't make sense.

Deciding When to Throw Numbers Out

Just as some years in the graph in Section 1 don't reflect a company's usual performance, some values in Section 3 might misrepresent typical PEs for the company. Because we use the average high and low PE ratios to estimate potential high and low prices five years out in Section 4, we want to make sure that those averages are reasonable and conservative.

For example, you might choose to eliminate PEs that are significantly higher or lower than others. The PEs might trend one way or the other, indicating that future values might not match those in the past. These errant values are called outliers—they lie outside the expected boundaries for the stock. Before you calculate the average values in Section 3, eliminate these outliers from the table and, *don't use them in your calculations*. Remember, if you purchase a stock based on

$$\text{Average low price} = \frac{13.4+23.7+31.5+30+34}{5} = \frac{132.6}{5} = 26.5$$

$$\text{Average PE} = \frac{\text{Average high PE} + \text{average low PE}}{2} = \frac{50.5 + 30.1}{2} = 40.3$$

Calculating the Current PE Ratio

You want to use the last four quarters of EPS data when calculating current PE. To use the last four quarters, add up the quarterly EPS from the last four formula above. The current PE is also called the "trailing PE" or "trailing twelve months PE".

$$\text{Current PE} = \frac{\text{Present price}}{\text{EPS for last four quarters}} = \frac{34.58}{.30+.34+.34+.39} = 25.2$$

3 PRICE-EARNINGS HISTORY as an indicator of the future

This shows how stock prices have fluctuated with earnings and dividends. It's a building block for translating earnings into future stock prices.

PRESENT PRICE **34.580**   HIGH THIS YEAR **45.000**   LOW THIS YEAR **33.290**

Year	A PRICE HIGH	B PRICE LOW	C Earnings Per Share	D Price Earnings Ratio HIGH A÷C	E Price Earnings Ratio LOW B÷C	F Dividend Per Share	G % Payoff F÷C X 100	H % High Yield F÷B X 100
1 1997	26.7	13.4	0.57	46.8	23.5	0.230	40.4	1.7
2 1998	43.0	23.7	0.67	64.2	35.4	0.250	37.3	1.1
3 1999	50.0	31.5	0.87	57.5	36.2	0.310	35.6	1.0
4 2000	49.3	30.0	1.02	48.3	29.4	0.360	35.3	1.2
5 2001	46.8	34.8	1.31	35.7	26.0	0.440	33.6	1.3
6 TOTAL		132.6		35.7	23.5		182.2	
7 AVERAGE		26.5		35.7	23.5		36.4	
8 AVERAGE PRICE EARNINGS RATIO			29.6	9 CURRENT PRICE EARNINGS RATIO	25.2			

Figure 12-02: Removing outliers in the price-earnings history.

price forecasts that use overly optimistic price/earnings ratios, the stock price might drop as the PE ratios return to their usual stomping grounds.

Some people would argue that most of Pfizer's PE ratios are outliers. The high PEs start in the mid 30s and shoot all the way up to 64.2. Even the low PEs are in the high 20s and low 30s. This example keeps only the lowest values for both high and low PEs for the last five years. Doing this results in a five-year average PE ratio of 29.6.

Descending PEs

When PE ratios start to drop, the average PE might not be representative of PE ratios to come. The average could be higher than the most recent year's value! To be conservative when PE ratios are steadily decreasing, choose a PE that is equal to or less than the PE in the most recent year. For example, if PEs are decreasing because competition is heating up or the market appears to be beginning a long decline, PE ratios could continue to fall for several years.

Pfizer's high PE ratios have dropped steadily from 64.2 to 35.7 since 1998. For example, in Figure 12-01, the average high PE is 50.5, even though the most recent year's high PE is only 35.7. In this case, you might choose the lowest value, 35.7, instead of the average value. Or, if you think things will get even worse, you might select a number even lower than that. For example, to reflect the decreasing PEs for Pfizer, you might use a high PE of 30 and a low PE of 18 when you fill in the forecast high and low PEs in Section 4 of the SSG.

Ascending PEs

When PE ratios increase, the average high or low PE is the conservative choice. Although PE ratios are headed up, they can't continue in that direction forever. (Remember what happened to the Internet stocks with PEs in the hundreds!) The average high or low PE is less than the most recent year's PE. This average PE might better represent the normal PE for the stock.

Elevated PEs

What do you do with PEs that are outrageously high? In a word, lower them. Is an average high PE of 50 reasonable? Or is it the result of market optimism, irrational exuberance, current industry favoritism or some other short-term effect?

The average PE ratio for the past five years is a more conservative number that can protect you from the temptation of expecting fabulous performance to continue forever. The bull market of the 1990s lasted longer than any other. PEs were inflated for more than five years. The average PE is a step toward recognizing that investors won't continue to pay inflated PEs.

Many long-time NAIC investors set personal guidelines for PE ratios. Based on years of experience, these successful investors limit the PE ratios that they use to no higher than 15 or 20. For beginners, these guidelines keep your studies conservative. You might not find as many stocks to buy, but the ones you do buy stand an excellent chance of meeting your expectations.

Section 4 of the SSG uses the numbers calculated in Section 3 to forecast potential high and low prices for a stock over the next five years. These prices then indicate whether the stock is a good buy at its current price.

CHAPTER THIRTEEN

SSG Section 4 - Risk and

You Don't Have to Be Evel Knievel

Risk and reward are forces you must balance if you are to invest successfully. You can't eliminate risk in investing. Money in your mattress might burn in a fire. Money in a certificate of deposit will almost certainly lose its purchasing power over time.

The only solution is to manage the risks you must take. Quality growth companies produce fewer surprises. Conservative judgment increases your chances of making money because you purchase strong companies at excellent prices. Scales tip in your favor only when the potential reward of your investment more than offsets the risk.

Forecasting High & Low Prices

Buy, Hold & Sell Zones

The Upside-Downside Ratio

It's All Relative

Reward

Section 4 of the SSG uses the output of the price-earnings history in Section 3 to determine the value of a potential investment. It's not enough for an investment to offer value. It must offer enough value to offset the risks it carries. For example, mature large companies frequently grow slow and steady—nothing too exciting, but dependable as all get out. These companies still carry some risk, but at a level that allows you to sleep at night while realizing a 7 to 10 percent return. Small companies, on the other hand, can face endless dangers—inexperienced management, competition, new technology, obsolescence and cash flow uncertainties. To prevail, you must demand more from your riskier investments. The higher the risk, the higher the return you should expect. With higher returns, your winners can offset the investments that didn't pan out.

Forecasting High & Low Prices

Risk consists of the magnitude and possibility of danger—how much a stock's price could fall and how likely the occurrence of that misfortune. Every step of an NAIC stock study aims to reduce the possibility of calamity.

Quality growth and conservative judgment filter out companies that might not make the grade. Section 4 of the SSG focuses on the magnitude of danger. If the stock price drops, how far might it fall?

Eyeing the Reward

The high price for the next five years is an estimate of how high a stock's price might go during that period. It doesn't tell you when that price might appear, or the path of a stock price that brings you there. It's a rough estimate of the reward if things go as you forecast in your stock study. The High Price–Next Five Years line on the SSG is equal to the highest

PE people might pay for the company, multiplied by the highest earnings that the company might generate. The trick is choosing the highest PE people might pay and the highest earnings that the company might produce.

PRICE FROM PE

When you have a price and EPS for a company, you can calculate the PE ratio—the price divided by the earnings. Section 4 uses an estimate of future PE to forecast a price. It's easy to understand if you look at the formulas.
PE = Price ÷ EPS
PE x EPS = Price

Back in Chapter 12, you read about calculating average PEs and eliminating outliers. This judgment, from Section 3, of the high PE impacts your calculation of the potential high price.

For example, Pfizer's PE ratios have been consistently high for the past five years, so even the average high PE appears inflated. In this example, you might choose to limit the high PE to your personal PE limit, such as 30.

High price =	High PE x High EPS	= 30 x 2.55	= 76.5

For growth companies where sales and EPS increase steadily each year, the highest EPS is the EPS five years in the future. Use the EPS from Section 1 where the EPS trend line crosses the right margin of the graph. For Pfizer, the original EPS from the trend line (back in Chapter 10) was $2.55.

Determining the Risk

The low price during the next five years is an estimate of how low the stock price might drop during that period. Although the high price uses one approach, there are four methods for determining the possible low price—each one appropriate for a different type of company or situation. Each method on the SSG has a letter prefix, (a) through (d), as shown in the headings below.

(A) AVERAGE LOW PE

The low price determination method for growth companies appears first because it's used most often. Almost the mirror image of the calculation for high price, low price five years out is the lowest PE possible during the next five years multiplied by the lowest EPS. *(See Success Tip above)*

Because EPS should increase each year in a growth company,

Success Tip!

Most of the time, you use method (a) to pick a low price. But, sometimes, this approach produces a low price higher than the current price. If the current stock price is already lower than your forecast low price, your forecast is already wrong and you must reduce your forecast low price even more.

the lowest EPS is also the most recent EPS produced. You can use the EPS from the last full year of data or EPS for the most recent four quarters. If you use the most recent full year of data, just grab that number from the EPS column of Section 3. To use the last four quarters, add up the quarterly EPS from the most recent four quarters in the lower left corner of the Value Line sheet. Remember that bolded numbers represent forecast of future earnings, not actual performance. For Pfizer, the most recent four quarters of EPS are the second quarter of fiscal year 2001 through the first quarter of fiscal year 2002.

Because Pfizer grows steadily, method (a) is the preferred

USING HIGH PE TO CHOOSE A LOW PE

When PE ratios from the last five years don't offer a clear answer, you might wonder how to choose a low PE. Often, high and low PE ratios fall into a pattern. For example, with Pfizer the low PE hovers around 60 percent of the high PE. One way to pick a low PE is to multiply the high PE by this high-to-low factor.
• Low PE = High PE x High-to-Low factor
• For Pfizer, the high PE is 30, chosen as a maximum cutoff
• Low PE = 30 x .60 = 18

The lowest PE ratio comes from the judgment you applied in Section 3 of the SSG, back in Chapter 12. For example, if PEs are decreasing, you might choose a PE even lower than the one from the most recent year. If PEs are increasing, the average low PE for the last five years is a more conservative number.

approach for selecting a low price five years out. This example uses the EPS for the last four quarters for the low EPS. The low PE results from multiplying the selected high PE of 30 by a factor. Pfizer's low PEs tend to be about 60 percent of the high PEs.

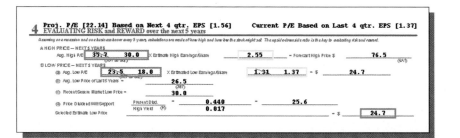

Figure 13-01: Selecting forecast high and low prices.

Low Price	= Low PE x Low EPS	
	= 18 x (.30 + .34 + .34 + .39)	= 24.66

In the high and low price area of Section 4, you have the opportunity to apply judgment to the high and low PEs for the next five years. For example, the high PE is 30 instead of the average high PE of 35.7 to reflect the dropping PEs in Section 3. The low PE is 18 instead of the average low PE of 23.5. Once again, this reflects the dropping PEs from Section 3.

(B) AVERAGE LOW PRICE OF LAST 5 YEARS

The average low price of last five years is best suited to cyclical and volatile companies. Business cycles in the past lasted about five years, so the average low price of the last five years represents a low price during the next business cycle. The last business cycle ran for more than a decade, so you must judge whether the recent low prices truly represent the lows of an entire business cycle.

(C) RECENT SEVERE MARKET LOW PRICE

The recent severe market low is useful for volatile companies. The low price of a volatile company during a serious market drop is a good indicator of the potential low price when the market takes another hit.

(D) PRICE DIVIDEND WILL SUPPORT

This low price is appropriate for high-dividend-paying companies. Dividends paid represent a yield earned on the money invested in stock. As the stock price goes down, the yield increases. When the yield is high enough, the stock becomes an attractive investment for the yield alone.

You calculate the low price supported by the dividend by dividing the current annual dividend per share by the highest yield in Section 3. The current dividend is the entry in the most recent year in the dividend column. The highest yield is the largest number in the % high yield column in Section 3.

You use the highest yield because dividing the dividend by the largest number in the % high yield column results in the lowest low price.

Low Price =	$\dfrac{\text{Present dividend}}{\text{High yield}}$	
	$\dfrac{.44}{.017}$	= 25.88

Buy, Hold & Sell Zones

With estimated high and low prices for the next five years, the next step is to find where the current price falls within that range. Dividing the range between estimated high and low price into three zones— buy, hold and sell— you can determine whether the stock might meet your objectives. If the price is near the low price you anticipate over the next five years, most of the potential price movement is up, which is more reward than risk. However, when the price is near the top of the range, the stock has to exceed your estimated high price to provide the return you expect—a risk that you don't want to take.

SIZING THE ZONES

It's simplest to divide the high-low price range into three equal zones representing buy, hold and sell. An alternative is to set the buy zone at the bottom 25 percent, the hold zone at the middle 50 percent, and the sell zone at the highest 25 percent. This alternative ensures that a price in the buy zone also provides a three-to-one upside-downside ratio, which is a reward measure discussed in the next section.

The top of the buy zone indicates the highest reasonable purchase price. Frequently, you'll see top companies in an industry out of the buy range. However, you can establish a watch list to see if the stock drops into your buy zone. Stock prices can drop because a company's performance is declining. However, prices drop regularly because of short-term events unrelated to that company— conflict in other countries, competitors with regulatory problems, and uncertainty over the next interest rate move. These price drops could give you the chance you're waiting for to buy a great company at a great price.

To create three equal zones, follow these steps.

1. Calculate the difference between the forecast high and low prices.

Price difference =	High price – low price	
	76.5 – 24.7	= 51.8

2. Calculate the size of the zones by dividing the price difference into thirds.

Price zone =	$\dfrac{\text{Price difference}}{3}$	
	$\dfrac{51.8}{3}$	= 17.3

3. Compute the top of the buy zone by adding the price zone to the low price for the next five years. The top of the buy zone is also the bottom of the hold zone.

Top of buy	= Low price + Price zone	
	= 24.7 + 17.3	= 42.0

4. Compute the top of the hold zone by adding the price zone to the top of the buy zone. The top of the hold zone is also the bottom of the sell zone.

Top of hold	= Top of buy zone + Price zone	
	42.0 + 17.3	= 59.2

5. The top of the sell zone is the high price for the next five years. Now that you have the top and bottoms of each zone, enter the values for the price zones in Section 4 of the SSG as demonstrated in figure 13-02.

C ZONING						
76.5 (4A) High Forecast Price Minus	24.7 (4B) Low Forecast Price Equals		51.8 (C) Range. 1/3 of Range =		17.3 (4C D)	
(4C) Lower 1/3 = (4B)	24.7	to	42.0	(B H)		
(4C) Middle 1/3 =	42.0	to	59.2	(Baxbx)		
(4C) Upper 1/3 =	59.2	to	76.5	(4A) (Sell)		
Present Market Price of	34.580		is in the	Buy	Range	

Figure 13-02: Calculating price zones as thirds of the price range.

The Upside-Downside Ratio

The upside-downside ratio compares the potential price increase to the potential price drop. It doesn't indicate the probability of the price going up or down. But it does show the magnitude of these possible changes. NAIC recommends an upside-downside ratio of at least three to one. A lower ratio, between zero and three, indicates that the stock is not currently in the buy range.

The potential increase in price is the difference between the forecast high price and the current price. The potential decrease is the difference between the current price and the forecast low price.

Upside-downside ratio =	Forecast high price − current price	=
	Current price − forecast low price	
	$\dfrac{76.5 - 34.58}{34.58 - 24.7}$	= 4.2

Pfizer's upside-downside ratio is 4.2, indicating that the stock is in the buy zone.

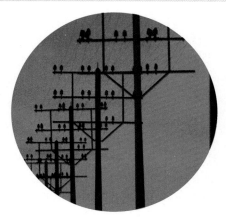

Abnormally High Upside-Downside Ratios

If the recommended upside-downside ratio is three, you might think that an upside-downside ratio of six or even higher represents an incredible buy. You would be wrong. The upside-downside ratio is the difference between the high price and the current price divided by the difference between the current price and the low price. The upside-downside ratio can increase if the current price is much lower than the high price.

However, it's far more common to see a big upside-downside ratio from the current price getting too close to the low price. As the current price approaches the estimated low price, the denominator of the ratio approaches zero, and the upside-downside ratio becomes

D UP-SIDE DOWN-SIDE RATIO (Potential Gain vs. Risk of Loss)						
High Price (4A) 76.5	Minus Present Price 34.580	=	41.9	=	4.2	To 1
Present Price 34.580	Minus Low Price (4B) 24.7		9.9		(4D)	

Figure 13-03: Upside-downside ratio and price zones.

infinity! If the current price closes in on the low price, it usually means that you didn't set the low price low enough. You're saying that no other bad news can affect this stock. The economy won't falter. No wars will break out. Nothing can make the company's EPS or sales worse. When you see a large upside-downside ratio, revisit your judgment in Section 3 and the forecast low price. You should probably reduce your forecast low price even further.

Negative Upside-Downside Ratios

Negative upside-downside ratios are even worse. They occur in two circumstances:

• The current price is LOWER than the estimated low price.

• The current price is HIGHER than the estimated high price.

In both cases, your forecast prices are wrong, because the stock price has already surpassed the values you selected. If the current price is lower than the forecast low price for the next five years, you must drop your forecast lower. When the current price is higher than the forecast high price, there isn't much to do besides look for another stock to study. The stock's price is extravagantly overvalued.

Price Target

The last part of Section 4 shows the potential price appreciation of the stock over the next five years. In most cases, you want a stock purchase to double in five years. Doubling the price is equivalent to 100 percent appreciation—you want the stock price to increase by the amount you paid for it. You can use this simple appreciation expectation to see if the stock comes close. If it doesn't, you don't have to complete the calculations in Section 5.

The potential price appreciation is the forecast high price divided by the present market price of the stock. You can review this calculation in Chapter 4 in the section "Showing Increases or Decreases as a Percentage."

Price appreciation =	Forecast High Price / Present Market Price	x 100 - 100 = %
	$\frac{76.5}{34.58}$ = 2.21	= 221-100 = 121%

The paper SSG form, Investor's Toolkit and NAIC Classic show this calculation for price appreciation. It's easy to do and gives you a nice estimate. Try it!

It's All Relative

Relative value doesn't appear on either the paper SSG form, or in the Beginner mode of *NAIC Classic*, but it is a valuable measure of risk (when properly used). Relative value is the ratio of the current PE ratio to the average PE ratio (adjusted by your judgment) for the last five years—it measures how much investors are currently paying for a stock compared to the average PE during the past five years. In NAIC methodology, relative value somewhere between .85 and 1.10 is ideal.

Relative value =	$\dfrac{\text{Current PE}}{\text{Five-year average PE}}$	=
=	$\dfrac{25.2}{29.6}$	= .85

Success Tip!

You can use the five-year average PE or your estimate of the company's normal PE for the relative value calculation. If you eliminate outliers in Section 3, remember to use the five-year average PE with the outliers eliminated. This example uses the five-year average PE with outliers removed as shown in Chapter 12.

When you buy a stock with a relative value over 1.10, you are paying a PE higher than the five-year average. You run the risk of PE ratios falling back to the company's more normal PE. When PEs drop and the earnings stay the same, the stock price drops. Even if EPS increases, falling PEs reduce the return you would otherwise enjoy.

On the other hand, a relative value below .85 could indicate hidden problems. You should try to find out why investors won't pay more for the company before you purchase.

Living Up to One's Potential

Only time will tell whether a company lives up to your expectations. If you could forecast the future with total accuracy, investing would be effortless. In the real world, stock studies are no more than a series of educated guesses. Some hold true, while others fall short. Each section of the SSG helps you filter out losers. Section 5 finally tells you whether a company has what it takes.

Dividends Amount to Something

Calculating Average Annual Return

Determining Compound Annual Return

ar Potential

Before you decide to purchase a company, you have to find out whether its return meets your objectives. The final section of the SSG unveils the potential return for a stock when purchased at its current price. Although the risk and reward measures in Section 4 hint at whether a stock offers good value, only Section 5 shows you the return you might achieve from both price appreciation and dividends.

Dividends Amount to Something

Dividends can seem like small potatoes when you see them come in a few pennies here or a few dollars there. But, companies that pay dividends usually pay them each quarter and those pennies add up over the years. Some companies reinvest all their earnings into the company to produce more growth—and investors hope that growth leads to higher stock prices, because that's the only return on their investment. When companies distribute earnings to shareholders as dividends, they contribute to the return you receive, regardless whether you reinvest the dividends in more company stock or use them to pay the electric bill.

Total return equals the return from both price appreciation and dividends. Price appreciation is easy to understand. But how do you calculate the return from dividends? Dividends are like interest paid on your initial investment. It makes sense to present the return from dividends in the form of yield—just like the yield banks pay on a savings account.

Present Yield

The present yield measures the yield from the most recent year's dividends, if you purchase the stock at its present price. This yield changes depending on the price paid for the stock.

Present yield =	$\dfrac{\text{Present year's dividend}}{\text{Current price}}$	
	$\dfrac{.44}{34.58}$	$= .013 = 1.3\%$

Average Yield

The average yield over the next five years represents the annual return you can expect dividends to contribute to total return. The calculation for average yield takes advantage of the average percent payout calculated way back in Section 3. Because percent payout indicates the percentage of earnings paid out as dividends, you compute the average dividends by multiplying the average EPS by the average percent payout. Then, you can divide the average dividends by the present price to compute the average yield.

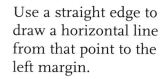

Year	A PRICE HIGH	B PRICE LOW	C Earnings Per Share	D Price Earnings Ratio HIGH A÷C	E LOW C÷C	F Dividend Per Share	G % Payout F÷C X 100	H % High Yield F÷B X 100
PRESENT PRICE 34.580				HIGH THIS YEAR 45.000		LOW THIS YEAR 33.290		
1 1997	26.7	13.4	0.57	46.8	23.5	0.230	40.4	1.7
2 1998	43.0	23.7	0.67	64.2	35.4	0.250	37.3	1.1
3 1999	50.0	31.5	0.87	57.5	36.2	0.310	35.6	1.0
4 2000	49.3	30.0	1.02	48.3	29.4	0.360	35.3	1.2
5 2001	46.8	34.0	1.31	35.7	26.0	0.440	33.6	1.3
6 TOTAL		132.6		35.7	23.5		182.2	
7 AVERAGE		26.5		35.7	23.5		36.4	

Figure 14-01: The Average percent payout in Section 3.

The only number you haven't calculated yet is the average EPS for the next five years. The average EPS is the EPS for the middle year of the five-year period. The simplest way to determine this number is to read it off the graph in Section 1. This is similar to the process used to determine the EPS five years in the future, described in Chapter 10.

 1. Mark the point where the EPS projection line crosses the third year in the future.

2. Use a straight edge to draw a horizontal line from that point to the left margin.

3. Mark the point where the horizontal line crosses the left margin.

4. Use the numbers on the scale in the left margin to determine the EPS three years in the future.

Average yield =	$\dfrac{\text{Average EPS x Average \% payout} =}{\text{Present price}}$	
	$\dfrac{1.96 \times 36.4\%}{34.58}$	= 2.1%

Calculating Average Annual Return

The average annual return is the return you receive during one year of owning an investment. It includes one year of price appreciation and one year of return from dividends. You can use the average price appreciation and the average yield to compute average annual return. The previous section determined the average yield from dividends.

So, all you need is the average price appreciation. The last part of Section 4 calculated the price appreciation for the next five years. To calculate the average price appreciation, just divide the total price appreciation by five. For Pfizer, the five-year price appreciation was 121 percent, so one year's worth of price appreciation is 24.2 percent.

Determining Compound Annual Return

To really see whether a company provides the return you want, you have to determine the compound annual rate of return. The Conversion Table in Section 5 shows simple return on the top row with compound return in the bottom row. Find the number on the top line closest to the average annual return. For Pfizer, 26.3 percent is closest to 26 percent.

Find the number below the simple return in the top row. Pfizer's 26 percent simple rate of return lines up with 18 percent compound rate of return. The rate of return should meet or exceed the minimum return you would expect for the company's size. Pfizer is a large company, so we should expect a

rate of return of 7 percent or more. Pfizer passes this test with flying colors.

Compound annual return identifies whether a company meets your objective for return. However, purchasing a stock is still more art than science. Before you decide to buy, it's a good idea to review all the sections of the SSG. Chapter 15 sums up the decision process.

Average annual return =	Average % price appreciation + Average yield
=	24.2 % + 2.1 % = 26.3%

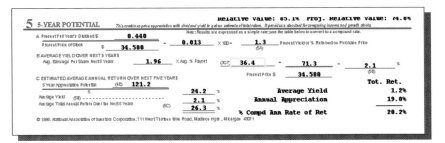

Figure 14-02: Section 5 of the SSG in Investor's Toolkit *doesn't contain the conversion table because the software calculates the compound rate of return for you.*

The software packages often calculate a slightly different compound annual rate of return than indicated by the conversion table on the paper SSG. For that reason, you should always prepare all your stock studies using the same tool, whether it is the paper form or a software package. Then you can be confident that you are comparing apples to apples.

CHAPTER FIFTEEN:

To Buy or Not to Buy

Nothing Personal

A decision whether or not to purchase a stock, is just business. A stock doesn't care whether you like it, pay too much for it, hold on to it too long or sell it too soon. But, buying a stock can be a long-term commitment, so you want to ensure that the two of you are compatible.

When you're just starting out, the SSG can take some time to complete. It's a good idea to summarize your findings when you're done. You can use this summary to make a decision, make a recommendation to your investment club or review your holdings.

Visual Analysis

The Final Word on Management

Is the Price Right?

Beyond the SSG

Summing Things Up

Whether you study stocks by yourself or collaborate with investment club members, organization and consistency produce stock studies that you can rely on. You need some kind of checklist to make sure you cover all the bases. As you gain experience, you can create your own list of items to check for every stock you study. As a beginner, you can use a pretty short list.

• What does the visual analysis tell you about the growth and consistency of a company?

• Does management seem competent? Are they delivering the performance you want?

• Does the outlook for the stock price make the stock suitable for purchase?

• What positive or negative influences does the company face?

• What issues or opportunities for growth exist for the industry?

The Stock Selection Guide and Report is a paper form that combines the SSG form with a two-page checklist where you can summarize your stock study results. If you plan to order these forms from NAIC, make sure to ask for the Stock Selection Guide and Report, not the Stock Selection Guide. NAIC Classic software includes an electronic version of the SSG Report.

Visual Analysis

A quick glance at Section 1 of the SSG tells you whether the company has grown strongly and consistently over the past 10 years. Remember to look for railroad tracks—almost parallel lines of sales and EPS growth—at an upward angle that indicates the growth at a rate you expect from a company of its size. In addition, make sure you can explain any values that don't fit the pattern or are significantly below or above the industry average. And, don't forget to document whether you would consider purchasing this stock based on the visual analysis. Here's a synopsis of questions for visual analysis:

Check Point	What to Look For
Have sales trended up, down or sideways?	Look for steadily increasing sales.
Has EPS trended up, down or sideways?	Look for steadily increasing EPS. EPS growth parallel to sales is ideal.
Has price trended up, down or sideways?	Stock price trending up with sales and EPS shows investor confidence in the stock. However, price can move sideways when the PE is in the high end of the range. As EPS increases, the PE returns to more reasonable levels. So, sideways trends might indicate that the price is ready to start heading up again or is still too high.
If sales are up, what has caused that trend?	Sales growth from new products, new uses for existing products and increasing same store sales (produced by management) are desirable because such growth can continue for long periods of time. Growth through acquisitions, building new stores and increasing market share is good, but can't continue forever.
Is the company growing fast enough for a company of its size?	Make sure that sales and EPS grow at least 7 percent for large companies, 12 percent for mid-sized companies and 15 percent for small companies.
Would you consider this stock based on the visual analysis?	Document whether you would investigate or discard this company as a candidate for purchase based on the results from your visual analysis.

Pfizer's sales and EPS growth rates in Section 1 of the SSG have been consistent and quite strong for a company of its size. In the past, the price trend was strong, which led to the stratospheric PE ratios you see in Section 3 of the SSG. The price has since dropped to a level more in line with the company's performance. Pfizer is an example of a company with increasing sales and EPS, but sideways price movement. The PE ratios (in Section 3 of the SSG in Chapter 12) began to drop in 1998 as price leveled off and EPS continued to increase.

The Pfizer annual report talks about a strong pipeline of new medicines, with 15 in line for regulatory approval over the next five years. It also has 94 compounds in development. The sharp jump in sales between 1999 and 2000 is due to the merger with Warner-Lambert. Although the sales growth rate settled back to previous levels, Value Line points out that efficiencies gained from the merger could boost EPS over the next few years.

The Final Word on Management

Good management can overcome many obstacles, whereas poor management can ruin companies with the best of prospects. Your first check for the abilities of management is in Section 1 of the SSG—strong and consistent sales and EPS growth. But, managerial competence also appears in steadily increasing profit margins and percent earned on equity (return on equity) in Section 2 of the SSG. As with sales and EPS in Section 1, make sure you can explain any outlying values or those that are significantly below or above the industry average. You can add your findings on management to Section 2 of the SSG report.

• Is management successfully growing the company?

• Is management improving profit margins steadily?

• Is management increasing the return on equity steadily?

• Does the management that produced a company's growth and quality still run the show? Are they still there, but ready to retire?

Pfizer's management has grown the company strongly for the past 10 years. The company's recent growth is a bit slower than in the past, but still good for a company of its size. Pfizer's profit margins have increased steadily and are well above industry average. The only downside here is that the current profit margins are tough to improve on. Pfizer has also increased percent earned on equity to numbers above industry average.

Is the Price Right?

A company might be a powerhouse of consistency and growth, but you still won't make money if you pay too much for its stock. Review PE ratios and past prices in Section 3, and forecast high and low prices for the next five years in Section 4, to see whether the stock price can increase enough to meet your objectives. Explain any outliers in PE ratios or price. Assess the upside-downside ratio to see if the odds of the price increasing are in your favor. *(See chart at right.)*

Pfizer's PE ratios have been coming down over the past several years. In many cases, this is a bad sign, but with Pfizer, the PE ratios are finally returning to normalcy and could be well positioned to begin to expand again. The upside-downside ratio indicates a buy at 4.2. The compound annual return of 18 percent (20 percent if you use the return calculated by software packages) is much higher than the 14.9 percent desired goal.

Check Point	What to Look For
Are PE ratios trending up or down?	PE ratios should be below the five-year average and trending upward. However, PEs that have moved sideways could indicate that they are ready to trend up again.
Are PE ratios significantly higher than the five-year average?	When PE ratios are above the five-year average, they could be about to head back down. And, decreasing PE ratios will dampen any return you might expect from increasing EPS.
Are the company's PE ratios above or below average in the industry?	PE ratios above the industry average often indicate an industry leader—a company in which investors have confidence.
What is the reasoning behind the choices for the forecast high and low prices?	Explain your choice for high PE over the next five years. Explain your choice for low price. If you use the low price for a growth company (option a), explain your choice for low PE and low EPS.
Where is the current price within the buy, hold and sell ranges?	Is the price in the buy range in Section 4 of the SSG? If you divide the price range into thirds for your price zones, remember that the top of the buy zone does not provide a three-to-one upside-downside ratio.
Does the upside-downside ratio indicate enough of a potential price increase to offset any price drop?	Look for an upside-downside ratio of at least three-to-one in Section 4 of the SSG.
What compound annual return might I receive if I purchase this stock at the current price?	The compound annual return in Section 5 of the SSG (which includes the return from price appreciation and dividend yield) should be at least 14.9 percent to achieve a goal of doubling your investment in five years.

Beyond the SSG

Many people mistake SSG calculations for a complete stock study. It is important to understand a company's prospects are often difficult to quantify. Before you act on some nice looking numbers in an SSG, review the qualitative features of a company. Keep looking for signs of strength and quality.

(See chart at right)

Pfizer is an established company with many well-known products. The company has 94 compounds in development and 15 medicines lined up for approval over the next five years. In addition to steady sales and EPS growth, Value Line data shows steadily increasing dividends over the past 10 years. Pfizer's annual report mentions that the company plans to increase its funding for research and development to discover new drugs—the source of every pharmaceutical company's growth. When drug patents run out, competitors can sell generic equivalents. A link from the Generic Pharmaceutical Association Web site to the Drug Patent Expiration List *(www.gphaonline.org/news)* shows drugs whose patents run out in the next three years. Pfizer has three drugs on the list, including Zoloft, which had almost $2 billion in sales in 2000.

Check Point	What to Look For
Has the company been in business for at least five years?	A company must have at least five years of history for you to forecast growth using the SSG.
Does it operate regionally, nationally or internationally?	The broader a company's region of operation, the more stable its performance might be.
How broad are its service or product offerings?	A company with limited services or products could get in trouble if their product becomes obsolete or a large company decides to compete.
How well known is the company and its products?	Well-known company names or brands might overcome competition that is lower price or higher quality.
Does the company pay dividends, and if so, how good is its dividend record?	Dividends can provide a significant portion of your return. If they do, you want a long and consistent record of dividends.
How does the company grow its business?	Look for growth strategies that can continue indefinitely—new products, new uses for existing products, increasing same stores sales.
Is competition increasing?	Competition can lead to lower profit margins or decreasing market share.
Are there economic, demographic or technological issues that might influence the future?	If competition is increasing, only invest in the industry leaders who can prevail over upstart competitors. Some industries move with the economy, so you should avoid purchasing cyclical companies like carmakers when the economy is heading for a downturn. Other industries benefit from demographic changes. For instance, health care companies benefit from an aging population that requires more health care.

Just as PE ratios can buoy prices or send them running, industry prospects can boost or bottom out the companies within an industry. Check for trends to see whether a company has to fight the industry current to succeed or can surf to success on a wave of prosperity.

Are there issues that affect the entire industry?

Will the industry benefit or be hurt by population, technology or regulatory changes?

What are the fundamental measures for the industry? (Some industries enjoy high profit margins and others low margins.)

How does the economy affect the industry?

How easy is it for new competitors to arise?

The drug industry benefits from the aging American population. As people grow older they require more health care, so drug companies have a larger market into which to sell. An industry overview provided by the Express Scripts web site *(www.express-scripts.com)* reports that managed health care programs prescribe drugs as an effective, lower-cost substitute for surgery. Because of this, drugs represent a growing percentage of heath care costs. The Generic Pharmaceutical Association web site *(www.gphaonline.org)* points out that generic drugs are popular because of lower cost but equal effectiveness. Generic drugs take business away from the brand name drugs as soon as the protection of a patent disappears. Drug companies must earn as much as they can during the 17 years of a patent on a drug.

The *Value Line* industry page reports that it now costs about $800 million to discover and market a drug today, which certainly makes it difficult for new competitors to get started. In many cases, small companies bring new drugs to market by teaming with larger companies. Pfizer has created many partner ships like this, so they benefit from the success of these smaller competitors.

Summing Things Up

You study stocks so you can make an investment decision. If the stock study doesn't show the pros and cons of the company clearly, it can be hard to decide. A cogent summary might show which way your analysis leans. The very first area of the Stock Selection Guide is a great example of a summary that supports a decision. You can mark the characteristics of a company as good, average or poor. When a company gets good marks in most of the categories, you have a stock to buy.

Reviewing the summary for Pfizer in the SSG, you can see that the company is a quality growth company with good prospects for the future. In addition, its price has dropped into a better buy range, mainly because Pfizer lowered expectations for the second quarter of 2002. With a long-term positive outlook, the stock seems to be a reasonable buy at the price on June 4, 2002.

It's always exciting to find a stock in the buy range. However, before you purchase a stock, you should check to see whether you are buying the best possible investment you can. To do this, you should compare the stock study results from several candidates from the same industry. You might find that another company in the same industry offers a higher quality, better return or less risk. Chapter 16 explains how to use the Stock Comparison Guide to uncover the best investment.

CHAPTER SIXTEEN:

Shopping for Stock

One from Column A, One from Column B

If you have trouble picking just one item on a menu, a combination plate could be the answer. NAIC recommends that you purchase a combination plate of stocks to diversify your portfolio and reduce risk. However, when you own more stocks than you can track, you run the risk of portfolio indigestion. With so much on your plate, some of your stocks might falter before you realize it. You're better off picking the best candidate an industry has to offer, then looking to another industry for your next purchase. The Stock Comparison Guide presents the results of several stock studies side by side, so you can pick the best of the bunch.

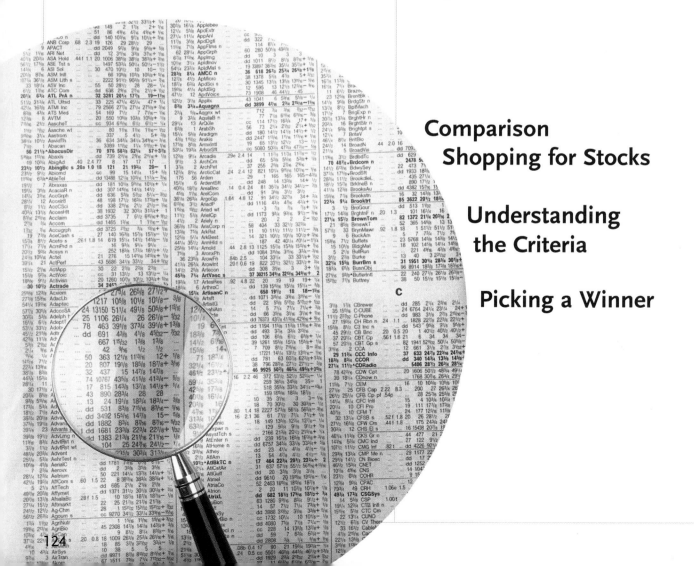

**Comparison
   Shopping for Stocks**

**Understanding
   the Criteria**

Picking a Winner

Shopping for a gift for someone you barely know is torture. How can you buy something they will like, when you don't know a thing about them? When you start investing, choosing a stock to buy is just as difficult. How can you decide on a stock if you haven't figured out the criteria that satisfy your needs? Are you risk-averse or prone to skydiving? Does the thought of one of your investments dropping by 30 percent give you the heebie jeebies? Would you rather see your portfolio grow more slowly to avoid a stock price roller coaster ride? Or are you willing to risk losing some money on an investment to try to grow your portfolio by 15 percent or more a year? After you understand your tolerance for risk, you can evaluate whether a company provides the right levels of risk and return for you.

Comparison Shopping for Stocks

Before you dive into the Stock Comparison Guide, take one last look at the SSGs you've prepared for the companies you're considering. Is one company charted on your Section 1 graph incredibly consistent while the others are as bumpy as a New York City cab ride?

Are numbers in Section 2, Evaluating Management, not just good, but great, while the other companies struggle with falling profit margins, casting doubt on past sales performance continuing into the future? You might decide to eliminate some of your candidates based on their demeanor in Sections 1 and 2 alone.

Getting Friendly with the Stock Comparison Guide (SCG)

If several stocks make the grade in your review of SSG Sections 1 and 2, you can use the Stock Comparison Guide to appraise the attributes of up to five companies side by side. The SCG uses information from SSGs you've already completed. If you use one of the NAIC software packages, the SCG is as easy as clicking on a menu and selecting some company names. If you prepare an SCG by hand, all you have to do is copy some data from your SSGs and perform a few simple calculations.

The SCG works best when you compare companies in the same industry. For example, you can't compare profit margins or debt ratios between industries because typical values can vary

widely—26 percent profit margins for drug companies versus 4 percent for grocery stores. However, you can still use the SCG as long as you keep those industry differences in mind. You could even use criteria such as profit margin, % earned on equity, and debt ratio by rating each company on whether its values are above or below its industry average.

You should update the SSG for every company you want to compare in the Stock Comparison Guide. A comparison won't be very effective if the measures have changed since you prepared the SSGs.

Understanding the Criteria

The Stock Comparison Guide begins with the more significant criteria—sales and EPS growth, profit margins and return on equity. But, there are influential criteria in every section. The NAIC software packages copy or calculate all the values in the SCG for you—and even select winners. However, you should understand what each criterion provides, so you can decide whether you want to use it in your decision.

Success Tip!

Most of the criteria reference the section of the SSG that supplies the data. For example, criterion 21, the upside-downside ratio, displays (4D) at the right end of its cell, referring to Section 4, item D, in the SSG.

Growth Comparisons

Growth comparisons are simple. The growth rates come from the historical and estimated rates that you enter below the graph in Section 1 of the SSG. The winner is the highest growth rate, whether you are measuring historical or projected growth, sales or EPS.

It's easy to spot the winners in the growth section. Scan each row for the highest number and circle it. Pfizer comes out ahead in growth comparisons with the highest growth rates for historical EPS, projected sales and projected EPS growth.

OUTCASTS IN GROWTH COMPARISONS

Although the highest growth rate in each row is a winner, you might not want to count every criterion in the growth comparison section of the SCG. Projected growth is more important than historical growth, because the projected growth is what will eventually deliver higher stock prices. For example, in the example SCG in Figure 16-01, Merck has the highest historical sales growth at 19.4 percent, but one of the lowest projected EPS growth rates at 8 percent.

GROWTH COMPARISONS (From Section 1 of the NAIC Stock Selection Guide)	Abbott Lab ABT	JOHNSON & JNJ	Merck MRK	Pfizer PFE	Schering SGP
(1) Historical % of Sales Growth	7.9 %	10.5 %	19.4 %	18.1 %	11.9 %
(2) Projected % of Sales Growth	9.0 %	10.0 %	10.0 %	11.0 %	7.0 %
(3) Historical % of Earnings Per Share Growth	11.5 %	14.0 %	13.8 %	19.0 %	16.5 %
(4) Projected % of Earnings Per Share Growth	9.0 %	11.0 %	8.0 %	14.0 %	7.0 %

Figure 16-01: Merck wins in historical sales growth, but loses where it counts— projected EPS growth.

MANAGEMENT COMPARISONS
(From Section 2 of the NAIC Stock Selection Guide)

(5) % Profit Margin Before Taxes (Average for last 5 Years)	(2A) Trend	25.8 DOWN	20.1 UP	26.0 DOWN	29.0 UP	30.2 UP
(6) % Earned on Equity (Average for last 5 Years)	(2B) Trend	35.9 DOWN	25.9 DOWN	41.7 UP	36.0 UP	41.4 DOWN
(7) % of Common Owned by Management		0.4	0.1	1.0	1.0	7.0

Figure 16-02: Management comparisons use the numbers from Section 2 of the SSG.

Management Comparisons

The SCG evaluates profit margins, return on equity and the percentage of stock that management owns. You use the five-year average values and trends for profit margin and % earned on equity from Section 2. Use the percentage from insider ownership in the SSG header for the percentage that management owns. Profit margins trending upward and higher than those of the competition indicate that management not only can contain costs and grow sales—but can do that better than the competition.

The return on equity, shown as % earned on equity in the SCG, represents the efficiency of the operation as well as the return on shareholder equity. Higher returns on equity indicate quality management. Upward trends not only show the skill of management, but are good indicators of possible stock price increases.

Criterion 7, % of Common Owned by Management, indicates whether management's interests are aligned with those of the shareholders. When company executives invest a portion of their assets in the company they run, they have strong incentives to manage the company well and see the stock price rise. In smaller companies, management might own a large percentage of the company stock. In very large companies, that same dollar level of investment might only produce one percent ownership.

(See Figure 16-02 above.)

You might approve of any SSG Section 2 numbers that are above industry average and trending up. When you complete an SCG by hand, you can circle only the highest number in each row or choose all the numbers whose trend is up. If you are using NAIC software, *Investor's Toolkit* takes the multiple winner approach, whereas *NAIC Classic* and *Stock Analyst PLUS!* pick one winner per row.

The NAIC software packages handle the % of Common Owned by Management differently. *Investor's Toolkit* displays management ownership for reference only; it doesn't count in the ratings. If you complete an SCG by hand, you can acknowledge overly high or low ownership in the company. However, growth rates, profit margin and return on equity are more important to investment success.

Success Tip!

Even in stock comparisons, growth and consistency must come first. Pay more attention to companies that win the growth and management comparisons, because they hold the key to successful investments. You can always wait for the price to drop into the buy zone.

Price Comparisons

The price comparisons in the SCG compare more than prices—they actually encompass measures from Sections 3, 4 and 5 of the SSG. These comparisons look at EPS, PE ratios, price zones, upside-downside ratio, yield and more. Unlike the growth measures, the winning values for some of the price comparisons aren't immediately apparent. Read on to find out what you should look for in these comparisons.

ESTIMATED TOTAL EARNINGS PER SHARE FOR NEXT 5 YEARS

The line (8) in the SCG for estimated total earnings per share for the next five years shows the sum of estimated EPS for the next five years. However, the winner is not the company with the highest total earnings, but the company whose current price is closest to those earnings. In effect, you are looking for the lowest PE ratio that results from dividing the current price by the EPS for the next five years.

To determine the winner for this measure, you must calculate the total EPS for the next five years. To do this, add up the EPS for each of the next five years. The method for obtaining a value for EPS from the Section 1 graph is described at the end of Chapter 10. You find the point where the EPS projection line crosses the vertical line for a year. Then, move horizontally over to the left margin of the graph and estimate the EPS value.

For example, using the graph in Figure 16-03, you can calculate total EPS for the next five years as follows. Note that this estimated number isn't much different than the $9.72 that *Investor's Toolkit* calculates, shown in Figure 16-04.

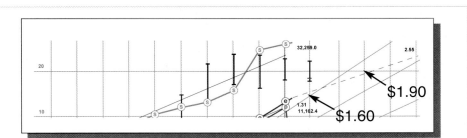

Figure 16-03: You can eyeball EPS for Pfizer from the Section 1 graph.

Year	EPS
2002	$1.60
2003	$1.75
2004	$1.90
2005	$2.25
2006	$2.55
Total	$10.05

The closer the current stock price is to this total, the more favorable is the price. You can use a table to calculate the winner for this SCG criterion. You're looking for the lowest PE ratio that results from dividing the current price by the total estimated EPS. As shown in Figure 16-04, Schering-Plough's $9.72 EPS is the winner because that results in the lowest PE—2.54.

Measures	ABT	JNJ	MRK	PFE	SGP
Current price	44.67	62.52	54.65	34.58	24.75
Total estimated EPS	12.26	13.13	19.89	10.32	9.72
Price / EPS	3.64	4.76	2.74	3.35	2.54

PRICE COMPARISONS
(From Section 3-5 of the NAIC Stock Selection Guide)

(8) Estimated Total Earnings Per Share For Next 5 Years			12.26	13.13	19.89	10.32	9.72
(9) Price Range Over Last 5 Years		High (3A) Low (3B)	24.90~57.20	20.80~53.40	39.00~96.70	13.40~50.00	15.90~60.80
(10) Present Price			44.67	62.52	54.65	34.58	24.75
Price Earnings Ratio Range Last 5 Years	(11) Highest	(3D)	33.20	36.00	37.60	35.70	32.30
	(12) Average High	(3D7)	30.70	30.80	33.00	35.70	32.30
	(13) Average	(3-8)	24.90	26.30	27.00	29.60	24.80
	(14) Average Low	(3E7)	19.10	21.80	21.00	23.50	17.40
	(15) Lowest	(3E)	16.50	19.40	17.90	23.50	16.10
(16) Current Price Earnings Ratio		(3-9)	23.80	32.90	17.40	25.20	15.70

Figure 16-04: PE ratio comparisons aren't as important as growth and management quality.

PRICE EARNINGS RATIO RANGE LAST 5 YEARS

This section enables you to review the price performance of each stock over the past five years and then judge which is more favorably priced for its present position in the market. Companies like these with long records of above average growth tend to sell at high P/Es, but their highs are usually not sustainable. Their average PEs may be more indicative of their highs in less speculative market conditions

(as in Fall of 2002). ABT and JNJ are selling at or above their average PEs and you should consider them more overvalued. MRK's and SGP's current prices are down considerably, suggesting more favorably values, after looking at their current PEs versus five-year average PEs. PFE's current PE is also below its average PE.

The next several criteria for estimated price zones are for reference only.

Success Tip!

Although higher PE ratios indicate investor confidence, they can also be dangerous. PE ratios that are higher than the five-year average ratio could drop back to levels that are more typical and drag the stock price down as well.

OTHER PRICE COMPARISONS

The remaining criteria in the price comparisons area of the SCG focus on the results from Sections 4 and 5 of the SSG. The present price range and the upside-downside ratio tell you whether the company is a buy, whereas the yield and combined estimated yield give an indication of the return you might receive if you buy the stock at its present price.

Clearly, you would like the present price range to be in the buy zone with an upside-downside ratio of at least three-to-one. However, when your candidates just aren't in the buy zone, you can pick a winner based on the growth and management criteria, add it to a watch list and postpone purchase until the price drops.

The current yield indicates the percentage return you receive from dividends if you purchase the stock at its current price. If you are looking for an investment that will provide some income, the winner in this row is the company with the highest yield. However, if you are only interested in long-term gains, you might eliminate the current yield criterion and focus on combined estimated yield or total return.

The paper version of the SCG uses combined estimated yield on line 23. The combined estimated yield is the estimated average annual return for the next five years from Section 5 of the SSG. It is the sum of the average price appreciation and average dividend. Although this number doesn't take compounding into account, you can still pick the winner on this line by looking for the largest number.

OTHER COMPARISONS

The Number of Common Shares Outstanding (24) is on the SCG form for reference only. Companies with a small number of shares might be more volatile than other companies. If you don't want stock prices that resemble Mexican jumping beans, you add a vote for companies based on the number of shares.

The lowest percent payout is preferable for line 26 of the SCG as long as the company has a high rate of return on invested capital. Companies that pay out little or none of their earnings as dividends have more money to fund future growth, which eventually leads to higher stock prices. It is important to check % earned on equity to be sure the company is really producing for the investor. Companies that pay out a high percentage of earnings as dividends will have trouble effectively growing the company.

		-Hold-	-Sell-	-Buy-	-Buy-	-Buy-
(20) Present Price Range	(4C5)					
(21) Upside Downside Ratio	(4D)	1.21	0.30	4.97	4.24	2.65
(22) Current Yield	(5A)	1.84	1.15	2.51	1.27	2.51
(23) Combined Estimated Yield	(5C)	8.08	4.33	16.94	26.35	15.12

Figure 16-05: Price comparisons for Sections 4 and 5 of the SSG.

NATIONAL ASSOCIATION OF INVESTORS CORPORATION

NAIC

INVESTMENT EDUCATION FOR INDIVIDUALS AND CLUBS SINCE 1951

Stock Comparison Guide

Prepared by ___ BJB, BJB, BJB, BJB, BJB

Date ___ 07/09/2002

NAME OF COMPANY

GROWTH COMPARISONS
(From Section 1 of the NAIC Stock Selection Guide)

	Abbott Lab ABT	JOHNSON & JNJ	Merck MRK	Pfizer PFE	Schering-P SGP
(1) Historical % of Sales Growth	7.9 %	10.5 %	19.4 %	18.1 %	11.9 %
(2) Projected % of Sales Growth	9.0 %	10.0 %	10.0 %	11.0 %	7.0 %
(3) Historical % of Earnings Per Share Growth	11.5 %	14.0 %	13.8 %	19.0 %	16.5 %
(4) Projected % of Earnings Per Share Growth	9.0 %	11.0 %	8.0 %	14.0 %	7.0 %

MANAGEMENT COMPARISONS
(From Section 2 of the NAIC Stock Selection Guide)

		Abbott Lab ABT	JOHNSON & JNJ	Merck MRK	Pfizer PFE	Schering-P SGP
(5) % Profit Margin Before Taxes (Average for last 5 Years)	(2A) Trend	25.8 DOWN	20.1 UP	26.0 DOWN	29.0 UP	30.2 UP
(6) % Earned on Equity (Average for last 5 Years)	(2B) Trend	35.9 DOWN	25.9 DOWN	41.7 UP	36.0 UP	41.4 DOWN
(7) % of Common Owned by Management		0.4	0.1	1.0	1.0	7.0

PRICE COMPARISONS
(From Section 3-5 of the NAIC Stock Selection Guide)

			Abbott Lab ABT	JOHNSON & JNJ	Merck MRK	Pfizer PFE	Schering-P SGP
(8) Estimated Total Earnings Per Share For Next 5 Years			12.26	13.13	19.89	10.32	9.72
(9) Price Range Over Last 5 Years		High (3A) Low (3B)	24.90~57.20	20.80~53.40	39.00~96.70	13.40~50.00	15.90~60.80
(10) Present Price			44.67	62.52	54.65	34.58	24.75
Price Earnings Ratio Range Last 5 Years	(11) Highest	(3D)	33.20	36.00	37.60	35.70	32.30
	(12) Average High	(3D7)	30.70	30.80	33.00	35.70	32.30
	(13) Average	(3-8)	24.90	26.30	27.00	29.60	24.80
	(14) Average Low	(3E7)	19.10	21.80	21.00	23.50	17.40
	(15) Lowest	(3E)	16.50	19.40	17.90	23.50	16.10
(16) Current Price Earnings Ratio		(3-9)	23.80	32.90	17.40	25.20	15.70
Estimated Price Zones	(17) Lower-Buy	(4C2)	33.80~39.80	30.80~41.10	47.10~58.38	24.70~37.65	19.00~24.25
	(18) Middle-Maybe	(4C3)	39.80~51.80	41.10~61.70	58.38~80.92	37.65~63.55	24.25~34.75
	(19) Upper-Sell	(4C4)	51.80~57.80	61.70~72.00	80.92~92.20	63.55~76.50	34.75~40.00
(20) Present Price Range		(4C5)	-Hold-	-Sell-	-Buy-	-Buy-	-Hold-
(21) Upside Downside Ratio		(4D)	1.21	0.30	4.97	4.24	2.65
(22) Current Yield		(5A)	1.84	1.15	2.51	1.27	2.51
(23) Combined Estimated Yield		(5C)	8.08	4.33	16.94	26.35	15.12

OTHER COMPARISONS

		Abbott Lab ABT	JOHNSON & JNJ	Merck MRK	Pfizer PFE	Schering-P SGP
(24) Number of Common Shares Outstanding		1,552.00	3,047.22	2,272.00	6,277.00	1,465.00
(25) Potential Dilution from Debentures, Warrants, Options		None	None	None	0.00	None
(26) Percent Payout	(3G7)	41.00	35.80	43.70	36.40	36.20
(27)		0.0 %	0.0 %	0.0 %	0.0 %	0.0 %
(28)		0.0 %	0.0 %	0.0 %	0.0 %	0.0 %
(29) Date of Source Material		6/4/2002	4/17/2002	6/4/2002	6/4/2002	6/4/2002
(30) Where Traded		NYSE	NYSE	NYSE	NYSE	NYSE

Figure 16-06: The complete drug industry SCG.

CHOOSING YOUR OWN CRITERIA

The SCG contains two lines, (27) and (28), where you can add other measures. There are so many possible criteria; it can be tough to decide. However, you might select your criteria based on the type of companies you are studying. For example, for high-growth companies with high PEs, you might choose the PE to Growth Ratio (PEG), a ratio of the PE to the EPS Projected Growth Rate. If the companies carry debt you might compare the debt to equity ratio. Relative value and projected relative value measure where the current or projected PE lies relative to the five-year average PE.

Picking the Criteria to Use

If you complete the SCG by hand, you can eliminate criteria simply by drawing a line through that row. If you use *Investor's Toolkit*, you can click the name of a criterion to toggle it on or off. In *NAIC Classic* and *Stock Analyst PLUS!* you can click in the cells for each company to eliminate criterion for that company. If you want to eliminate the criterion from your ranking, just turn off every cell in that row.

Picking a Winner

After you eliminate criteria you don't want, circle the winner in each row. Then, count the number of circles for each company. In most cases, the company with the most circles wins. However, make sure to check for companies that don't make the grade in growth and management comparisons, but do well in PE or relative value. These companies are selling at a discount because their growth and quality is lacking.

Pfizer is a clear winner in this SCG, with winning numbers in growth, management, PE and combined estimated yield. Merck is an interesting competitor.

Although its growth rates aren't attractive, it provides the highest upside-downside ratio, but still falls short in the ultimate measure—the combined estimated yield. It just goes to show that you have to consider all the factors before you hook up with a stock for your portfolio.

Now that you've learned how to analyze and choose a stock to buy, you're probably raring to add stocks to your portfolio. The next section of this handbook tells you how to find companies to study, purchase stocks, and manage your portfolio to maximize your return.

CHAPTER SEVENTEEN:

Finding Companies to St

Sifting the Wheat from the Chaff

With more than 10,000 companies traded publicly, the problem is not finding companies to study, but choosing the companies worth studying. Your time is precious so you don't want to waste it studying a stock that isn't even close to being an investment candidate. To make matters worse, there seem to be more advice-mongers trying to tell you about stocks that will make you rich than there are stocks to buy. Fortunately, there are resources to winnow study prospects from the stock market field.

Sources of Ideas

An Introduction to Stock Screening

As a beginning investor, whether you invest by yourself or with members of an investment club, you don't really need more than 15 to 25 stocks in your portfolio. So, you only need a handful of ideas to get started. After your portfolio is established, you can continue to troll for other ideas that might improve on what you already have.

Sources of Ideas

There are plenty of sources for good investment ideas. It should be easy to avoid the temptation of bad ideas. But, just in case, here's a review. Mail, e-mail, newsletters, or Web sites that claim to have the names of stocks that will multiply so many times in the next so many days are so much piffle, poppycock, bunk, baloney, hogwash, hot air, tripe and tommyrot. As the saying goes "If it sounds too good to be true, it probably is." Likewise, avoid hot tips from your friends. Even if they have found a hot prospect, they probably won't tell you when the investment is about to head south.

Instead, focus on sources that point you to prospective investments that are easy to understand and follow, and will produce growth consistently over long periods of time. What's more, you can be your own best advisor. Peter Lynch, the guy who produced legendary returns in the Fidelity Magellan fund, believes that the average investor can beat the professionals, and many NAIC investors do just that. Simply pay attention to the stores at the mall with the stuff your kids can't live without, the restaurant chain that you and your friends visit each week and the companies where you and your club members work.

NAIC Can Help

You can count on NAIC to provide a variety of sources for ideas about companies to study. One advantage of NAIC's sources is that most of the potential stocks are in the ball-park for the criteria you want— quality, consistent growth and good value.

• *Better Investing* Stock to Study: Each month, *Better Investing* magazine presents an overview of a company and its industry. There's no guarantee that it meets your particular criteria or that its price is in the buy zone by the publication date, but it's worth your study.

• *Better Investing* Undervalued Stock: Each month, *Better Investing* magazine features a company that appears to sell for less than it should. These stock studies not only highlight a potential investment for the value-minded investor, but help you learn to differentiate short-term trends from more serious long-term influences.

The term "undervalued" is the original term for what Wall Street now calls "value stocks."

• *Better Investing* 100: Every April, *Better Investing* magazine presents the list of the 100 stocks held most widely by NAIC investment clubs and individual members. These stocks might not meet your objectives and could be too pricey for purchasing. However, any that pique your interest are worth some study, given the vote of confidence from numerous NAIC investors. NAIC set up an index based on these stocks in 1998 (going back to 1988) and it has consistently out-performed the major stock indices.

• NAIC model clubs: Many NAIC local chapters host a model club that meets and runs like a regular investment club— finding, researching and studying stocks. You can get ideas for stocks to study and learn more about the fine points of NAIC stock analysis.

• NAIC local and national events: Local events, such as Investor Fairs, or national events like CompuFest and Convention, offer a plethora of educational seminars, many of which discuss companies that you might want to study.

Publications and the Media

Financial magazines such as *Business Week*, newspapers, and financial Web sites such as Multex Investor *(www.multexinvestor.com)*, Money Central *(moneycentral.msn.com)* and Quicken *(www.quicken.com/investments)* are good sources of ideas for investments. However, you might have to sift through some distractions to find what you want. You can scout for hints about individual companies or opt for pointers to industries that are poised to prosper in the future. Many financial publications focus on shorter timeframes than NAIC investors do, so look for stories about companies that strike a chord with your long-term investor psyche.

INDUSTRY TRENDS ON THE INTERNET

Many Web sites include industry overviews and news. Multex Investor provides free industry investing reports *(www.industryin-vestingreports.com/default.asp)* which discuss current influences in the industry and some provide ideas for investments within that industry. CNN's Financial Network Web site *(www.cnnfn.com)* offers Industry Watch, featuring news stories on different industries. Some brokers also provide industry overviews as part of their service.

Spotting industry trends can be easy. You can find oodles of articles about the industries that benefit from the aging of the baby-boomer generation: health-care, pharmaceuticals, medical services and supplies, recreation, and financial services. But, sometimes, industry trends can be hard to spot, particularly when it comes to technology. You never know what technical marvel will turn our world topsy-turvy—computers, personal computers, the Internet, genomics, nanotechnology and more. The best advice is to keep looking and watch trends that seem to be heating up.

You might be able to search business databases at your local library or your library system's Web site. If you can't find the site online, ask the reference librarian at your library for instructions. For example, the EBSCOHost database includes abstracts, indexes and searchable full text for thousands of general, business and healthcare periodicals. In the Jefferson County Colorado library system, you can reach this database at agate.jefferson.lib.co.us/jcpl/useful.cfm#ebsco. You must enter your library card number to access the database, so you'll need to find the link within your local library system.

An Introduction to Stock Screening

Stock screening is a great way to find stocks that meet your criteria. When you screen for stocks, you enter the criteria that you want to meet or exceed and then let your computer or the Web site you use find all the companies that match. For example, you can search for companies that meet the NAIC guidelines for sales growth, EPS growth, PE, pre-tax profit margin, return on equity, and debt-to-equity ratio. You might screen for large or small companies or companies in a particular industry if you want to diversify your portfolio. An excellent stock screen is also published in *Better Investing Bits*, NAIC's computer magazine (available to members online).

Success Tip!

If you don't own a computer or haven't connected to the Internet, you might be able to use one at a local library or community center.

An NAIC-Style Stock Screen

You can take your pick from any number of Web sites that offer screening. Each one works a little differently, but the basic idea is the same. You enter criteria, minimums, maximums, or both, and then ask the screening tool to find the stocks that match. The list below shows Web sites that offer the more popular online screening tools. You can also use a software program such as *STB Investors Prospector* to find stocks.

• Quicken:
www.quicken.com

• Money Central:
www.moneycentral.msn.com

• Multex Investor:
www.multexinvestor.com

• Wall Street Research Net:
www.wsrn.com

A stock screen that uses NAIC methodology might include criteria for sales and EPS growth, PE, pre-tax profit margin, return on equity, and debt-to-equity ratio. You might add criteria for company size and industry to satisfy your portfolio diversification. And, if you are looking for some current income, you could add criteria for dividend yield.

PFIZER PE COMPARISONS

Criteria	Minimum	Maximum
Five-year sales growth rate	11%	
Five-year EPS growth rate	11%	
PE trailing 12 Months		30
Sales in millions	$4,000	
Industry (Pharmaceuticals) Yield		1%
Return on equity	15%	
Debt to equity ratio		33%

This screen defines a minimum of 11 percent for five-year sales and EPS growth. This ensures that the company is growing fast enough for a large cap company. If the stock screen you use supports it, you might also add a criteria for growth in the last quarter to check that growth is still strong. Setting a cap on PE helps weed out stocks that are overvalued. However, this measure isn't infallible. Setting sales to a minimum of $5,000 million targets large companies. A maximum yield of 1 percent restricts the screen results to companies that still reinvest earnings into growing the company. A return on equity of at least 15 percent identifies companies that provide a good return on the money share-holders have invested—and offer an above industry average value to boot (for pharmaceuticals). Limiting the debt to equity ratio to less than 33 percent finds

companies whose capitalization is mostly from stock. Too much debt can spell disaster if a company falls on hard times. Debts must be paid regardless of a company's income. Even worse, if a company goes bankrupt, the debt holders get first crack at company assets. Shareholders only receive money if there is anything left over.

Modifying a Screen

If the first set of results is too large—or too small—you can modify your requirements until you get a manageable number of stocks to study. For example, you might shoot for a screen that returns four to 10 companies, depending on whether you are studying alone or with an investment club.

A computerized stock screen only sees black and white. If a company just misses meeting the criteria, you won't see it in the results. When you use a computerized screen, set your criteria a little looser to catch the companies that are close. For example, a company growing at 10.9 percent won't appear in a screen that demands a minimum growth rate of 11 percent. A growing company that is currently overvalued won't show up in a screen that limits the PE to below 20.

(See Success Tip at right)

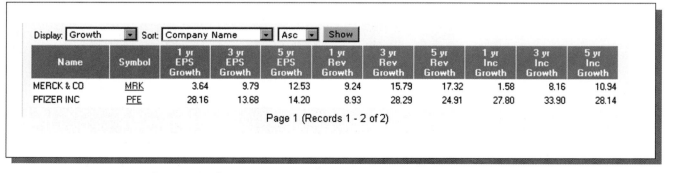

Name	Symbol	1 yr EPS Growth	3 yr EPS Growth	5 yr EPS Growth	1 yr Rev Growth	3 yr Rev Growth	5 yr Rev Growth	1 yr Inc Growth	3 yr Inc Growth	5 yr Inc Growth
MERCK & CO	MRK	3.64	9.79	12.53	9.24	15.79	17.32	1.58	8.16	10.94
PFIZER INC	PFE	28.16	13.68	14.20	8.93	28.29	24.91	27.80	33.90	28.14

Display: Growth   Sort: Company Name   Asc   Show

Page 1 (Records 1 - 2 of 2)

Figure 17-01: The results from the NAIC style screen using Quicken.com's screening tool.

Remember that growth and consistency are critical. If you must tighten your criteria to decrease the number of results, first tighten the criteria that focus on growth trends—strong and consistent sales and EPS growth and return on equity.

Screening with Value Line

You can also use sections in the Value Line Investment Survey to screen stocks. The lists for Industries In Order of Timeliness and Timely Stocks in Timely Industries appear in Part 1 of the Value Line

Summary and Index. Although Value Line timeliness focuses on three to six months in the future, you can use these lists to find stocks to study—as long as you complete an NAIC stock study and a Stock Check List or SSG before you decide to buy. For example, industries that the baby boomers use should be timely now. Electronics, Medical Services, Securities Brokerage, Advertising, Drug, Medical Supplies, Financial Service, and Drugstore have all placed in the top 25% of the list in recent times.

CHAPTER EIGHTEEN

How to Buy Stock

They Call It the Stock Market, Don't They?

Unless you're a successful entrepreneur, you can't grow your own stocks. You have to buy them. Like groceries, you can buy stocks directly from the source or go through a middleman. Similar to the seemingly infinite selection of products at the local grocery *store, you can choose from a plethora of brokers, accounts and types of orders. Don't let the selection intimidate you. After you pick a stock to buy, finding someone to sell it to you is a snap.*

How to Pick a Broker

DRIPS & Dollar-Cost Averaging

The Right Type of Account

Placing Your Order

How to Pick a Broker

Brokers were once "one size fits all". Today they come in all shapes and sizes. With full-service brokers, you pay hefty commissions and receive deluxe treatment—you don't just get someone to buy and sell stock for you. Full-service brokers offer financial planning, in-house research, stock recommendations and a broker who, in theory, only recommends investments that fit your objectives. Discount brokers offer lower commissions and fewer services. Deep discount brokers buy and sell stocks and that's about it.

Account Minimums

Brokers might require a minimum amount of money before they'll open an account for you, trade on your behalf and charge you a commission for the privilege. If you're just getting started, you can opt for a firm with no minimum balance requirements. However, even brokerage houses with high account minimums might waive the minimum if you agree to an automatic monthly investment plan. Automatic investment plans have a secondary benefit in that they keep money flowing into your investments. You won't be tempted to skip a deposit into your investment account.

Commissions

Brokers might charge from $5 to more than $100 per trade. In addition, brokers might charge different amounts for online orders, telephone orders, market orders or limit orders. Commissions can vary based on how many shares you trade and whether you buy stocks listed on a stock exchange or over-the-counter. After you decide how you want to place your orders, look for the broker who offers a reasonable fee for those services. If you plan to trade online, look for brokers who offer additional means of placing a trade. You wouldn't want to miss a great buy because you couldn't log in to the broker's Web site.

RATING THE BROKERS

You can compare different brokerage houses from magazines or Web sites by checking their broker ratings. For example, *Business Week* and *Kiplinger's Personal Finance* magazine both include articles reviewing the current broker picks. Gomez Associates' Web site *(www.gomez.com)* offers broker rankings based on different type of investors—buy and hold, day traders, and more.

Today, most brokers offer online services. With online investing, you can choose from more levels of service, a wide range of commissions, a never-ending array of fees, some hidden—and the ability to trade stocks in your jammies. To choose the right broker, you need to know what your options are and what is most important to you.

If you reinvest your dividends, go directly to the company you want to buy to see if it has a dividend reinvestment plan and check NAIC's Low Cost Investment Plan covering over 150 companies.

Other Fees

Fees for services other than stock trades could add up to more than you save on low-cost commissions. Some brokers charge to issue a stock certificate, send a copy of your statement, wire funds, manage your account and even close your account. Don't just choose the broker with the lowest commissions. If price is important, figure out how much your account will cost you each month, including fees and commissions, and pick the broker with the lowest overall cost.

Services

Brokers do more than buy and sell shares. Some provide valuable investment information, including news, research reports, buy and sell recommendations, and free real-time quotes. They might offer accounts with check writing, automatic rollover of cash to a money market account and automatic fund transfers.

Some brokers only offer online access, whereas others offer online and telephone trades along with local offices. Verify that a broker offers access you want and see whether trades cost more if you use the telephone or show up in person, instead of

trading online. Unless you always place limit orders, you want your broker to execute your orders and cancellations quickly and accurately. If you use an online broker, make sure the broker is reliable, even on busy days. And, look for brokers who charge the online commission rate if you have to telephone to place an order because you can't log in to their site.

Some of the deep discount brokers skimp on providing tax information. Check to see that they provide the level of tax documentation you want.

What About Mutual Funds and Other Securities?

If your portfolio is a smorgasbord of securities—stocks, bonds and mutual funds—you probably want a brokerage "supermarket." These firms not only trade stocks and bonds, but also sell scores of mutual funds, often with little or no transaction fee. If you use mutual funds in addition to stocks, see how many funds the broker offers and how many are available without transaction fees.

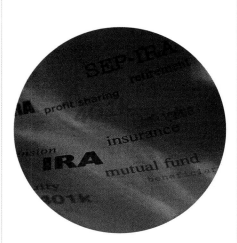

If you decide you want service and low-cost, two brokers might just be the solution. If your IRA account meets the account minimum for a broker with great research and services, transfer your IRA account to them. Then, open a brokerage account for your small regular investments with a firm with no minimum balance, low commissions and free dividend reinvestments.

Customer Service

Life is too short to spend entire days on hold. If you spend all your time trying to correct an error in your account, you won't have time to find those great investments. Whether you need some hand holding or could teach Warren Buffett a thing or two, your broker should provide prompt, polite and results-oriented customer service. Call a broker several times before signing up to see how responsive they are.

A Regular Schedule of Investments

Dollar cost averaging means investing a fixed amount of money in a stock at a regular interval. You buy fewer shares when the price is high, and more shares when the price is low, reducing your average price paid over time. These regular contributions to your investment accounts are great for building wealth, even if you love to spend money.

Payroll deductions and automatic transfers to an investment account protect your hard-earned money from your spending self. You get the benefits of dollar cost averaging and you might think twice before taking money out of savings.

Dividend Reinvestment Plans (DRIPs)

You can buy stocks directly from many companies through their dividend reinvestment plans. To enroll in a DRIP, you usually need only one share of stock in the company. After that, many companies reinvest your dividends in your name without charging any fees or commissions. Others have a fee that is usually less than any broker's fee.

BUYING THAT FIRST SHARE

In the past, broker commissions were cost prohibitive for the purchase of single shares or dollar cost averaging. Investing $25 doesn't make sense when the minimum brokerage commission is $40. Even today's discount commissions, which can be as low as $7, are more than 25% of a $25 contribution. But now, you can purchase these lone shares through discount brokers without paying a fortune in commission. If you can't meet the account minimum for a brokerage account, you can buy shares directly from the hundreds of companies that offer direct stock plans (DSPs).

In addition to reinvesting dividends in DRIPs, you can often buy additional shares of stock with a small investment and little or no commission. At this point you refer to them as Optional Cash Purchase (OCP) or Direct Stock Purchase (DSP). These additional purchases occur on a regular schedule, such as the last day of the month or the quarter. You can send in a check just before the purchase date; the company purchases your shares, and you then receive regular account statements documenting what you own and your transactions. You can learn more about these programs by reading the free online book on the DRIP Central Web site (www.dripcentral.com.) The NAIC Low Cost Investment Plan also gets you started with stock purchases for very low fees. The number of stocks in the NAIC program is limited, but you only pay a one-time setup fee to buy shares from any of the companies in the program.

You can't specify the day to buy or sell with Dividend Reinvestment Plans, so you can't control how much you pay to buy a stock or how much you get when you sell. DRIPs are best when you plan to hold stocks for the long term, so a few dollars difference in the buy or sell price won't matter.

averaging an affordable solution. You choose the amount you want to invest each week or month, the stocks you want to buy and how much you want to buy of each. With a preset schedule of investments, you pay commissions such as $4 for a single recurring trade or $12 for as many recurring trades as you want in a month.

These companies can provide these commissions because they pool all their client purchases and make a bulk purchase of each stock at set times of the day. They get a bundle of small commissions from their clients, but pay one commission for the one large order they place. Sharebuilder (*www.sharebuilder.com*) and Buy and Hold (*www.buyandhold.com*) are two of the better-known sites. For more information on these online services and online brokers, see the *NAIC Computerized Investing & the Internet Handbook*.

Getting Ultra-Low Commissions

If the administration of multiple DRIP accounts is too much for you, you might like online services offering commissions so low that they make regular investing and dollar cost

The Right Type of Account

Although some brokers focus on specific types of clients and services, many of the brokerage houses today try to satisfy a broad range of investors. Frequently, you'll find an overwhelming choice of account options, but they all boil down to two things: services and taxes.

Brokers and Their Services

With a basic brokerage account, you can buy and sell stocks and store the holdings in your portfolio. You can still use a basic brokerage account if you buy mutual funds and bonds. However, in this situation, you should use one of the "supermarket" brokers, such as Charles Schwab & Co., that offers many mutual funds without charging commissions on your purchases.

If you build up cash before investing, look for an account that sweeps your cash into a money market fund. That way your money earns interest while you wait.

Most of the larger brokerage houses come up with catchy names for their accounts, and the catchier the name, the harder it is to figure out what the account offers. Request information from the broker about their accounts or read about them online to see whether the services meet your needs.

What's in a Name? If you want other services, such as check writing or a debit card attached to your investment account, go for a brokerage account with cash management features. These cash management accounts usually sweep cash into a money market fund. In addition, some of them even offer banking services such as online checking, bill payment and access to ATMs. Keep in mind that these cash management accounts often carry higher account minimums and fees than regular brokerage accounts, so make sure the convenience is worth the cost.

Accounts and Taxes

Everyone knows that taxes can take a big chunk out of the money you make, whether it's your salary or your investment returns. The tax rates on capital gains, particularly long-term ones, are lower than the tax rates on ordinary income. Even so, why give up any money to taxes unnecessarily? Most, but not all, tax-advantaged accounts revolve around retirement. These accounts are aptly titled. They have an advantage because you pay less in taxes on the money you make in them. Of course, nothing to do with taxes comes without strings attached. Your eligibility for these accounts depends on your annual income.

Individual Retirement Accounts (IRAs) come in several forms. With a traditional IRA, your contributions might be tax-deductible if your income is low enough. More importantly, your earnings in the account aren't taxed until you withdraw funds from the account so you can let the compounding work to grow your nest egg. In a Roth IRA, you use after tax dollars when you contribute to the account. However, this type of IRA has several advantages after you get past the non-deductible contribution. Earnings in the account are tax-free, thus you pay no taxes when you withdraw your money. In addition, you can continue to contribute to your Roth IRA past age 70, and you don't have to start withdrawing funds when you reach a specific age.

SAVING FOR EDUCATION

A more recent addition to the tax-advantaged stable is the Coverdell Education Savings Account. As a parent or guardian, you set up and manage this savings plan for a minor. Contributions grow tax-free until they are withdrawn, and the child won't owe tax if the withdrawal is for qualified education expenses.

If your children earn income, they can start investing for retirement in a custodial Roth IRA. If your children start investing for retirement early, they won't have to save as much to enjoy long and fun-filled golden years.

Placing Your Order

With low-commission services, you set up your purchases on a fixed schedule. The broker actually places orders consolidated from all the scheduled requests of its clients. However, when you buy stock in a regular brokerage account, you can choose among several types of orders.

Market Orders

You use a market order when you want to buy or sell a stock immediately at the price of the stock the moment your order reaches the market. When you use a market order, you know that the trade will occur, but you won't know the price until after the trade executes. For example, you place a market order to buy Freeblesnaps, Inc. at 10 a.m. on Tuesday, when its stock price is $33.25. Your order will most likely execute by 10:05 A.M. on Tuesday, but the price may be lower or higher than the $33.25 it was when you placed the order. If a stock is in your buy range, you might issue a market order if you don't expect the stock price to change dramatically in a short period of time.

Limit Orders

If you're willing to wait for the price you want, you can place a limit order to buy or sell a stock only when it reaches the price you set. However, the order won't execute if the price doesn't reach that limit, so there is no guarantee that your order will execute. For a buy limit order, the price you get will be at or below your limit, whereas the price for a sell limit order is at or above your limit.

When prices are changing quickly, you can use a limit order to make sure that you don't buy or sell at a price different than you expect. If you are buying in this situation, you can place a limit order at the highest price you are willing to pay, which is also above the current ask price. If you are selling, you limit the order to the minimum price you are willing to accept. In the figure below, the order has a duration of GTC. This stands for Good 'Til Cancelled. A Good 'Til Cancelled order remains in effect until you cancel the order, or a length of time set by your broker passes, usually about 60 days.

Stop limit orders constrain your losses if a stock price begins to drop dramatically. They can also protect your profit by selling a stock if it increases to a price you set. A stop limit order buys or sells at the market price, only when the stock price is at, or past, the stop price that you specify.

As soon as you complete your first purchase, you own a portfolio—albeit a rather limited one. Soon, you'll need to manage that portfolio to keep it growing robustly.

Order Entry (Step 1 of 3)

Symbol: pfe   Symbol Lookup

Action: Buy

Quantity: 100

Order:
- Market Order
- Limit $ 34.25
- Stop $
- Stop Limit
  Enter both fields above.

Timing: Good Until Canceled

[Clear]   [Review Order]

Optional
Dividend Reinvestment
- Yes
- No

Special Conditions*
- Minimum qty.
- Do not reduce
- All or none

*Non Market Orders only

Figure 18-01: You can specify a limit price on a purchase so you only buy the stock if it drops below the price you specify.

CHAPTER NINETEEN

Managing Your Portfolio

Make the Most of Your Money

Some investors spend inordinate amounts of time fretting over buying new stocks. If they assume that buy and hold means buy and forget, they could be in for trouble if companies in their portfolio take a turn for the worse. Smart investors manage their portfolio to make sure that every dollar invested pulls its weight.

Portfolio management covers a lot of ground—it can increase your returns, increase your portfolio quality, reduce financial risks and unite your stock holdings with your investment goals. You might think it takes a lot of effort to achieve all these results, but the basic concepts of portfolio management are quite simple. Putting those concepts into practice isn't hard, although it does require some practice to perfect. This chapter is merely a brief introduction to portfolio management. To learn more, read NAIC Using Portfolio Management Wisdom.

An Overview of Portfolio Management

What You Need to Know

Using NAIC Tools to Maximize Portfolio Performance

An Overview of Portfolio Management

A good portfolio might contain 15 to 25 quality growth stocks (more or less depending on how many you can follow) diversified by size and industry. See Chapter 3 for more information on NAIC guidelines for diversification. Just like a magnificent garden, an impressive portfolio requires planning, careful construction and regular maintenance.

Ideally, you identify your investment goals—be they capital appreciation or current income, high or low risk, desired annual return or other criteria—before you even begin to buy stocks. Only then can you construct a portfolio that matches your objectives. You also should strive to set criteria for purchasing stocks so you know when you find a winner. Sure, you're looking for quality growth stocks selling at an attractive price, but it's helpful to create a checklist. For example, you might specify what you want in terms of sales and EPS growth rates, profit margins, return on equity, upside-downside ratio, relative value and/or total return.

Success Tip!

Even if you built your portfolio before setting these standards, it's not too late. You can always start to adjust your holdings after you determine your criteria.

With defined criteria, you can compare stocks you own and the results they offer to the standards you set. It's easy to identify the actions you need to take—whether you sell, hold or buy more. Even more important, there's no need for second-guessing. It's easy to understand the reasons behind your actions. For example, as long as a company meets your criteria for growth and consistency, it's easy to hold tight when the real problem is a down market or an industry that is out of favor. When those short-term influences disappear, your solid stock should bounce right back.

MAKE THE MOST OF YOUR MONEY

As your portfolio grows, portfolio management becomes increasingly important. At the start, your monthly contribution is a significant addition to your portfolio. A $50 contribution is 10% of the value in a $500 portfolio. However, when your nest egg reaches $100,000, you should focus more energy on maximizing the return on your $100,000, not deciding where you will add the .05% that your $50 represents.

Just about every game plan has an offense and a defense, and investing is no different. In portfolio management, defense is your first step. You can't appreciate your flowers if weeds are overrunning your portfolio. You want to get rid of stocks whose financial performance starts to deteriorate or that simply don't live up to your expectations. Declining financial measures, such as slowing growth and EPS or declining profit margins, eventually affect stock price. If you're paying attention to these signs, you can sell before the stock price dramatically reduces the value of your portfolio.

When you finish weeding, you can start on offense—feeding your portfolio to achieve faster growth, higher quality, less risk or better diversification. Depending on your objectives, you might strive to replace slower growers with more vigorous stocks. Or, you might exchange one stock for another of better quality. For example, you could sell a stock growing erratically at 15 percent for one that produces consistent 15 percent growth. If some of your stocks have skyrocketed, while the prices for others took a nap, you could sell overvalued stocks to buy more of those that represent a good value. Or, you might just decide to buy more of a solid stock that has dropped to an attractive purchase price. Of course, every situation is unique. You must decide what to do based on the stocks you own and current events.

What You Need to Know

A freshly completed SSG can separate potential winners from also-rans. However, time marches on and making management decisions means tracking a company's performance. Tracking a stock does not mean watching its incessant price fluctuations day and night. Price is important, but a company's financial performance is the key to your buy, hold and sell decisions.

Tracking a stock doesn't require a lot of time. Once a month, you should update the prices for all the stocks in your portfolio. Remember, you don't want to agonize over price changes. You use these prices more for watching the trends in the PE ratio. During this monthly checkup, you can see if any companies announced quarterly results. If they did, update your SSGs with the sales, EPS and possibly pre-tax profit for the most recent quarter.

You can use the trends in sales, EPS, pre-tax profit and PE to determine whether you need to act. In addition, you should always keep on the lookout for news on the stocks you own. Good news might not require a quick response, but if a company announces a fundamental long-term problem, you want to review it and make a decision as to how likely the company's growth is to resume.

Using NAIC Tools to Maximize Portfolio Performance

Using the SSG and the Stock Comparison Guide diligently and with conservative judgment, you have a great chance of buying winners—at least four out of every five stocks you purchase—and achieving the returns you want. But, you can increase your chances of success even further by managing your

portfolio on a routine basis. Watching trends is central to portfolio management, whether it's sales growth, EPS, pre-tax profit, PE ratios or the proximity of your forecasts to actual performance. NAIC offers several tools to help you decide how to manage your portfolio.

If you use one of the NAIC software packages and update sales, EPS and pretax profit each quarter, you don't have to do any additional calculations to produce NAIC PERT reports.

NAIC's Portfolio Management Guide (PMG) highlights a stock's price and PE compared to your forecasts for high and low price and PE. You shouldn't buy, sell or hold just because of the current price and PE. However, a quick scan of the PMG might indicate a stock to examine more closely for potential purchase or sale.

You can use the report forms from NAIC's Portfolio Evaluation and Review Technique (PERT) tool to help you track the performance and analyze trends of the stocks in your portfolio. PERT reports show recent growth rates and trends, so you can see whether a company is still performing as you expect. (PERT reports were reviewed in Chapter 3.) If the growth rates start to decline, you should watch the company to see if the trend continues.

Success Tip!

Your first check on the PERT report is whether the company's EPS for the last 12 months is close to your forecast for EPS growth. If it isn't, look at the quarterly growth trends. If the trends for the company aren't what you expect, you might want to reevaluate your SSG and lower your forecasts. With lower forecasts, the company might change from a buy to a hold, or even from a hold to a sell.

If company growth trends look good on the PERT report, you can check the value measures it displays, such as PE, relative value, PE as a percentage of growth rate, upside-downside ratio and the annual rate of return. If the value measures also look good, you might consider purchasing more of that stock.

The PERT Portfolio Trend Report shows quarterly percentage changes for the last two quarters as well as for the last 12 months. You can check these to see if recent performance is still on track or not. If the last two quarters are declining and further research indicates an undesirable long-term trend, start looking for another company for your portfolio. You can also use the PERT trend report to review each company's potential total return, the percentage it represents in your portfolio and the overall percentage of investment in small, medium and large companies. You can use this report to find the slow growers that you might want to replace or the strong performers that you want to augment with more shares. Or, you can check for stocks that take up too much of your portfolio and identify whether you should try to replace those with companies of a certain size to improve your diversification.

Success Tip!

Investor's Toolkit and Stock Analyst PLUS! both offer a challenge tool to see if a new contender might be a better investment than an existing company in your portfolio. These tools show you how the challenger fares, taking into account your broker's commission and taxes you pay if your investments are in a taxable account.

The PERT Worksheet A (PERT-A) shows trends in performance of one company at a time. It can provide an early warning of deterioration in quarterly and trailing 12-month sales, EPS and pre-tax profit. When pre-tax profit margins drop, EPS often follows. By watching these trends on PERT-A, you might be able to sell a stock before its declining performance appears in the stock price.

On the other hand, if a stock price drops or just sits in one place, you can check to see if the company's fundamentals are still good. If they are, you don't have to worry. In fact, that might be your signal to buy more.

CHAPTER TWENTY:

The Art of Selling

They're Stocks, not Children

People often struggle with selling. Your possessions become familiar; you grow close. Selling seems like such a mercenary thing to do. But the stocks in your portfolio aren't your kids. You bought your stocks to make money, and eventually you will have to sell a few of them to collect—or protect—your winnings.

Reasons to Sell

The Do's and Don'ts of Selling

Sell Signals

The High Price of Selling

Selling seems more difficult than buying; that's because it is. You're faced with TWO good decisions— selling a stock for the right reasons and replacing the stock you sold with one of less risk and greater potential. To make matters worse, when the stock is in a taxable account, the new stock usually must gain at least 37 percent just to break even! No wonder Warren Buffett says the best time to sell is NEVER.

Reasons to Sell

Selling is inevitable. If you're lucky enough to win the lottery every year, you might be able to hold your stocks and let your kids do the selling. However, even if you don't need the money, you usually have to sell a stock that doesn't live up to your expectations. Otherwise, your portfolio could flounder or even drop in value. The trick to selling is to be cool and logical. You must sell for the right reasons or you might sell the wrong stock, or sell the right one at the wrong time.

Go Ahead. Use Your Money!

The reason most people invest is to make money to spend on things— a new home, kids' toys, college, retirement and big kids' toys. When these life events come along, you have to sell your stock. If your funds are in an investment club, you might have to sell stock to pay departing club partners. There's nothing wrong with selling stocks to use the money. However, you want to sell the right stocks—the ones with the least potential or greatest risk. Keep reading to find out how to identify these stocks.

Deteriorating Financials

Companies that were once the zenith of strength can begin to deteriorate financially. When this happens, you can shield your portfolio from serious damage by selling the company before the stock price drops too far. You can identify signals such as slowing growth, increasing debt or declining profit margins in the SSG or PERT reports. But, some of the signs, such as management changes or product line problems, require keeping tabs on company news. Deteriorating financials can include:

- Sales or EPS growth slowing below the level you expect
- Declining profit margins
- Excessive or increasing debt
- Adverse management changes
- Intense increase in competition
- Product mix or pipeline decline
- Products falling out of favor or becoming obsolete
- Customer base shrinking or dependency upon one major customer

The Opposite of Buy Signs

Another way to distinguish a stock to sell is by looking for the opposite of the reasons you buy. When you buy, you want growth, quality, increasing profit margins and return on equity, PE ratios lower than the five-year average, an upside downside ratio of at least three-to-one, and a projected total return of a certain amount. Here are some possible sell signals:

- Growth slows or stalls
- Profit margins decline
- Management's results lack consistency
- PE is significantly higher than five-year average
- Upside-downside ratio is below one
- Projected total return drops below the level you expect.

You certainly don't want to rush to call your broker if a stock you own exhibits one sell symptom, but you should start to watch more closely. When the symptoms multiply, make your decision.

Diversification

Maintaining the diversification of your portfolio might require some selling. Companies that do incredibly well can expand to comprise a large percentage of your portfolio. Selling for diversification is a study in equilibrium. For safety, you don't want one stock representing the bulk of your portfolio, but you don't want to sell your winners too quickly. Typical guidelines are no more than 4 to 7 percent of your portfolio in one company. There's a Wall Street adage that says, "every good portfolio has at least one outstanding stock."

Improve Portfolio Quality

Eventually, you will own a portfolio of stocks. But, will you sit on your accomplishments? No! You can still search for stocks of equal or better quality with higher reward and less risk than those you currently own. If you find better replacements, you might sell existing stocks to improve the quality of your portfolio. For example, you might sell an existing stock in favor of one with higher upside potential. Or, you might replace a current holding for a stock with a similar return because the new stock is much less risky.

Exceptional performers often end up priced higher than they are worth. In addition to upsetting your diversification, these stocks become much higher risks. They just don't offer that much upside potential. You don't want to sell these companies too quickly, but at some point other companies become more attractive. One solution when you have a fast growing overvalued stock is to sell a fraction (like one quarter or one third) and start a new growth stock.

MAKING ROOM FOR WINNERS

If a winner starts to hog your portfolio, one solution is to add more money to your other holdings in the portfolio. But, you might not be so fortunate to have a spare $1,000 or $10,000 lying around. In that case, you might sell part of your holdings in the company to bring the percentages back into line. You also might consider bending your portfolio percentages a little— perhaps to 10 percent to allow your winner room to excel. However, this tactic increases the risk in your portfolio, so make sure that the company's performance is worth the potential risk.

The Do's and Don'ts of Selling

Investors often avoid selling. You spend all this time learning how to buy stocks; you don't want to undo all that work by selling them! But not selling can lead to poorer portfolio returns. Make sure that you don't succumb to some of these common mistakes.

Waiting Too Long To Sell

Investors often become emotionally attached to their stocks. When a company strikes a chord, you might overlook its obvious flaws. When a company's financial measures begin to decline, it's time to admit that your forecasts didn't pan out and sell. Psychologically, you won't like to admit that you made a mistake. Many investors hold onto a stock until it returns to the buy price, rather than taking a loss. You should consider that another stock might provide that same return in much less time!

Success Tip!

Remember that a loss on a stock in a taxable account carries a tax advantage. Sell your losers to offset capital gains on your winners.

Selling Too Quickly

Some investors have the opposite problem. They sell too soon. Somehow, letting stocks percolate doesn't seem right, as if investing is about taking constant action. That's actually called day trading. If you're itchy to take action, keep yourself busy studying stocks and let your good performers grow in your portfolio!

Other investors sell because the price has dropped or gone up too far. If nothing bad has happened to the company, a lower price is more a buy signal than one to sell. On the other hand, a price that rises above your forecast high price doesn't necessarily mean that a company is at the end of its run. You should check the company's growth rates and update your stock study. If the company is still growing vigorously, you might need to adjust your forecasts, as the company might still be reasonably valued.

A stock price that stands still is also a challenge for an investor. Sometimes a stock will sit for several years only to shoot up in a short period. If a company is still growing and there are no negative influences, be patient. The stock price will likely catch up.

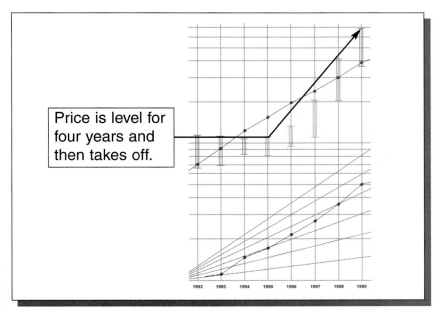

Price is level for four years and then takes off.

Figure 20-01: Price can sometimes level out, but it will catch up to a company's growth in time.

Bad news scares many investors—but if it is just a temporary phenomenon, such as a short-term increase in supply costs, the ensuing price drop is an excellent buying opportunity.

You shouldn't rush to sell just because an analyst downgrades a stock. Use your own judgment and only sell if the stock study shows sell signals. Stock market drops and industry declines can cause price drops in good stocks. If a company still meets your tests, don't sell.

Insiders selling stock doesn't reveal as much as does insiders buying. When insiders buy, they see their stock as an excellent investment. However, they could sell for many reasons, to: diversify their own portfolios, meet SEC requirements or fund personal expenditures. Of course, major insider selling could be an indication of problems on the horizon. You should always do some research if you see a flurry of insider sales.

Choosing a Stock to Sell

When you sell stock to generate cash, you have several ways to choose which stock to sell. This section provides a quick introduction, but you can learn more by reading the *NAIC Using Portfolio Management Wisdom Handbook*.

1. **Adjust Diversification:** If your portfolio diversification is out of whack, you can sell some or all shares of a company whose value has overrun the percentage of your holdings that you set for it.

2. **Maximize Potential Return:** You can also sell companies with the least attractive potential return. The PERT Portfolio Trend Report, mentioned in Chapters 3 and 19 (and your SSG study), show estimated EPS growth, projected average return and total return figures for your stocks. The stocks with the lowest total return offer the least promise and are good candidates for selling. If you choose this approach, remember that you hold some stocks with lower total return because of their safety and you could increase the risk in your portfolio by selling these lower performers.

3. **Improve Quality:** If you want to improve the quality of your portfolio, look at the graphs in SSG Section 1 for the companies you own. Hold onto the companies with the rock steady sales and EPS growth. Consider selling companies whose growth bounces around. You can also use the Stock Comparison Guide to compare management capabilities using the numbers from Section 2 of the SSG.

Sell Signals

The Rule of Five says that one out of five investments will not perform to our expectations, no matter how good they look when we first study them. Revenues and earnings growth can slow and profit margins can drop for any number of unforeseen reasons.

You can get an early warning by reviewing sales, EPS and pre-tax profit each quarter. Slowing sales and EPS growth lead to slowing stock price growth and sometimes price drops, if investors expected too much from a company. But, pre-tax profit is the best early warning sign. When the pre-tax profit margin drops, a company keeps less of the money it brings in. If it doesn't match the drop in pre-tax profit margin by cutting costs in some way, earnings will drop—and that is a sure step to a drop in price. If you catch these drops in profit margin, you often have time to sell before the price falls. On the other hand, if sales, EPS and profit are steady or still growing, you know that a price drop is due to market fluctuations and could present a buying opportunity. The *NAIC Using Portfolio Management Wisdom Handbook* goes into more detail on how to watch your stocks for sell signals. The following steps are a brief introduction.

Update your stock studies at the end of each fiscal quarter.

1. Check for a decline in sales growth of more than one quarter. When sales decline over time, check for potential long-term impacts such as increased competition, industry or regulatory issues, and technology changes.

2. Check for a decline in pre-tax profit growth for more than one quarter. Investigate the cause to determine whether this trend will continue.

3. Check for a decline in EPS growth. You should use 12-month trailing EPS to eliminate declines from seasonal variations. Even if the share price hasn't fallen too far, continued reductions in earnings will slash the price soon enough.

4. Check whether the company meets your growth forecasts. If the 12-month trailing EPS consistently falls below your estimate, you should revise your stock study, because lower EPS will reduce the forecast high price and total return in your stock study.

The High Price of Selling

As you study stocks, you will come across candidates that look very appealing. Typically, you can't just plunk down extra cash to buy this new gem. If you have to sell a stock to buy a new one, the new stock has to outperform your existing holding enough to cover commissions and in some cases taxes, and still provide the return you expect. When all is said and done, a new purchase in a taxable account might have to increase by almost 37 percent (in simple price appreciation) just to break even! *Investor's Toolkit* and *Stock Analyst PLUS!* both provide a tool called the *Challenger* or *Challenge Tree* to show you whether a stock is worth the work.

You have to keep track of your buying and selling. In the next chapter, you'll learn a little bit about keeping records, whether for yourself or your investment club.

CHAPTER TWENTY ONE

Keeping Records

Someone Wants to Know

Even if you don't care about what's going on in your portfolio, someone else will—whether it's the other members in your investment club or the IRS. At a minimum, you have to keep records of purchases and sales, dividends, and capital gains so you can report income and losses (or gains) on your tax return. But keeping good records goes beyond taxes. You should care about the return your portfolio provides. If it doesn't meet your objectives, you need to take action—if you want to pay for that college education or retire early.

**What You Need when
You Invest by Yourself**

**Keeping Records
for an Investment Club**

Keeping records and tracking portfolio performance is not fun if you're using pencil, paper and calculator. If you own more than a couple of stocks and mutual funds, and reinvest your dividends, you might bypass important record keeping steps if you don't use a computer. Organized records are a must whether you are working manually or electronically.

What You Need when You Invest by Yourself

Keeping records for your own portfolio is tax and portfolio management. The government wants its share of your investment earnings. Even more important, you need to know how your portfolio is doing and what changes might make its performance even better. If you use a computer, products such as *NAIC Personal Record Keeper, Quicken* and *Microsoft Money* can help track your activities and simplify tax time. Although PERT reports help you decide what actions to take to manage your portfolio, these other products provide more in-depth views into portfolio diversification—by asset type, industry and company size.

Tax Records

You pay taxes on dividends and capital gains in any taxable investment account. Dividends are easy. You just need to keep a list of the dividends you receive from each company that you own. Then, on Schedule B (Form 1040) for your federal tax return, you list the companies that paid you dividends and the annual dividend for each company.

You don't have to keep on top of these records with quite as much fervor for your tax-deferred or tax free accounts. You only need to keep track of how much money you deposited in the account.

For capital gains, you need a little more information. To calculate your capital gain, you need to know your sales price and the cost basis (the price you paid plus other fees such as commissions). In addition, you also need to know the dates you bought and sold the stock to determine whether your capital gain counts as short term or long term.

Portfolio Management

The first measure for your portfolio is the compounded annual return. If your portfolio isn't meeting your objective for return, you have some work ahead of you. See Chapters 19 and 20 to learn more about buying and selling stocks in your portfolio. Even if your return is satisfactory, you should also review your diversification by company size and industry.

Keeping Records for an Investment Club

Investment clubs are groups of people who pool their money to invest in stocks. Record keeping for investment clubs is a little more complicated because you have to track more than tax transactions and portfolio perform-ance. The members also want to know how much their portion of the club portfolio is worth. Fortunately, there are resources that make club accounting more palatable. After all, even the club treasurer wants time to study stocks. You can use *IClub Central's Club Accounting* software or you can perform club accounting chores online with NAIC Online Club Accounting (*www.naic-club.com*).

Club Taxes

Investment clubs are usually partnerships. If you obtain a Federal Tax ID number for the club, you can transfer the tax obligations of the club to each of its members. After closing the books at the end of the year, the club treasurer prepares a Form 1065 Schedule K-1 for each person who belonged to the club at any point during the year. The treasurer files the K-1 with the IRS and distributes copies to each member for their own taxes.

Success Tip!

It's a good idea
to specify how the club
handles these situations
in the club by-laws, so
everyone knows
what to expect.

Members, Valuation & Withdrawals

Members pool money in an investment club and purchase stock. Similar to a mutual fund, each member owns a number of units in the club based on how much they contribute and the current value of the units. The unit value changes when the treasurer recalculates the club worth. If some members contribute before the valuation of the club and others contribute after (which usually means they paid late), members might receive different numbers of units for their contribution. The treasurer has to keep track of when members pay, the value of the units at payment time and the number of units each member receives.

If a member leaves a club for any reason, the club has to pay the departing member their portion of the club valuation. The club can pay the member in cash, stock or a combination of the two. Paying a member in cash or stock can produce different tax implications for the departing and remaining members. For example, paying a departing member with stock doesn't produce any taxable gain in the club. The departing member will have to pay taxes on the capital gains when selling the stock. If the club has to sell stock to pay cash to the departing member, those capital gains are taxable to every member of the club. *NAIC Investment Club Accounting Handbook* offers all the details on accounting for investment clubs.

Portfolio Management

Fortunately, portfolio management for a club isn't much different than what you do as an individual. You still monitor whether the returns meet the club's objectives and make buy and sell decisions to improve portfolio performance. You also make adjustments to diversification. In fact, the only difference is that more people have to agree on the objectives and the actions taken to meet them.

CHAPTER TWENTY TWO:

The Annual Report

Digging for Gold - and Dirt

At first glance, annual reports might seem overwhelming. Some of them seem to blather on forever. However, when you know the secret, you can glean the information you need without letting them consume your weekends. Although you often have to read between the lines to find out where companies have fallen short, you can unearth both the good and bad news from annual reports—which is just what you need to forecast a company's prospects.

You don't have to read annual reports cover to cover. In fact, you're better off extracting key items and using the time you save on more research and judgment.

Anatomy of an Annual Report

What to Look for and What to Ignore

Where to Obtain Annual Reports

An annual report tells you what a company's been up to during its last fiscal year. You can use the annual report to find out what the business is all about, what the company is working on or trying to achieve, as well as the nitty-gritty of its financial performance. Depending on a company's attitude, this report could be anything from easy to read and forthright to rambling and vague. Some annual reports contain a lot of fluff—pictures, philosophical sidebars and self-aggrandizing. But you can still mine valuable facts when you know where to look.

If you prefer Shaker style to Louis the Fourteenth gilding, you might prefer the SEC-driven version of the annual report, the 10-K. The Securities and Exchange Commission requires companies to disclose a host of financial data for each fiscal quarter and fiscal year. The 10-Q is the quarterly report, whereas the 10-K covers an entire year. These bypass the shiny paper and color pictures and include the SEC required disclosures. Often, you'll find straightforward detail about a company's financial performance, how it runs its business, and a little bit about the people who manage the company (including how they are compensated.) You can also learn about the industry in which the company operates and the opportunities, issues and risks that it faces. For example, the 10-K identifies legal proceedings in which a company is embroiled.

Anatomy of an Annual Report

- **Letter to Shareholders:** The president or CEO writes this communication to the company's shareholders. It might hype a company's fabulous performance or address recent problems, but basically it must tell the truth.

- **Corporate profile:** This section can be heavy on the fluff. However, you can learn a lot about a company's business and strategies in this section. It might describe its business divisions or explain its harder-to-understand products. If a company is doing well, it might focus on its vision or philanthropic initiatives.

- **Auditor's report:** The auditor's report presents the auditor's opinion of the company's financial position presented in the annual report. Auditors do not express opinions about the value of a company or its suitability as an investment.

- **Management discussion and analysis:** In this section, company management comments on past results as well as future prospects. They discuss factors that influence performance, such as competition, costs, inflation, currency exchange rates and accounting policies.

- **Financial statements and notes:** Every annual report provides an income statement, balance sheet and statement of cash flows for the company. You might see a variety of other, more specific, statements. For example, Pfizer includes a statement of shareholders' equity, unaudited quarterly performance, and a summary of the past 10 years of financial performance. The notes to the financial statements are the grittiest of the nitty-gritty. These notes discuss the finer points of financial performance in addition to explaining any exceptions to the statements.

- **Personnel:** Some annual reports include information about a company's officers and board of directors.

What to Look for and What to Ignore

The corporate profile is often little more than a marketing tool for a company. These are the pages with colorful pictures, heartwarming stories and glowing descriptions of business units and product lines. You can learn more about a company's products, businesses and initiatives in the corporate profile but be prepared for a rose-colored view.

Letter to the Shareholders

Letters to shareholders come in as many varieties as there are presidents and CEOs. Some leaders will include hard numbers, whereas others prefer to stick to less quantitative statements. When a CEO makes projections of the future, you should judge whether those forecasts seem reasonable or overly optimistic in the light of the factors that will influence the company in the future. Analyze what the CEO has to say about those influential factors—the market, industry trends, company strategies, R&D efforts or other items. For example, if the letter to the shareholders forecasts 25 percent growth in the future while also mentioning stiffening competition, you might question their assertions.

In addition to analyzing management's forecasts, you

should also scrutinize their explanations of past performance, particularly if there have been problems. The first check is whether the CEO talks about the company's problems at all. If they sweep issues under the table, you should question how much to trust anything the CEO says. Then, examine the explanations for poor performance. If they seem more like rationalizing than valid excuses, you can either dig deeper to understand the problems or move on to a company with more forthright disclosures.

In many cases, the letter to shareholders steers clear of hard numbers, but you can still consider the tone of the correspondence. Is the CEO positive about the future, confident in making projections, or defensive about problems and cautious to forecast anything?

Pfizer's letter to shareholders doesn't predict the company's future growth rates. However, the CEO is extremely positive— "another record year," "a remarkable year," "most valuable pharmaceutical company," "largest privately funded bio-medical research organization," and "our fast growing capabilities." In addition, he does throw out some numbers when it comes to the company's drug pipeline—94 new compounds in development, 68 projects for expanding the use of current products, 15 new medicines in line for regulatory approval in the next five years.

Pfizer also talks about the touchy-feely stuff. The company offers award-winning training to its sales representatives. It works to make its internal R&D best in class, but also forges alliances with other companies, such as the joint venture with IBM and Microsoft to create software and services to reduce paperwork for physicians.

Auditors' Report

Auditors' reports tend to follow a standard format describing the company and auditor's responsibility for preparing and reviewing the financial statements. Don't expect to hear the auditors endorse a company as a good investment. They also don't come right out and say "these folks are shady."

However, ANY kind of modification to the standard verbiage of an auditors' report is a red flag. Likewise, a qualified opinion is a warning. In this case, qualification expresses reservations about the financial reports, not the competence of the auditor. If the auditors' report includes any notes, make sure to read those.

The auditor's report for Pfizer follows the boilerplate without any unusual language.

Management Discussion & Analysis

This section provides a no-nonsense review of past results and future prospects with an emphasis on numbers. Typically, the management discussion and analysis covers the results of company operations, capital resources and liquidity.

The management discussion does more than list the numbers. It usually explains why the values are increasing and decreasing—which can be great material for your forecasts of future growth rates.

The management discussion and analysis section might appear under pseudonyms. For example, Pfizer refers to this section as the Financial Review.

Some companies might break down revenues by business unit, geographic area or product line. You can find out where the company is doing well and where it lags and why. Then, if the company announces a sale of a business unit or product line you can tell if they are getting rid of dead wood or key components. If a company does business overseas you can check the impact of currency exchanges on the results. This section might

include more detailed information on products. For example, Pfizer not only breaks down revenues in numerous ways, it also describes recent product approvals and developments.

You can also read about expenses, such as rising or falling costs, inflation, interest, taxes and in some cases, restructuring charges. For example, because of the recent merger with Warner-Lambert, Pfizer includes restructuring charges, but also talks about how its increase in R&D funds is offset by administrative cost savings. Look for trends in expenses—are they going up or down? Read more to determine whether the current trend is likely to continue. Remember, the more money that goes out in expenses, the less there is in earnings for shareholders.

The section on capital resources discusses whether a company has enough money to operate. You can turn to this section for the numbers you need to calculate debt and liquidity ratios, such as debt to equity and the current ratio for the company. It typically includes cash, short and long term debt, as well as other sources of funding such as lines of credit.

You might also find additional sections covering competition, risk management strategies, foreign currency exchange issues, interest rate risk or legal proceedings. Pfizer discusses the pricing pressures on pharmaceuticals in light of possible Medicare reform. The government could command price controls on prescription drugs directly or by increasing the number of people receiving health care through managed care organizations. On the other hand, Pfizer doesn't mention any significant legal proceedings.

The outlook section can be very useful, as long as you are confident that company management presents reasonable estimates of future performance. You might find forecasts for future sales and earnings growth, profit margins or other fundamental measures. In Pfizer's case, the goal is for double-digit revenue growth and 15 percent diluted EPS growth. The company also projects merger-related costs savings of $1.7 billion by the end of 2002, which will help earnings.

The GAAP principles have, and will continue to, evolve over time. They ensure that financial data are presented fairly and are comparable between different companies. In addition, certified public accountants must state whether the financial statements they prepare follow GAAP.

Financial Statements & Notes

The section for financial statements and notes is hard-core content. Financial statements follow a prescribed format according to the rules of Generally Accepted Accounting Principles (GAAP). With most companies, these statements are a reasonable representation of the financial state of the company.

Notes to financial statements discuss accounting policies, provide finer detail and identify exceptions to the statements. For example, Pfizer elaborates on the merger with Warner-Lambert, including the restatement of results of operations, merger-related costs and discontinued operations. Financial statements, introduced in the next two chapters, include:

- Balance Sheet (or Consolidated Balance Sheet)
- Income Statement (or Consolidated Income Statement)
- Cash Flows (or Consolidated Statement of Cash Flows)

Where to Obtain Annual Reports

Annual reports are easy to obtain whether you use a computer, the Internet, telephone, or pencil and paper. The number for investor relations usually appears on the Value Line company sheet. You can call investor relations to request an annual report. In fact, you might ask for an investor packet, which might contain the annual report, the SEC 10-K report, the most recent 10-Q, analyst reports and perhaps a list of competitors.

If you use the Internet, you can obtain the annual report and SEC filings from a variety of sources. If you are looking for these reports for only one company, you can start at the company Web site. Almost every company has an investor relations section where you can obtain investment related information. For example, on Pfizer's web site *(www.pfizer.com)*, you can click a link called Investing in Pfizer. From the investor relations area, you can obtain the annual reports for the past three years plus the most recent 10-K and 10-Q reports. You can also read (or listen to) recent press releases.

The Annual Report Service Web site *(www.annualreportservice.com)* provides online access to many (but not all) annual reports. For example, Pfizer does not participate in Annual Report Services' site. For the companies that do, you can choose between downloading an electronic version and requesting a hard copy of the report to be mailed.

For SEC filings, you can go to their Web site by searching the EDGAR database *(www.sec.gov/cgi-bin/srch-edgar/)*. EDGAR stands for Electronic Data Gathering and Retrieval. A SEC reports site that you might find more user-friendly is Free Edgar *(www.freeedgar.com)*.

After you obtain your first annual report, continue with the next chapters to learn more about deciphering the financial statements it contains.

CHAPTER TWENTY THREE:

The Income Statement

At The Heart of Finances

Financials are all about comparisons. Numbers by themselves don't tell us much, but begin to spill the beans when put into a frame of reference. Seventy-five degrees could be downright toasty in Point Barrow, Alaska in January and refreshingly cool in Death Valley, Arizona in July.

Similarly, financial numbers for a company are hard to judge by themselves. By comparing similar values in financial statements from year to year for the same company or between different companies, you can determine whether a prospective investment is attractive or not.

Accounting —
Art Not Science

Viewing Income &
Expenses over Time

A Snapshot of
Company Finance

Fun Things to Do
with Financial Statements

and Balance Sheet

The income statement and balance sheet offer two views of company performance. The income statement shows how a company makes money, where it spends money and how much is left over during a period of time. The balance sheet is a snapshot of what a company owns and owes and of the shareholders' investment in the company on a specific date. The balance sheet shows whether a company uses debt or stock to fund growth.

Accounting—Art Not Science

Many people think that accounting is tedious and tiresome. Just because it deals with numbers, they reason that it must follow immutable mathematical rules. Our financial calculations don't use a specialized form of addition, subtraction, multiplication or division. Because of the financial creativity some companies have exercised much too frequently in recent years, standardization in accounting allows investors to compare the financial health of two or more companies with some level of confidence. Still, there is creative art to categorizing money, goods and expenses.

The Financial Accounting Standards Board (FASB, pronounced fazz-be) develops, maintains and adjusts the accounting standards known as Generally Accepted Accounting Principles (GAAP). Financial reports, for internal use within a company, do not have to conform to GAAP—they can appear in any format the company wants. However, the financial statements presented to those outside the company, such as investors, must conform to GAAP.

THE ORIGIN OF FINANCIAL STATEMENTS

After the stock market crash and the Great Depression, Congress passed legislation to prevent similar disasters from occurring in the future. The Securities Act of 1933 requires companies to provide investors with financial and other information about the securities they sell to the public.

The Securities Exchange Act of 1934 governs the operation of securities markets and brokerage firms, including rules for purchasing securities on margin and investor access to current financial information. This act also created the Securities and Exchange Commission (SEC) to oversee compliance.

These two securities acts define modern financial reporting, specifying the format for financial statements: standard contents, disclosure requirements and reporting frequency. The SEC requires unaudited financial information each quarter—the ever-popular Form 10-Q. Companies file detailed annual reports, Form 10-Ks, which are audited by independent third parties.

Some accounting concepts take some getting used to. For example, a building purchase expenditure shows up as an asset on the balance sheet, whereas expenditures for office supplies appear as costs on the income statement. Some companies recognize revenue when they receive payment, but other companies might recognize revenue over a period to match the corresponding expenses of a project. In the beginning, you don't have to dig too deep into these conundrums. Conservative judgment in your stock studies goes a long way to cover your inexperience. But, over time, you'll absorb these details and apply them as you examine companies for investment.

Viewing Income & Expenses over Time

The income statement, also known as the profit and loss statement, shows the results of company operations over a period. Whether for a quarter or an entire year, the income statement shows revenues generated and expenses incurred during the period—in effect, how a company makes and spends its money over time. By dividing the earnings by the number of shares outstanding, the income statement also shows the earnings per share (EPS).

Success Tip!

The PDF formatted annual reports for Pfizer are on its Web site. You can compare these simplified financial statements below to the actual 2001 reports.

Some companies might include additional lines to further delineate revenues and costs, but the following table shows the basic ingredients of an income statement. The first column in the table includes letter labels, referenced by the calculations. The numbers in the table are from Pfizer's 2001 results.

AN INCOME STATEMENT TEMPLATE

	INCOME STATEMENT:	2001
	Sales or revenues	$32,259
	Cost and expenses	–$21,930
	Income before tax	$10,329
	Taxes	–$2,561
	Other deductions or additions	$20
a	Net income	$7,788
	PER SHARE NUMBERS	
b	Shares outstanding (diluted)	6361
c	Earnings per share = (a/b)	$1.22
d	Dividends per share =	$0.44
e	Price per share	$34.58
	Yield = (d/e)	1.3%
	PE ratio = (e/c)	28.34

Sales or revenue: The money coming in from products and services sold, interest earned or income from selling assets.

Costs: The costs of running the company, including producing and distributing what a company sells. These costs could include the components of a product, salaries for employees, benefits, travel expenses, research and development, or marketing, to name a few.

Success Tip!

Accounting principles require that financial reports record revenues and related expenses in the same period. This can result in expenses appearing in the income statement before the bills are actually paid. It might seem like a strange thing to do, but it more accurately reflects what the company truly earned during a period. For example, if a company has to buy components in bulk for its products, but sells the products over a few years, costs at the beginning would outstrip sales, whereas costs would seem inordinately low for the rest of the time.

Income before tax (Pre-tax profit): Sales minus costs.

Taxes: The portion that goes to Uncle Sam and the state. **Other deductions or additions:** You might see other types of deductions or additions in the income statement. For example, Pfizer shows some income from discontinued operations. This is income produced by parts of the business that the company no longer operates.

Income after tax: The amount left over after costs and taxes are subtracted.

Net income: A company can distribute net income to owners as dividends or reinvest to grow the business. The more income given to owners (stockholders) in a dividend, the less is available to reinvest and grow the company.

Yield =	Dividends per share / Price per share	$.44 / $34.58	= 1.3 %

Dividends: The money the company pays out to its shareholders.

Shares outstanding: The number of shares issued to all shareholders. Diluted shares include those that could be issued in the future, such as for employee stock options.

EPS: Net income divided by the number of shares outstanding. EPS shows how much of the company's earnings are attributable to each share of stock.

Dividends per share: The money the company pays out to each share.

Price: The price that people are willing to pay (or bid) or receive (or ask) for their shares of stock. In other words, the price at which buyers and sellers agree to exchange shares.

Yield: Yield is what the dividend per share represents as a percentage of the current price for a share of the stock, and could be compared to the yield on a savings account or certificate of deposit.

From our Pfizer SSG, the following example demonstrates the calculation for yield.

PE ratio: A measure of what investors are willing to pay for one dollar of a company's earnings.

A Snapshot of Company Finance

The balance sheet is a snapshot of what the company owns (assets), what it owes (liabilities) and the shareholders' investment in the company (shareholders' equity) at a point in time. It is called a balance sheet because the shareholders' equity and total liabilities always balances with the total assets.

Some companies might include additional lines for finer detail about assets and liabilities, but the following table shows the basic ingredients of a balance sheet. The first column in the table includes letter labels, referenced by the calculations. The numbers in the table are from Pfizer's 2001 results.

Assets: Things that the company owns and uses to generate revenue, such as cash, accounts receivable, prepaid expenses, inventory, land and equipment.

Liabilities: What the company owes, such as unpaid expenses, accounts payable, estimates of future expenses (pensions), value of monies received but services not yet provided (deferred income), or debt used to acquire assets.

Shareholders' equity: The investment of the shareholders in the company—much like an individual's net worth. Shareholders' equity is what is left after you subtract liabilities from assets.

Success Tip!

The balance sheet might dramatically overestimate or understate the value of some assets and liabilities, because it doesn't show fair market value. Unless values are measurable, such as when they are sold, they don't appear on the balance sheet.

Some assets purchased in the past, such as land or art, could be worth much more today, whereas other assets are worth much less. In addition, the value of a global brand name doesn't appear on a balance sheet. Liabilities can also be hidden, such as a tobacco company's future obligations from lawsuits. Hidden liabilities can depress the stock price, whereas understated assets could make the stock price seem overvalued.

BALANCING THE BOOKS

	BALANCE SHEET:	2001
	Current assets	$18,450
	Long-term investments	$5,729
	Property, plant and equipment	$10,415
	Goodwill	$1,722
	Other	$2,837
	Total assets	$39,153
	Current liabilities	$13,640
	Long-term debt	$2,609
	Deferred taxes	$452
	Other liabilities	$4,159
	Total liabilities	$20,860
	Shareholders equity	$18,293

Fun Things to Do with Financial Statements

Most of what you need to know about a company before you buy it is on the SSG. But, you can detect early warnings as well as potential good news by analyzing ratios of a company's numbers. These numbers usually come from the income statement and balance sheet, although a few ratios of interest use values from the statement of cash flow. The following is a quick introduction to some of the ratios you can use to further evaluate your investment prospects.

You're already familiar with a few ratios calculated using numbers from the income statement and balance sheet. Pre-tax profit on sales and return on equity in Section 2 of the SSG are key ratios computed from financial statement entries.

• **Current ratio**: The current ratio measures the liquidity of a company's short-term assets—does the company have enough short-term assets to pay off its short-term liabilities? Generally, a current ratio of two-to-one or more is preferable. Current assets and liabilities appear on the balance sheet.

Current ratio =	$\dfrac{\text{Current assets}}{\text{Current liabilities}}$	$= \dfrac{\$18,450}{\$13,640}$	= 1.35

• **Quick ratio**: The quick ratio measures the ratio of assets that are readily converted into cash. A current ratio of two-to-one or more is preferable.

Current assets and liabilities appear on the balance sheet. All the numbers for the quick ratio appear on the balance sheet.

Quick ratio =	$\dfrac{\text{Current assets} - \text{inventory}}{\text{Current liabilities}}$	$= \dfrac{\$18,450 - \$2,741}{\$13,640}$	= 1.15

• **Receivable turnover**: The faster a company converts its credit sales to cash, the better it can operate, pay bills and earn money. Receivables turnover represents the number of times in a period that accounts receivable are turned into cash and higher numbers are preferable to low. Increases in accounts receivable or the corresponding decrease in receivable turnover is a warning sign. It might be due to ineffective collection practices, but it could also come from a company aggressively shipping products to customers to boost declining sales. You can use the accounts receivable from the previous two years to calculate the average. Sales come from the income statement and accounts receivable appears on the balance sheet.

Receivable turnover =	$\dfrac{\text{Sales}}{\text{Average acct. receivable}}$	$= \dfrac{\$32,259}{(\$5,337 + \$5,489) / 2}$	= 5.96

• **Inventory turnover**: Inventory turnover is the number of times a company replaces its inventory during a period and higher numbers are preferable. If inventory turnover is low or declining, a company might have aging or obsolete inventory —and that can lead to a write-off against income in the future.

Inventory turnover =	$\dfrac{\text{Cost of goods sold}}{\text{Average inventory}}$	$= \dfrac{\$5,034}{(\$2,741 + \$2,702) / 2}$	= 1.85

CHAPTER TWENTY FOUR

The Statement of Cash

Cash Is King

Your posh pad on the outskirts of town might be the envy of your friends, but if you can't pay the mortgage, you have a cash flow problem.

Companies are no different—they run on cash. In fact, many financial experts consider cash flow (not sales, earnings or profit) to be the best measure of a company's financial health.

Anatomy of the Statement of Cash Flow

How the Statement of Cash Flow Works

What to Look for in Cash Flow

Flow

The income statement shows sales, profit and earnings for a company over a period of time, whereas the balance sheet is a snapshot of assets and liabilities. If you can read a cash flow statement, not only can you link the income statement to the balance sheet, you can spot problems or opportunities ahead of the crowd.

Anatomy of the Statement of Cash Flow

The income statement and balance sheet both feed the statement of cash flow. Although the income statement displays revenue and costs, accounting practices turn many items on both the income statement and balance sheet into funny money. The cash flow statement is like a financial detective; it follows the cash flowing in and out of a company.

Companies can obtain cash from three different sources. Cash from operating activities is the cash a business generates or uses. Excess cash generated from the ongoing operations of a company is ideal, because it shows that the business can sustain itself. On the other hand, cash from investing activities indicates investments or divestitures, both internal and external. For example, investing activities include buying or selling assets such as buildings, or investing company money in the stock market. Selling an asset could impact future sales and earnings. It also adds a gain or loss to the income statement, which can artificially and quite temporarily improve or reduce the company's earnings. Cash from financing activities shows cash coming in from the outside—from banks, investment capital firms or shareholders. A company can finance an investment or raise funds for operations with cash from issuing stock or debt. Financing investments is OK if those investments help a company grow—and typically companies in their start-up phase do use these sources of cash. However, when you notice that an established company is financing operations, you have spotted a red flag. Dig deeper into the management discussion and analysis in the annual report to find out why a company can't generate enough cash from operations to run itself.

Company cash isn't quite the same as greenbacks in your wallet. With the advent of discounted cash flows and leveraged buyouts, accounting rules now disconnect revenues and expenses from cash. In effect, a dollar of revenue does not equal a dollar of cash. To sort out this tangle of ephemeral finance, there are a few simple rules to determine whether something provides or consumes cash.

Sources of Cash

• An increase in either a liability or equity account is a source of cash. For example, when someone loans you money, you can spend it on something. Cash comes in, but your debt increases in the amount of the borrowed funds. Similarly, when a company issues stock, it receives money for those shares, but its equity account increases.

• A decrease in an asset account is also a source of cash. When you sell an asset, you receive money, but the value of the asset account decreases. Accounts receivable is the money that customers or other parties owe a company. When a customer pays their bill, cash comes into the company, but accounts receivable declines by the amount of the payment.

Uses of Cash

• A decrease in a liability or equity account uses cash. A company must spend cash to pay off debt or buy back stock it has issued.

• An increase in an asset account uses cash. A company spends money to buy fixed assets or produce inventory.

How the Statement of Cash Flow Works

The statement of cash flow links the income statement and the balance sheet. It starts with net income from the income statement and ends with cash from the balance sheet. It attempts to explain changes on the balance sheet not resulting from transactions recorded in the income statement.

The following table is a simplified version of the Pfizer 2001 statement of cash flows. Sources of cash appear as positive numbers, whereas uses of cash are negative.

In the example for Pfizer, the company produced $9,291 million from operations and spent $7,225 million on investments.

It spent another $2,096 million on financing, mainly paying dividends. Because the cash from operations almost matched the decreases in cash from investing and financing, Pfizer's cash started the year at $1,099 million and ended the year at $1,036 million.

STATEMENT OF CASH FLOW:	YEAR ENDED 12/31/2001
Operating Activities	
Income from operations	$7,752
Depreciation	$1,068
Sales of equities	–$17
Deferred taxes	$217
Increase in accounts receivable	–$30
Increase in inventory	–$102
Prepaid and other assets	$132
Accounts payable and accrued liabilities	–$201
Other items	$647
Net cash from operating activities	**$9,291**
Investing Activities	
Purchase of property, plant and equipment	–$2,203
Sales of property, plant and equipment	$68
Purchases of short-term investments	–$14,218
Redemptions of short-term investments	$12,808
Purchases of long-term investments	–$3,713
Sales of equity investments	$80
Other investing activities	–$47
Net cash from investing activities	**–$7,225**
Financing Activities	
Proceeds from long-term debt	$1,837
Repayments of long-term debt	–$151
Increase in short-term debt	$2,351
Decrease in short-term debt	–$526
Common stock issuances	$62
Purchases of common stock (buy back)	–$3,665
Cash dividends paid	–$2,715
Stock option transactions	$711
Net cash from financing activities	**–$2,096**
Adjustments	$96
Cash at beginning of year	$1,099
Cash at end of year	$1,036

What to Look for in Cash Flow

Many investors ignored mundane financial measures, like earnings, to justify buying dot-com companies. Sanity has returned and these same investors, wiser and most likely poorer, now scrutinize company sales, earnings and cash flow.

• Did cash increase or decrease during the period? Decreasing cash could lead to additional financing activities. If a company must continually increase debt or issue more stock, the values of your shares eventually will suffer. Read the management discussion to find the reason for decreasing cash.

• Is net income on the income statement close to the value of cash from operating activities? If it is, the company's earnings are primarily from operations and have more substance. If not, find out why.

• Are net income and cash from operations growing at a similar rate? When cash from operations growth begins to lag behind net income growth you are seeing an early warning of problems to come.

• Are accounts receivable increasing faster than sales? When a company can't collect what it is owed, it doesn't bring cash in. Accounts receivable increase, which uses cash, so the statement of cash flow shows a negative number for accounts receivable.

• Are inventories growing faster than sales or cost of goods sold? Increasing inventories might mean slowing demand or products falling out of favor. Buying inventory takes cash, so increasing inventory shows up as negative on the statement of cash flows. Compare the growth of inventory on the cash flow statement to the growth of sales on the income statement.

• Has cash flow from operations remained negative for too long? Eventually, the company has to learn to support itself from the cash it generates from operations.

• Is a company raising cash by selling assets? Assets often produce growth, so selling assets is the worst way to raise cash. It also often means that the company can't borrow any more money, so check for high levels of debt.

There you are. Not only have you learned to study stocks and build a portfolio, you now can read financial statements and use the results to make even better investment decisions.

PRE-TAX PROFIT MARGIN WORKSHEET

a. Year										
b. Net profit										
c. Tax rate as a decimal										
d. 1 – Tax rate										
e. Pre-tax profit (b/d)										
f. Sales										
g. Pre-tax profit on sales (e/f)										
h. Percent pre-tax profit margin (X 100)										

PERCENT EARNED ON EQUITY WORKSHEET

a. Year			
b. EPS			
c. Book value per share			
d. Percent earned on equity (b/c) X 100			

Glossary

For a handy and completely thorough glossary for investors, pick up a copy of Wall Street Words: An Essential A to Z Guide for Today's Investor *by David L. Scott (Houghton Mifflin, 1997). For online glossaries, start with About.com's web page for glossaries (beginnersinvest.about.com/cs /glossary1/index.htm). This page provides links to over a dozen different financial and business glossaries. Find the one you like the best and add a bookmark in your browser.*

10-K—Annual report that contains audited financial information about a publicly traded company's performance for a fiscal year. Required by the SEC.

10-Q—Quarterly report that contains unaudited financial information about a publicly traded company's performance for a fiscal quarter. Required by the SEC.

Accounts receivable turnover—Number of times during an accounting period that a company converts sales into cash (calculated by dividing annual sales by average value of receivables).

Annual Report—A report that covers a company's financial and operating results for one fiscal year. Includes summary of performance, comments about the future, and audited financial statements such as income statement, balance sheet, cash flow statement, and auditor's report.

As reported—Data presented as reported by a company in its audited financial statements.

Asset management account—A brokerage account that includes trading securities, checking, credit or debit card, automatic sweep of cash balances into a money market fund, margin loans, and in some instances, online banking services.

Asset—An item with monetary value, whether tangible like real estate or intangible like goodwill, owned by a company.

Auditor—Person who inspects a company's financial records and reports his or her opinion of their accuracy.

Automatic reinvestment—Using money from dividends or capital gain distributions to purchase additional shares of a stock.

Balance sheet—Company financial statement that shows assets, liabilities, and shareholders' investment in the company as of a specific date.

Beta—Measure of volatility of a stock compared to that of the stock market as a whole. A beta of 1.1 indicates a stock is likely to change 110 percent when the stock market changes by 100 percent.

Bond—A long-term debt security issued by a company or a governmental unit. The purchaser of a bond earns interest on his or her money and receives the amount invested if he or she holds the bond until it matures.

Book value—Total assets minus total liabilities are recorded on the balance sheet of a company. Same as shareholders' equity or net worth.

Capital expenditure—Money spent to acquire a long-term asset, which will depreciate over its lifetime.

Capitalization—The types and amount of financing a company uses to obtain funds, including common stock, preferred stock, long-term debt, and retained earnings.

Cash flow—Cash generated or consumed by a company during a period. Cash flow is net income after taxes with non-cash expense such as depreciation added back in.

Certificates of deposit (CD)—A savings vehicle where the holder of the CD deposits money with a financial institution, receives interest for the length of the CD, and the original deposit back upon maturity.

Commission—The fee a broker or agent charges to make a trade.

Common stock—Stock that represents ownership of a company. However, holders of notes, bonds, or preferred stock have claims to the assets of a company before common shareholders.

Compound annual growth rate—Annual growth rate that takes into account the original investment and earnings from previous compounding periods. Comparable to compound interest at a bank where the bank pays interest on money, and then pays interest on the original deposit plus interest already earned.

Current asset—Assets that might be converted to cash within one year.

Current liability—Debt due within one year.

Current ratio—A measure of a company's ability to pay off short-term obligations. The ratio of current assets divided by current liabilities.

Cyclical stock—Stock in a company whose performance is significantly affected by the economy.

Debt—Obligation to pay an amount to a creditor, lender, or bondholder. Also called liability.

Debt to Equity Ratio—Ratio of debt to equity owned by the shareholders.

Declared dividend—Dividend authorized by the board of directors of a company.

Depreciation—A non-cash expense that appears on a company's books to indicate the reduction of an asset's value.

Dilution—A reduction in the equity ownership in a company represented by a share of stock because of the issuance of additional shares.

Director—A member of the board of directors of a company, who might also be an executive of that company.

Direct stock purchase plans (DPPs or DSPs)—A plan where investors can buy stock directly from a company without a broker. Also known as a Direct Investment Plan (DIP).

Disclosure—The requirement for a company to report its performance.

Discount broker—A broker that charges low commissions and usually provides fewer services.

Diversification—Purchasing securities whose performance is not linked over time, such as stocks in different industries or different size companies. Diversification reduces risk in a portfolio.

Dividend—A taxable distribution of a company's earnings to share-holders.

Dividend reinvestment—Purchasing more shares in a company using the dividend paid out.

Dividend Reinvestment Plans (DRIPs)—A plan where investors can reinvest dividends directly through the company to buy more shares of stock without a broker.

Dividend yield—Yield provided by the annual dividend, calculated by dividing the dividend of a stock by the market price.

Dollar-cost averaging—Lowering the average cost of a company's shares by buying shares with a fixed amount of money on a regular schedule. You buy more shares when the price is low, fewer shares when the price is high.

Download—Copying a file from a Web site to your computer.

Earnings estimate—An estimate of a company's earnings by financial analysts.

Earnings per share (EPS)—The net income of a company minus preferred dividends paid divided by the number of average shares outstanding. EPS represents the portion of the earnings to which one share of common stock is entitled.

Economic risk—The risk to investments from an overall downturn in the economy.

Education IRA—A tax-deferred account used to save for tuition.

Equity—Ownership in a property or corporation. Shareholders equity is the total assets of a corporation minus the total liabilities.

Exchange rate—The ratio of one currency to another. Exchange rates can affect the earnings of a company when it does business overseas.

Expense—Costs incurred by a company.

FASB—The Financial Accounting Standards Board is an independent accounting organization that sets standards for financial accounting.

FDIC—Federal Deposit Insurance Corporation is a federal agency that insures the deposits at commercial banks up to $100,000 per depositor.

Financial analyst—A person who assesses financial investments.

Financial planner—A person who helps individuals prepare and manage a plan to achieve financial objectives.

Financial statement—A report of financial performance for a company.

Fiscal year—The twelve months designated as the annual reporting period for a company.

Full-service broker—A broker who offers other services, such as financial planning, stock research, analysis, and recommendations, in addition to executing stock trades.

Fundamentals—The basic financial measures of a company including revenue growth, EPS growth, dividend payout, profit margin, and PE ratio.

Fundamental analysis—Estimating the value of a stock by evaluating fundamental measures.

GAAP—Generally Accepted Accounting Principles are guidelines evolved over time that help companies present financial data fairly and comparably to other companies.

Good until cancelled order—An order to buy or sell a stock at a specific price that remains in effect until canceled by the customer or executed by the broker.

Gross profit—Revenue of a company minus the cost of goods sold.

Growth rate—Annual rate of growth, either actual or estimated.

Home page—The first page that appears when accessing a Web site.

Import—Transferring data into an application, such as importing data from a Web site or financial application into a stock analysis program.

Income statement—A financial statement that shows revenues, expenses, and net income for a period.

Index—A measure of some portion of the financial markets, such as the Standard and Poor's 500 index or Dow Jones Industrial index.

Inflation—The overall increase of prices for goods and services.

Inflation risk—The risk from inflation eroding the purchasing power of your money.

Insider—A person, such as a director or executive, with information about a company that is unavailable to the public.

Interest—The money paid by a borrower to a lender for the use of the lender's money.

Internet—A network of computers that connect to each other.

Inventory turnover—The number of times a company sells and replaces its inventory during a period. Calculated by dividing the cost of goods sold by the average value of inventory.

Investment club—A group of people who pool their money to invest and learn more about investing.

Investment objective—The goal for an investment, such as income or capital appreciation.

Liability—An obligation to pay an amount of money to another party. Also called debt.

Limit order—An order to buy or sell a security at a specified price or better. The order does not execute unless the stock reaches or passes the limit price.

Limit price—The price specified for a limit order. A limit price for a buy order is the highest price the investor will pay, whereas a limit price for a sell order is the lowest price the investor will accept.

Market order—An order to buy or sell a security at the best price currently available.

Market price—The current price at which a stock trades.

Market risk—The risk that a particular investment will turn bad.

Mutual fund—An investment where an investment advisor or fund manager invests money for fund shareholders to achieve an investment objective.

Mutual fund family—A number of mutual funds offered by the same mutual fund company.

Mutual fund supermarket—A broker that offers a variety of mutual fund and mutual fund families.

NASDAQ—A computerized dealer system that shows price quotations for stocks traded in the over-the-counter market.

Net worth—Total assets minus total liabilities as recorded on the balance sheet of a company. Same as shareholders' equity (or book value).

New York Stock Exchange—A market where buy and sell orders for stocks listed on the exchange are executed.

Normalized—Data that is adjusted to eliminate nonrecurring gains or losses to better reflect ongoing performance of a company.

Operating income—The income (revenues minus expenses) obtained from business operations. Excludes item such as gains from selling a business unit.

Payout ratio—The ratio of net income a company pays to shareholders as dividends.

PE ratio—Price earnings ratio is the ratio of stock price to a measure of a company's earnings (last fiscal year, last four quarters, projected). Represents the confidence or concern investors have in a company.

PEG ratio—PEG ratio is the ratio of PE to a company's growth rate. A PEG ratio is an indication of whether a company's price might be reasonable given its rate of growth. Guidelines for maximum PEG ratio range between 1.5 and 2.

Portfolio—A collection of investments owned by an individual or company.

Portfolio management—Buying and selling all or part of the holdings in a portfolio to improve performance, increase quality, reduce risk, or improve diversification.

Preferred stock—Shares that convey ownership in a company and provide a claim to earnings and assets of the company prior to the claim of common shareholders.

Pretax profit—Profit before taxes are deducted.

Price appreciation—The increase in the price of an investment.

Profit margin—The percentage of profit to annual sales. Represents the amount of money a company gets to keep from each dollar it brings in.

Quick ratio—A harsh test of a company's ability to meet short-term obligations, calculated by dividing current assets excluding inventory by current liabilities.

Rate of return—The annual return as a percentage of the original investment amount.

Ratio analysis—Comparing financial measures of a company or measures of one company to another to determine whether a company's results are acceptable or at risk.

Reinvestment risk—The risk that interest rates will be lower when a CD or bond matures.

Retirement account—An investment account for saving for retirement where contributions might be exempt from tax and earnings grow tax-deferred.

Restated—Data that is modified due to changes in a company's structure or previously unknown information. Companies restate their numbers to reflect the changes from an acquired company or divested business unit.

Return on equity—The return a company earns on shareholders' investment in the company.

Revenues—The total dollars from sales, services, or other sources for a company.

Roth IRA—An Individual Retirement Account where contributions are taxed, but all withdrawals in retirement are tax-free.

SEC—A federal agency that enforces U.S. securities laws.

Share—One unit of ownership in a company.

Shareholder—An individual or organization that owns shares in a company.

Shareholders' equity—The investment by shareholders in a company, including the amount invested and profits.

Statement of cash flow—A financial statement that shows how a company obtains and spends cash during a period.

Stock—Ownership in a company.

Stock screen—A tool for eliminating stocks that do not meet specific criteria, such as EPS growth rate, debt/equity ratio, or dividend yield.

Stock split—An increase or decrease in the number of shares without a corresponding change in assets so that shareholders equity remains the same.

Stop price—Price specified in a stop order at which the order executes. A stop price for a buy order indicated the highest price at which an investor is willing to buy. A stop price for a sell is the price at which an investor will sell to avoid further losses.

Tax-advantaged retirement accounts—Retirement accounts that provide tax breaks for saving, such as shielding contributions from current taxes, or tax–free withdrawals.

Tax-deferred—Income where taxes are not paid until a later date.

Tear sheet—A printed page from Standard and Poor's stock report binders.

Technical analysis—Trying to determine the future price of a security based on price, price changes, and trading volume.

Ticker symbol—The abbreviation for a company on stock quotation systems.

Total return—The annual return from dividends and price appreciation.

Unaudited statement—A financial statement that has not been audited by a CPA.

Unrealized capital gain—The increase in the value of an asset that has not yet been sold.

Value investing—Investing in stocks where the stock price doesn't fully reflect the fundamental performance of a company.

Watch list—A list of stocks that you create to monitor for potential purchase or sale.

Web site, Web page—A Web site is a collection of Web pages. A Web page is one within a site.

Write off—Eliminating the value of an asset from the balance sheet by charging an expense equivalent value shown on the balance sheet for the asset. Companies might write off obsolete inventory, obsolete assets, or bad loans.

Yield—The annual return for an investment expressed as a percentage, calculated for stocks by dividing the dividend by the purchase price.

Index

INDEX

Dividends up, greenhouse gas emissions down. The next quarter matters. So does the next quarter century.

BP's investment strategy is to create value. Our 2002 dividends, which are set in U.S. dollars, increased 9% over the previous year. In the last 20 years, our dividends have increased by an average of 4% per year above inflation. Yet we believe profits and responsibility can go hand in hand.

Today, BP is the combined energies of British Petroleum, Amoco, Castrol and ARCO, with over 100,000 employees in over 100 countries, serving around 13 million customers worldwide every day. To learn more about our performance and strategy, visit www.bp.com/investor_centre

In 1997, we recognized the risks of global climate change, and set a target to reduce our own greenhouse gas emissions. Through technology and better management of energy use, we achieved our target 8 years ahead of schedule, at no net cost and with substantial economic gains to our business.

bp

beyond petroleum™